Volume 18

Ema Toyama

Missions of Love
Ema Toyama

Story

Yukina and Shigure's love missions began as research for a novel, but now Yukina has finally realized that her feelings for Shigure are true love. Meanwhile, Hisame has discovered that Yukina is the novelist Yupina, and threatens Yukina that if Shigure were to find out about it, he would never forgive her. In the midst of it all, Yupina and Dolce are scheduled to appear on TV for a public showdown, and Hisame appears to be plotting something...?

Characters

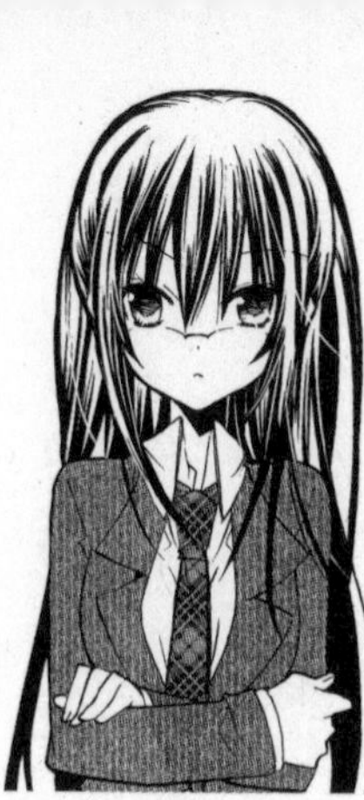

Shigure Kitami
The ever-popular, yet black-hearted, student body president. He made a game of charming all the girls and making them confess their love to him, then writing it all down in his student notebook, but Yukina discovered his secret!

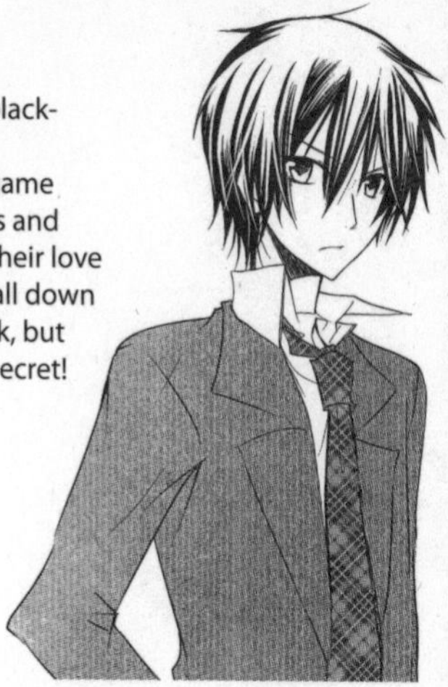

Yukina Himuro
A third-year junior high student who strikes terror in the hearts of those around her with her piercing gaze, feared as the "Absolute Zero Snow Woman." Only Akira knew that she is also the popular cell phone novelist Yupina, but…

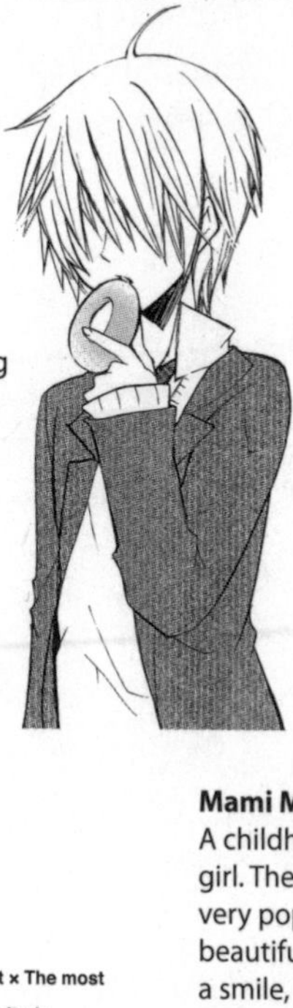

Akira Shimotsuki
Yukina's cousin and fellow student. He loves to eat. He is always nearby watching over her. They were boy-friend and girlfriend for a while, but now they have reverted to their former relationship.

XX me!

It is time for love.
Secret cellular phone novelist × The most popular boy in school.
Love mission of absolute servitude.

Mami Mizuno
A childhood friend of Shigure's. A sickly girl. The teachers love her, and she's very popular with the boys. She's a beautiful young girl who always wears a smile, but deep down, her heart is black. She has confessed her love to Akira.

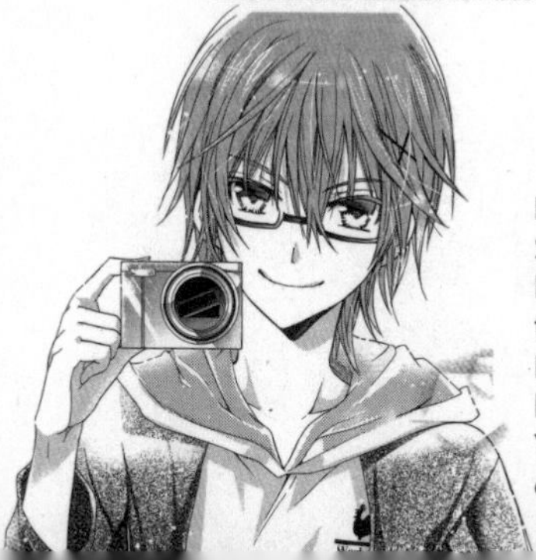

Hisame Kitami
Shigure's brother, one year his junior. He is actually the cell phone novelist Dolce. After Mami rejects him, the revelation that Yukina is Yupina sends him out of control…

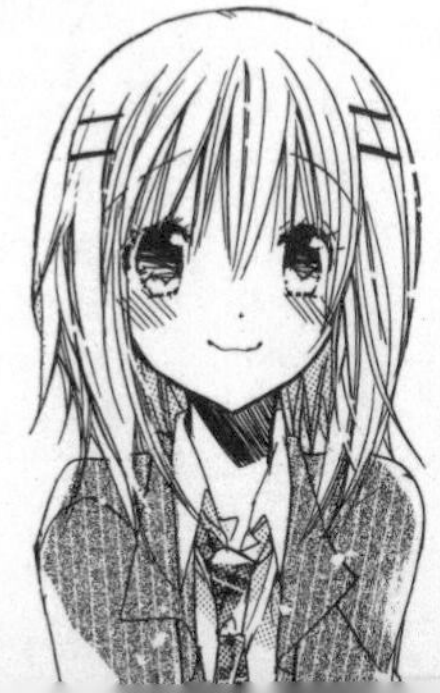

MISSIONS OF LOVE

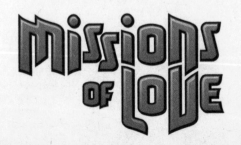

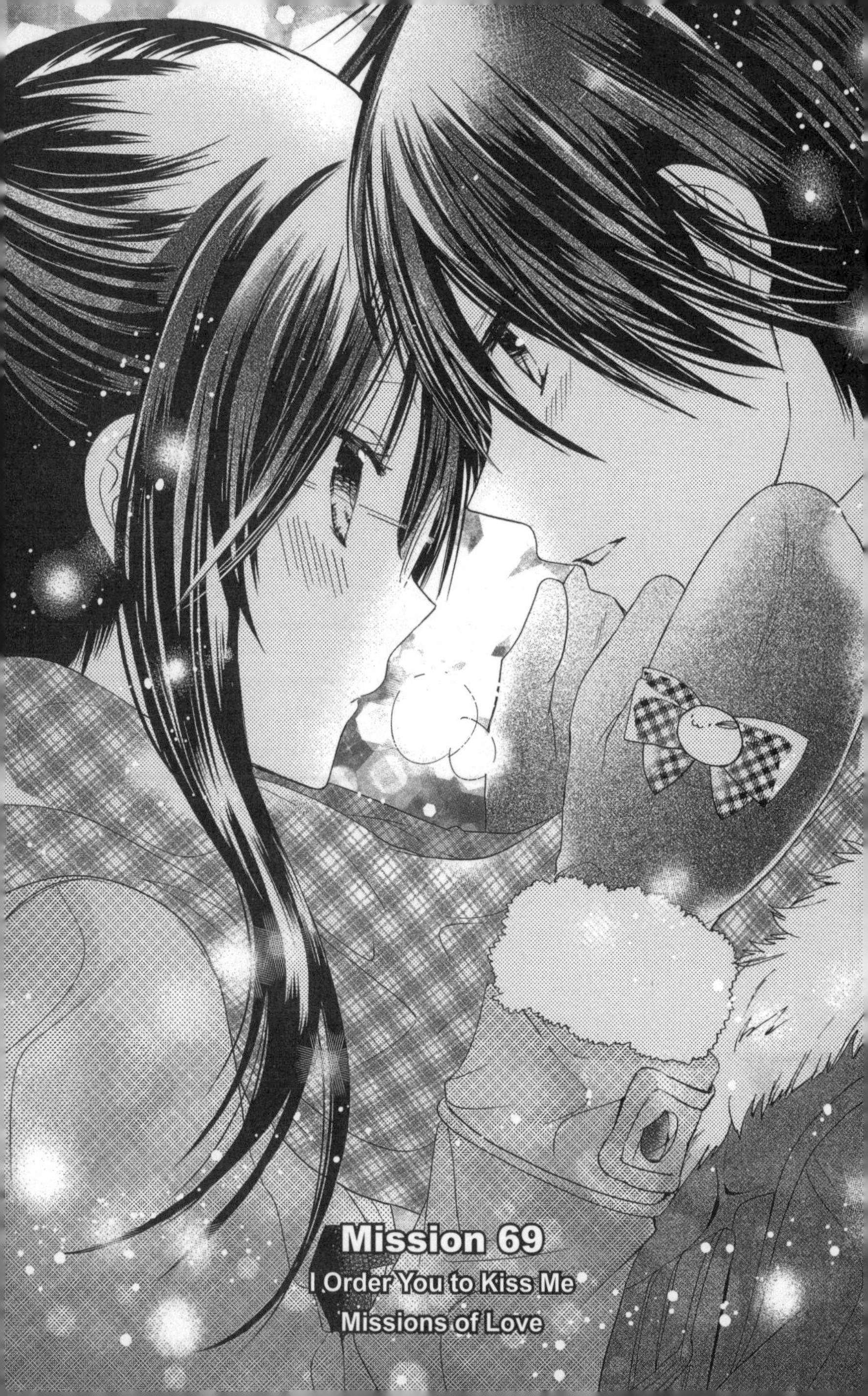
Mission 69
I Order You to Kiss Me
Missions of Love

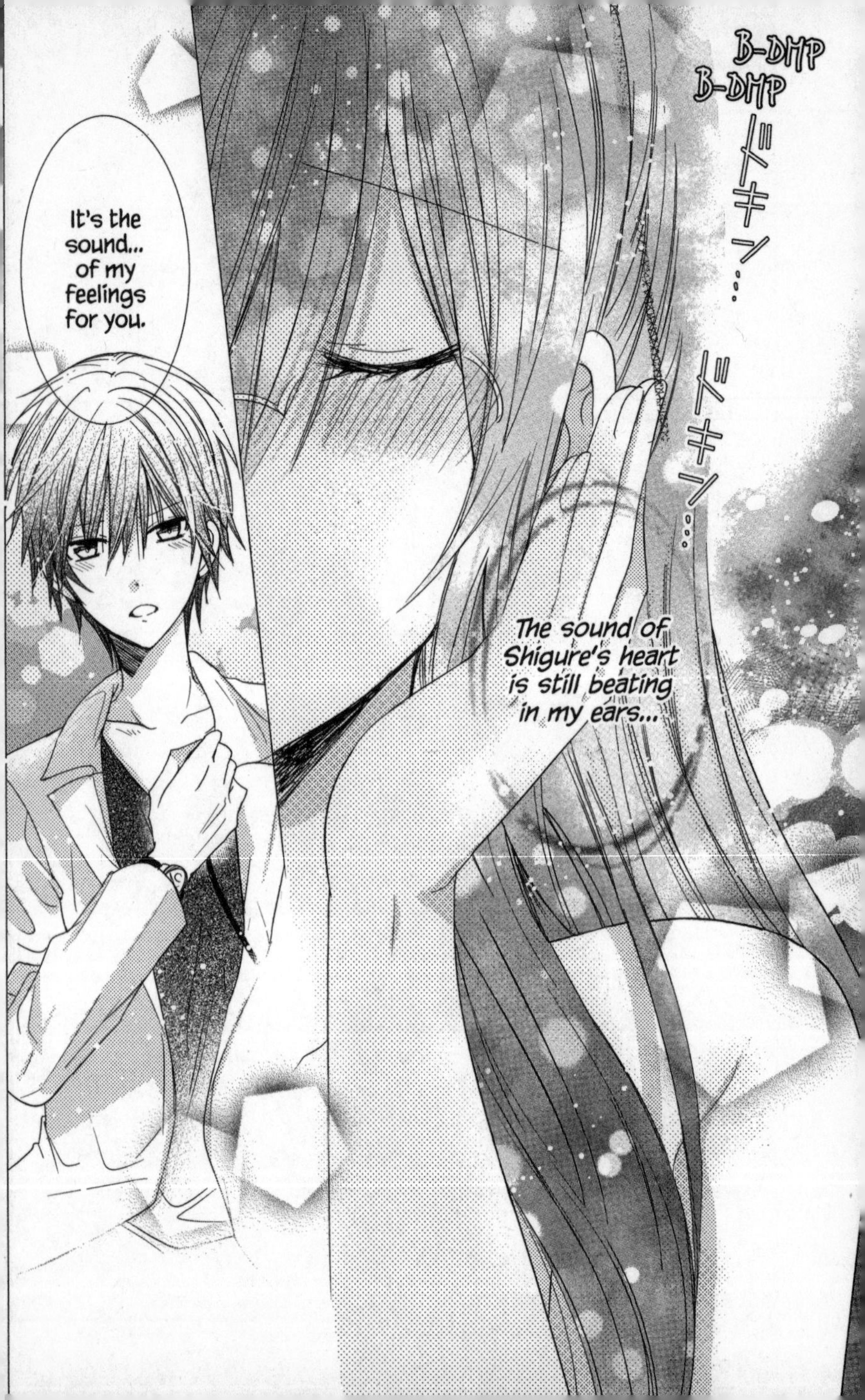
B-DMP
B-DMP
ドキン…
ドキン…
The sound of Shigure's heart is still beating in my ears...
It's the sound... of my feelings for you.

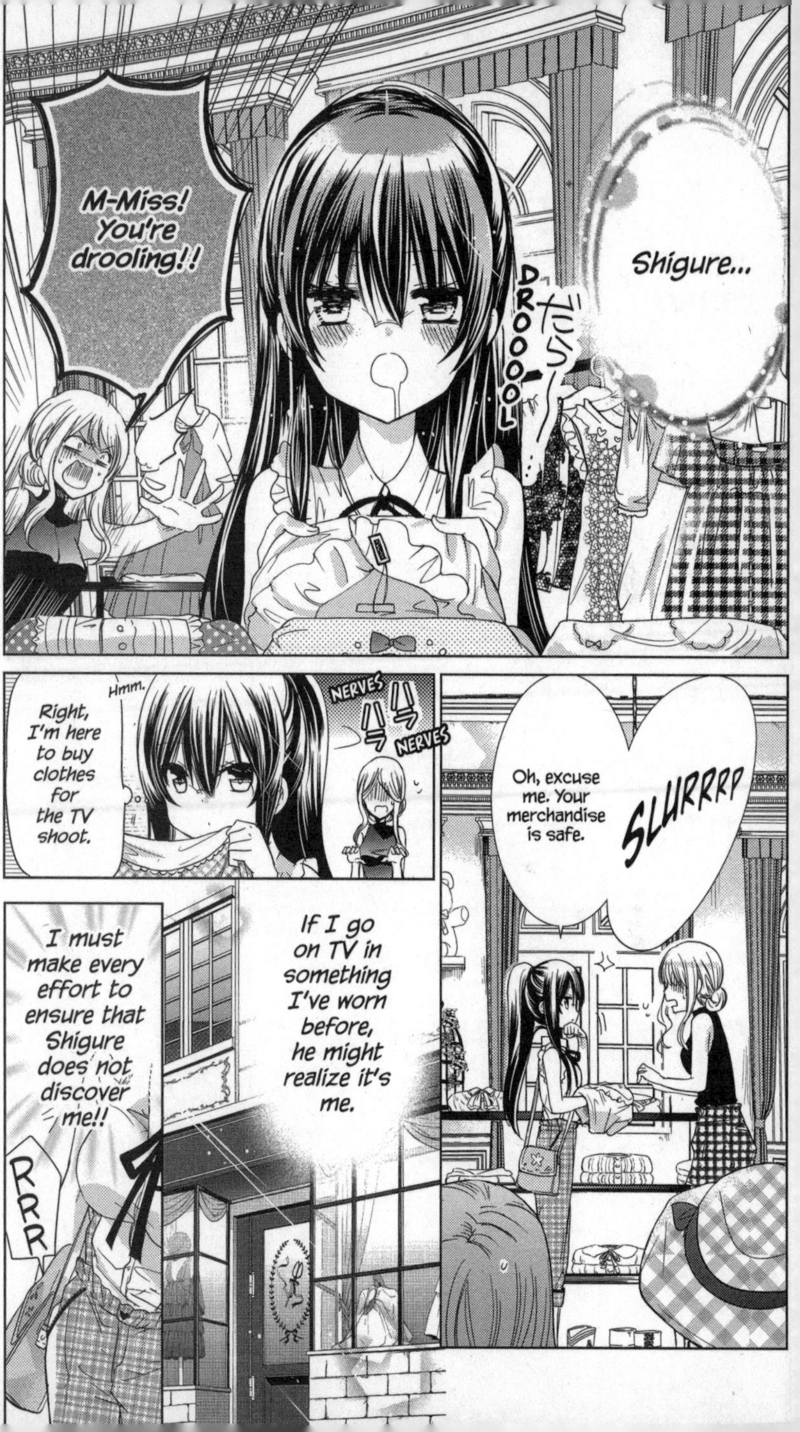
Shigure...
DROOOOOL
M-Miss! You're drooling!!
Oh, excuse me. Your merchandise is safe.
SLURRRP
NERVES
NERVES
Hmm.
Right, I'm here to buy clothes for the TV shoot.
If I go on TV in something I've worn before, he might realize it's me.
I must make every effort to ensure that Shigure does not discover me!!
RRR

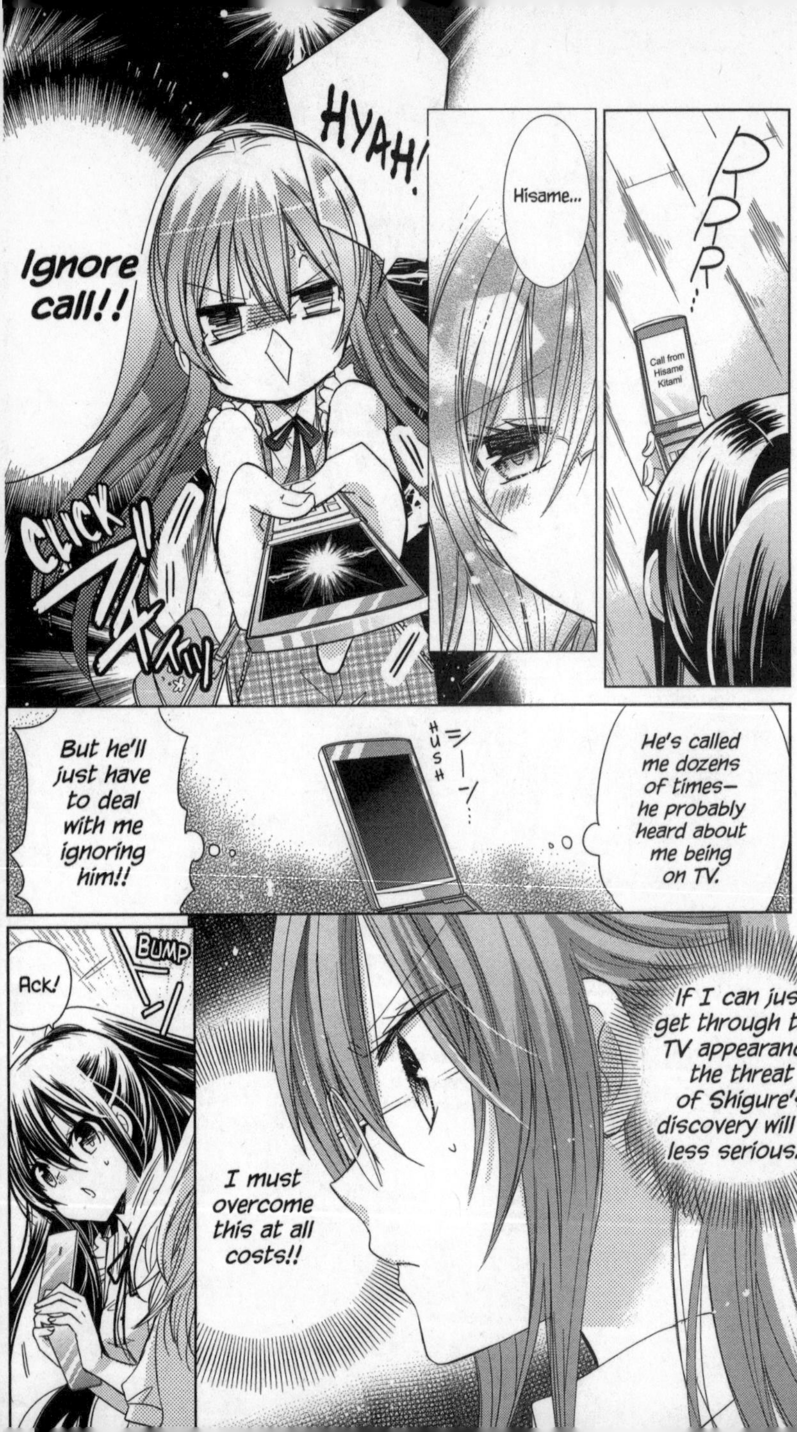
RRR...
Call from Hisame Kitami
Hisame...
HYAH!
Ignore call!!
CLICK
He's called me dozens of times—he probably heard about me being on TV.
HUSH
But he'll just have to deal with me ignoring him!!
If I can just get through this TV appearance, the threat of Shigure's discovery will be less serious...
I must overcome this at all costs!!
BUMP
Ack!

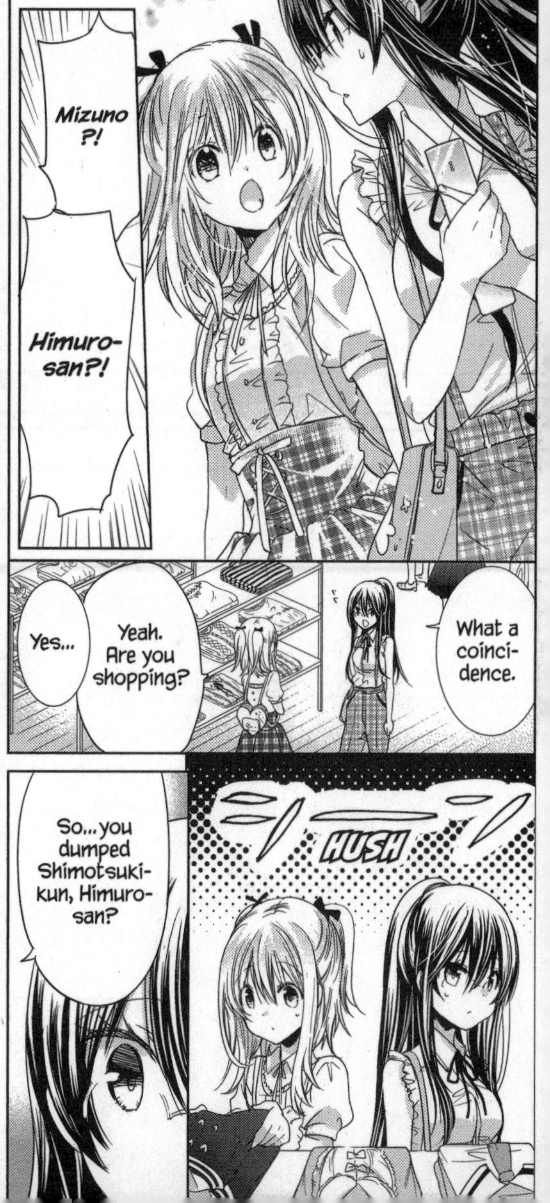
Ah...
Mizuno ?!
Himuro-san?!
What a coinci-dence.
Yeah. Are you shopping?
Yes...
HUSH
So...you dumped Shimotsuki-kun, Himuro-san?

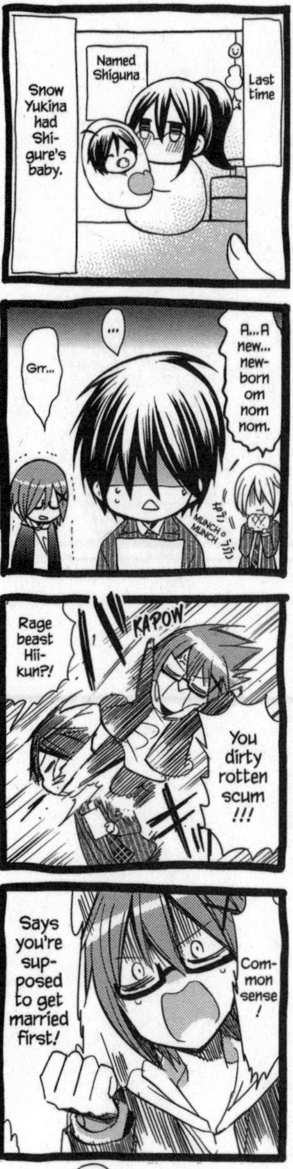
Last time
Named Shiguna
Snow Yukina had Shi-gure's baby.
A...A new... new-born om nom nom.
...
Grr...
MUNCH MUNCH
KAPOW
You dirty rotten scum !!!
Rage beast Hii-kun?!
Com-mon sense !
Says you're sup-posed to get married first!
How principled.

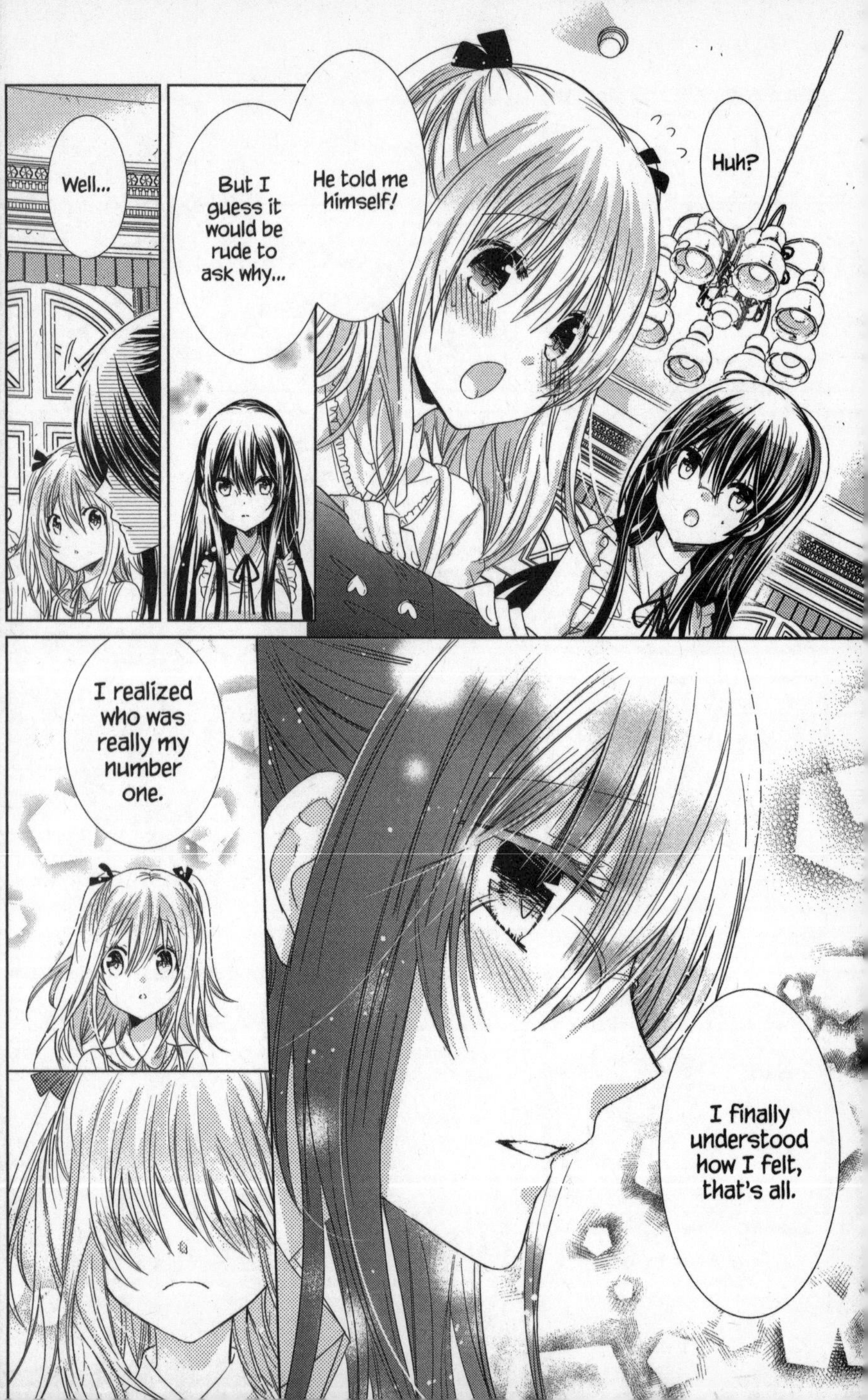
Huh?
He told me himself!
But I guess it would be rude to ask why...
Well...
I realized who was really my number one.
I finally understood how I felt, that's all.

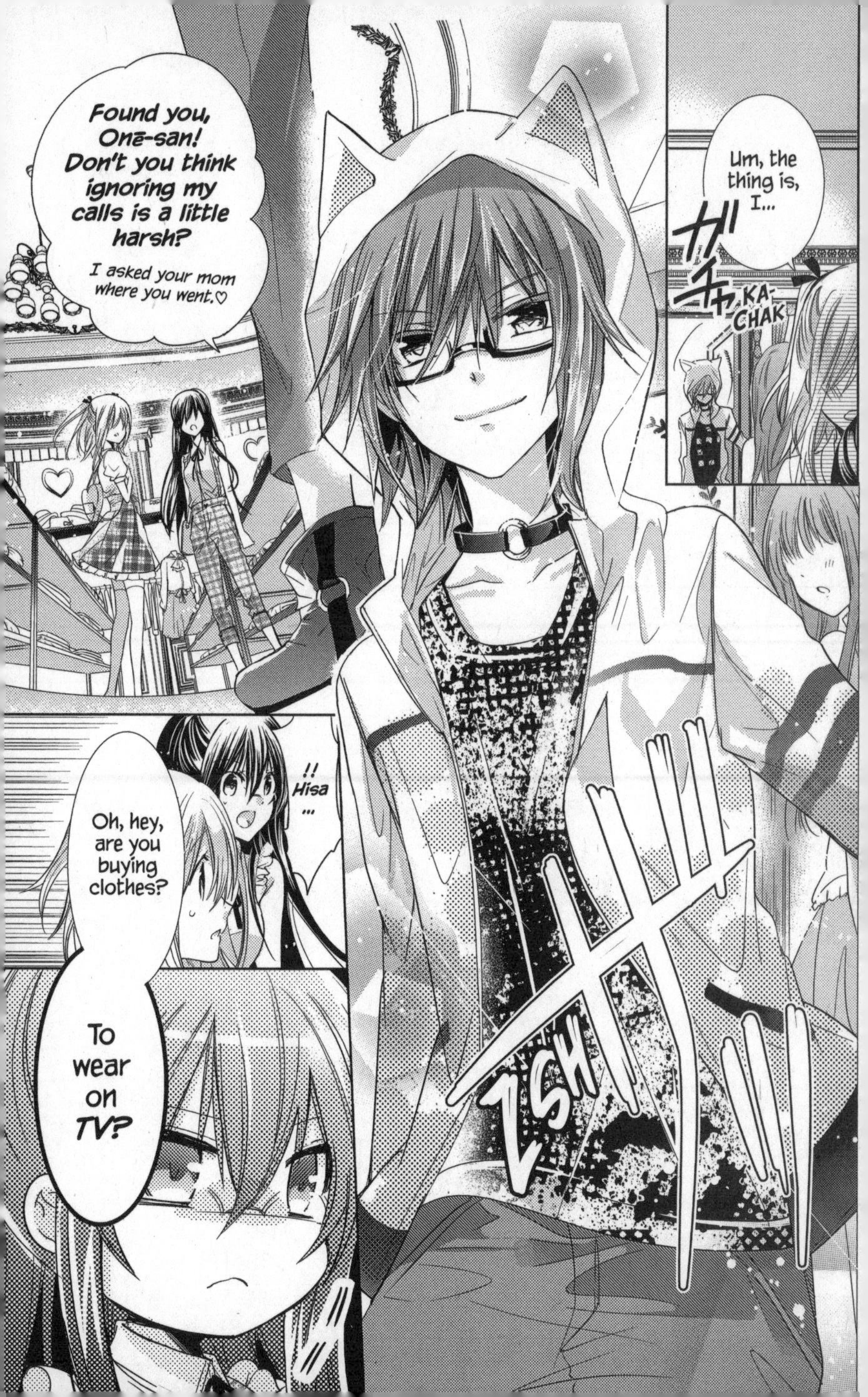

Um, the thing is, I...
ガチャ KA-CHAK
ZSH
Found you, One-san! Don't you think ignoring my calls is a little harsh?
I asked your mom where you went.♡
!! Hisa...
Oh, hey, are you buying clothes?
To wear on TV?

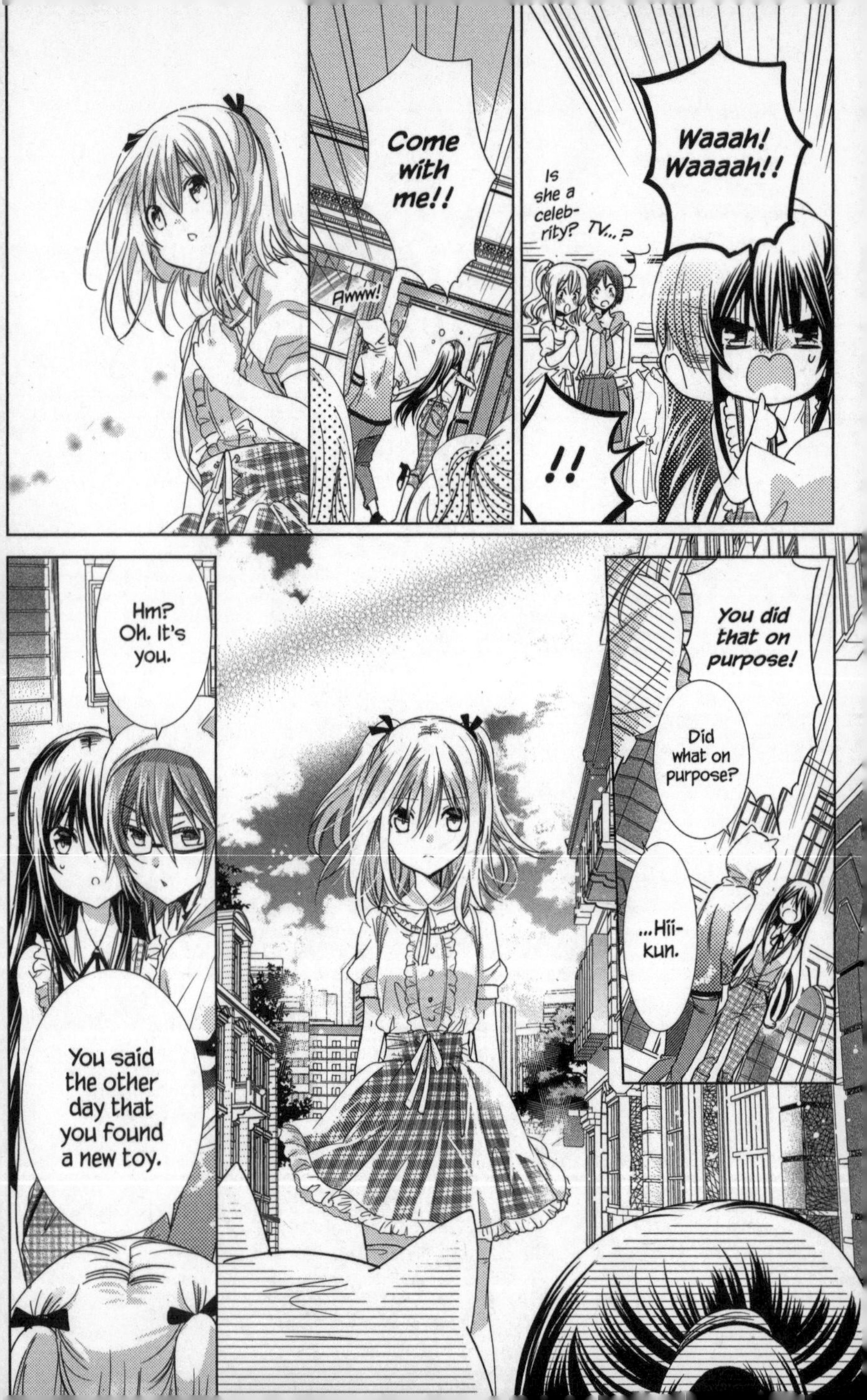
Waaah! Waaaah!!
Is she a celebrity? TV...?
!!
Come with me!!
Awww!
You did that on purpose!
Did what on purpose?
...Hii-kun.
Hm? Oh. It's you.
You said the other day that you found a new toy.

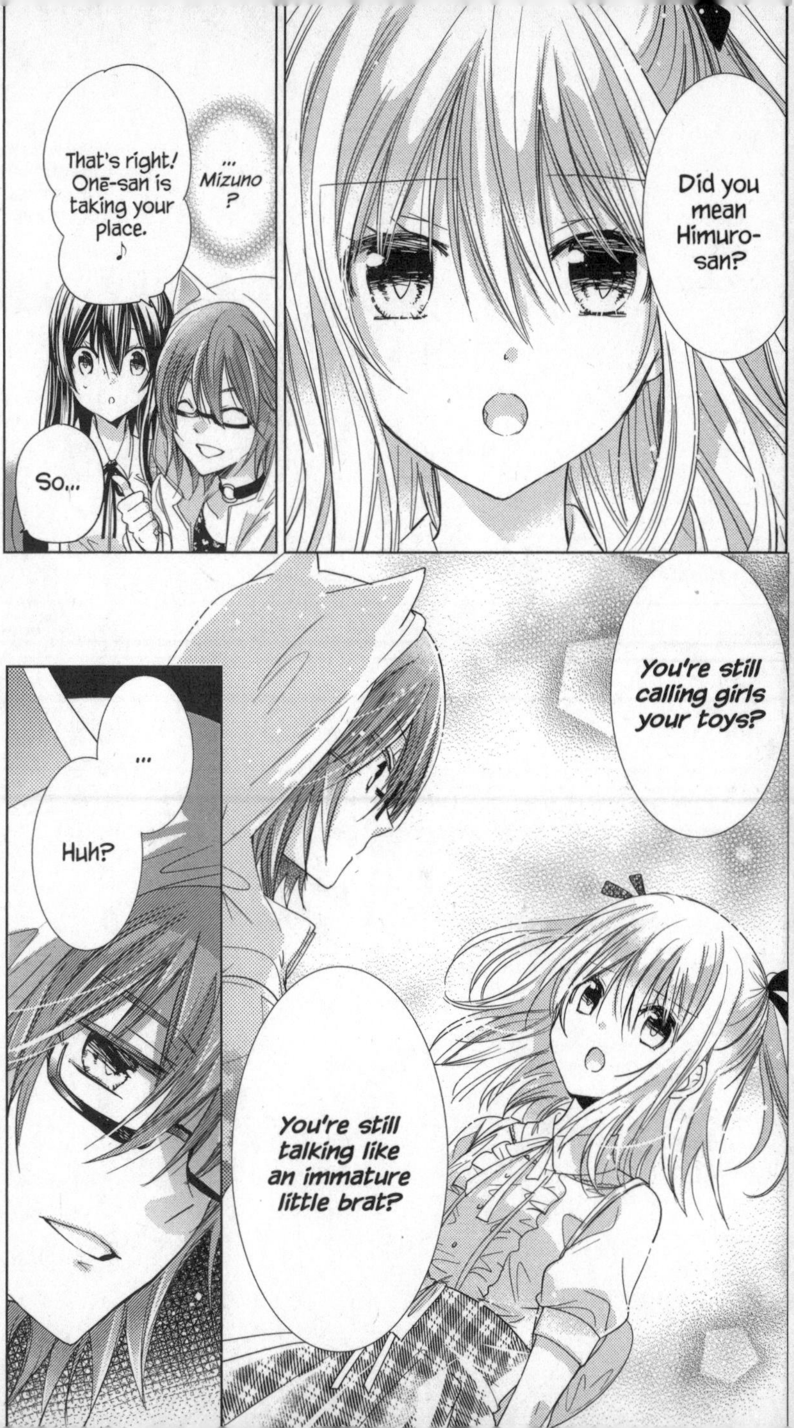
Did you mean Himuro-san?
... Mizuno?
That's right! One̅-san is taking your place. ♪
So...
You're still calling girls your toys?
...
Huh?
You're still talking like an immature little brat?

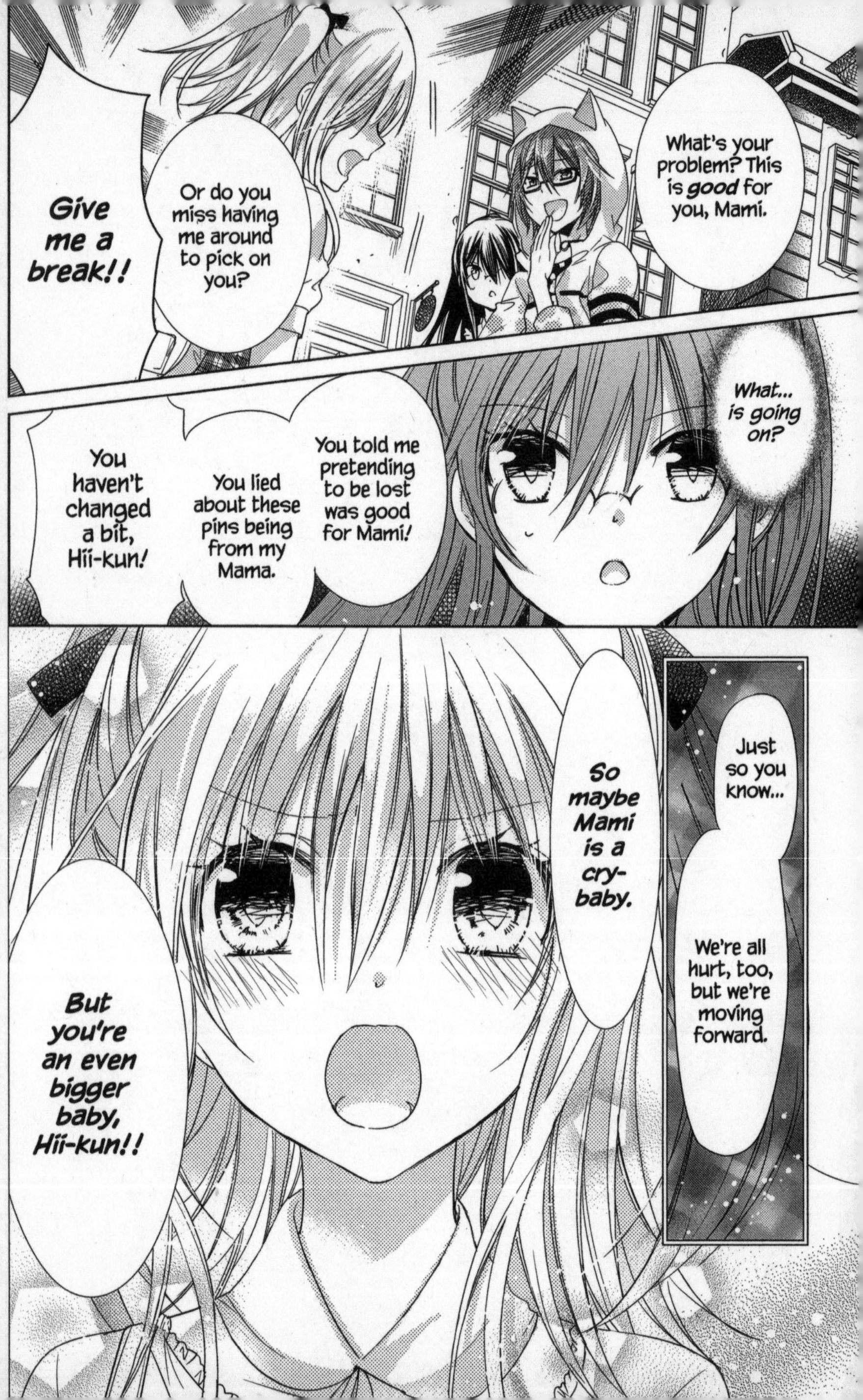
What's your problem? This is *good* for you, Mami.
Or do you miss having me around to pick on you?
Give me a break!!
What... is going on?
You told me pretending to be lost was good for Mami!
You lied about these pins being from my Mama.
You haven't changed a bit, Hii-kun!
Just so you know...
We're all hurt, too, but we're moving forward.
So maybe Mami is a cry-baby.
But you're an even bigger baby, Hii-kun!!

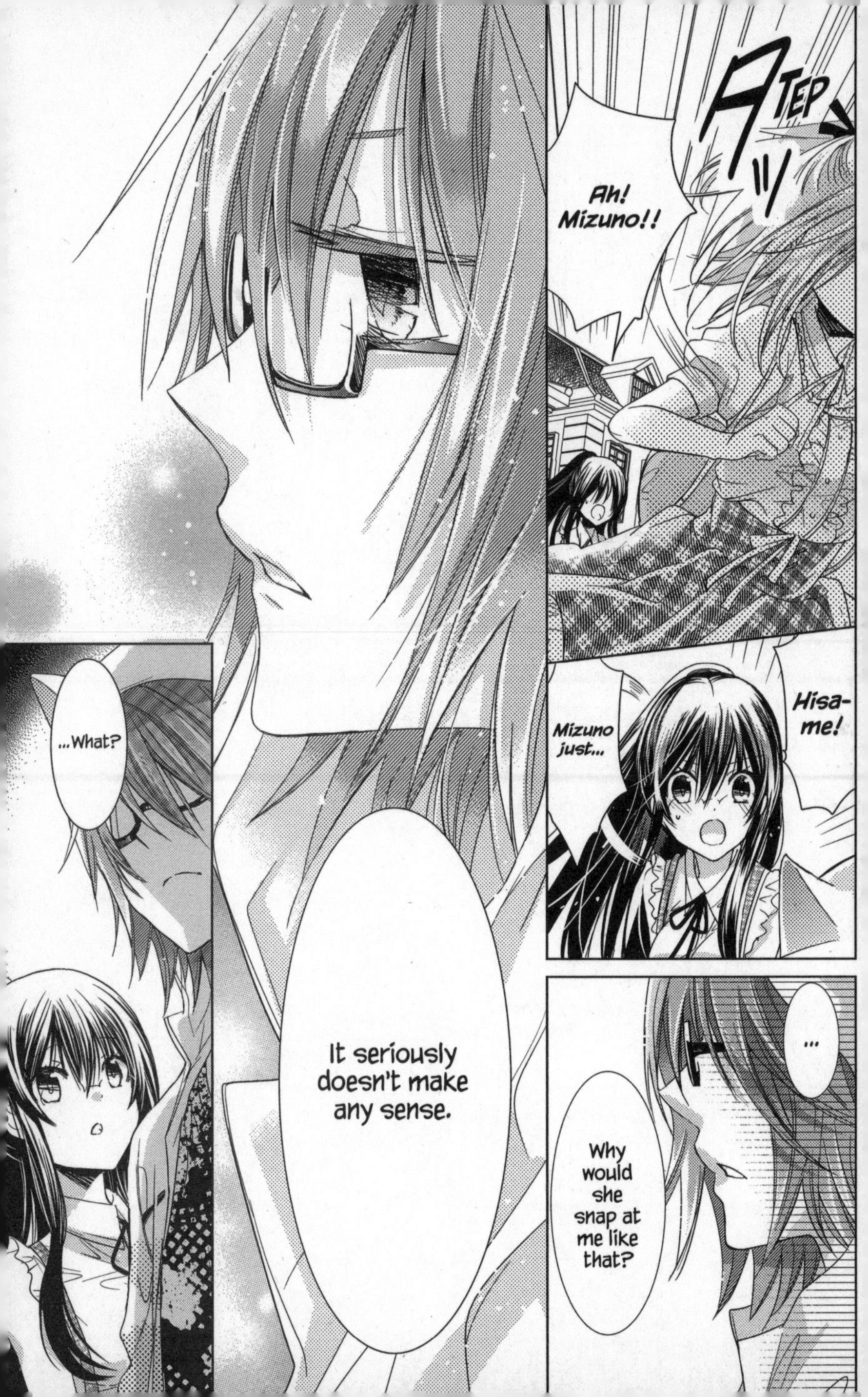
TEP
Ah! Mizuno!!
Hisa-me!
Mizuno just...
...
Why would she snap at me like that?
It seriously doesn't make any sense.
...What?

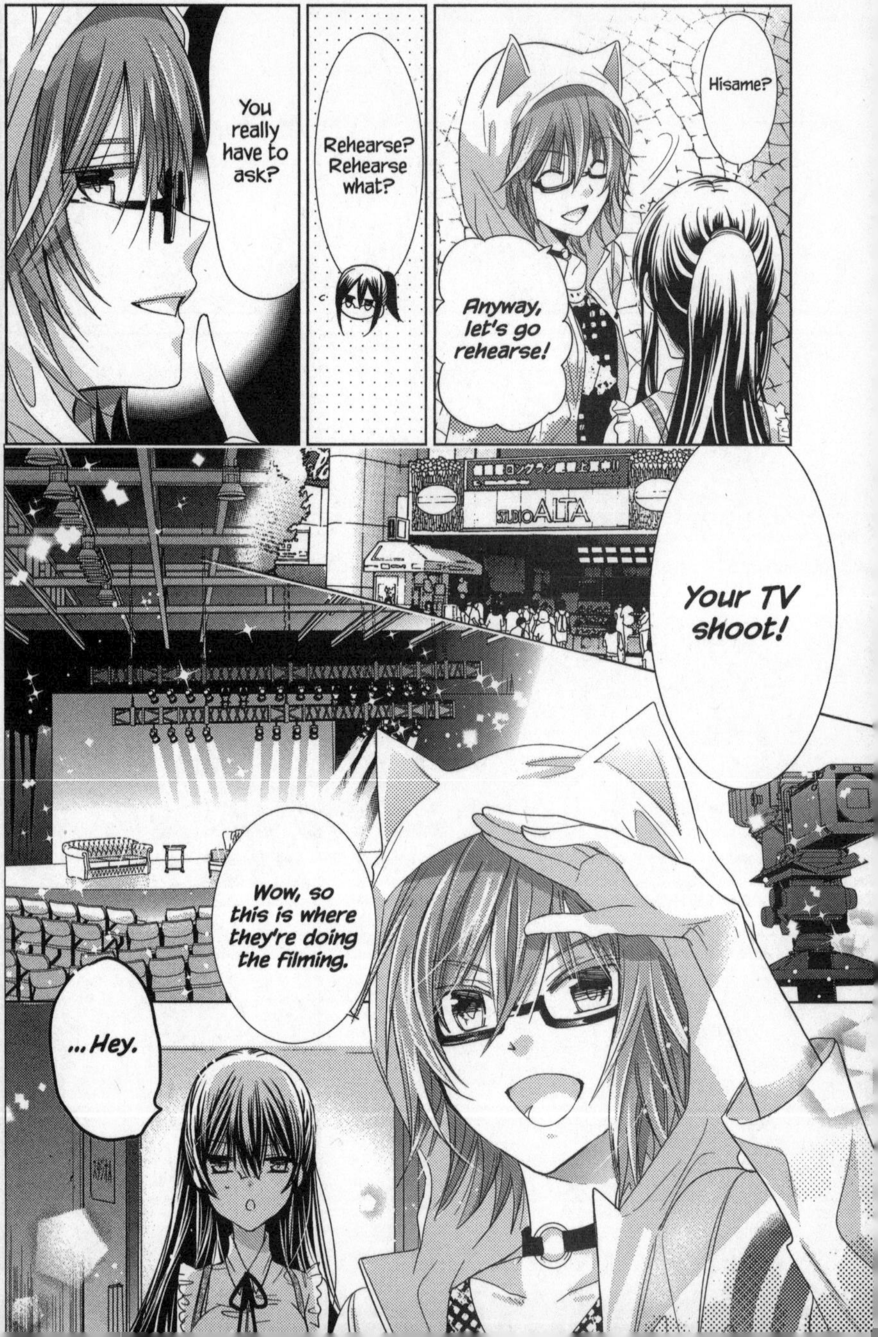
Hisame?
Anyway, let's go rehearse!
Rehearse? Rehearse what?
You really have to ask?
STUDIO ALTA
Your TV shoot!
Wow, so this is where they're doing the filming.
...Hey.

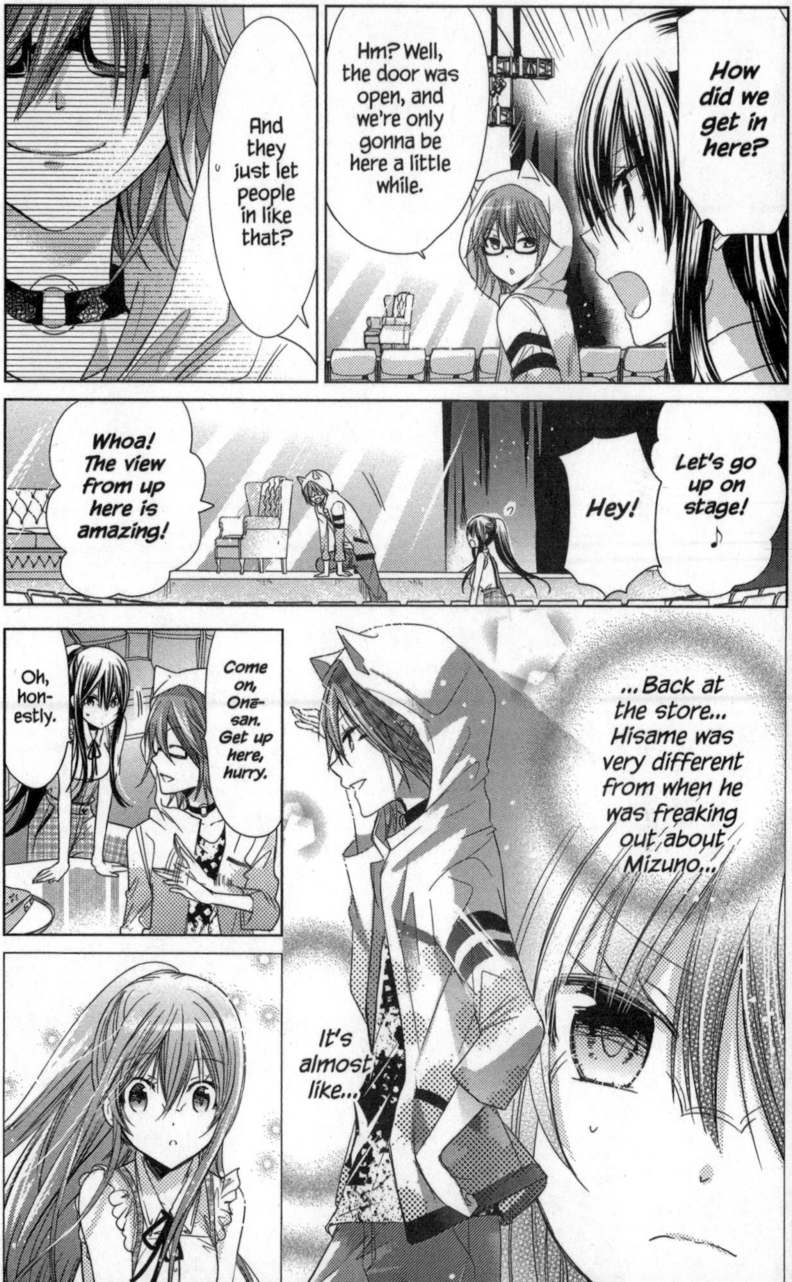
How did we get in here?
Hm? Well, the door was open, and we're only gonna be here a little while.
And they just let people in like that?
Let's go up on stage! ♪
Hey!
Whoa! The view from up here is amazing!
...Back at the store... Hisame was very different from when he was freaking out about Mizuno...
Come on, One-san. Get up here, hurry.
Oh, hon-estly.
It's almost like...

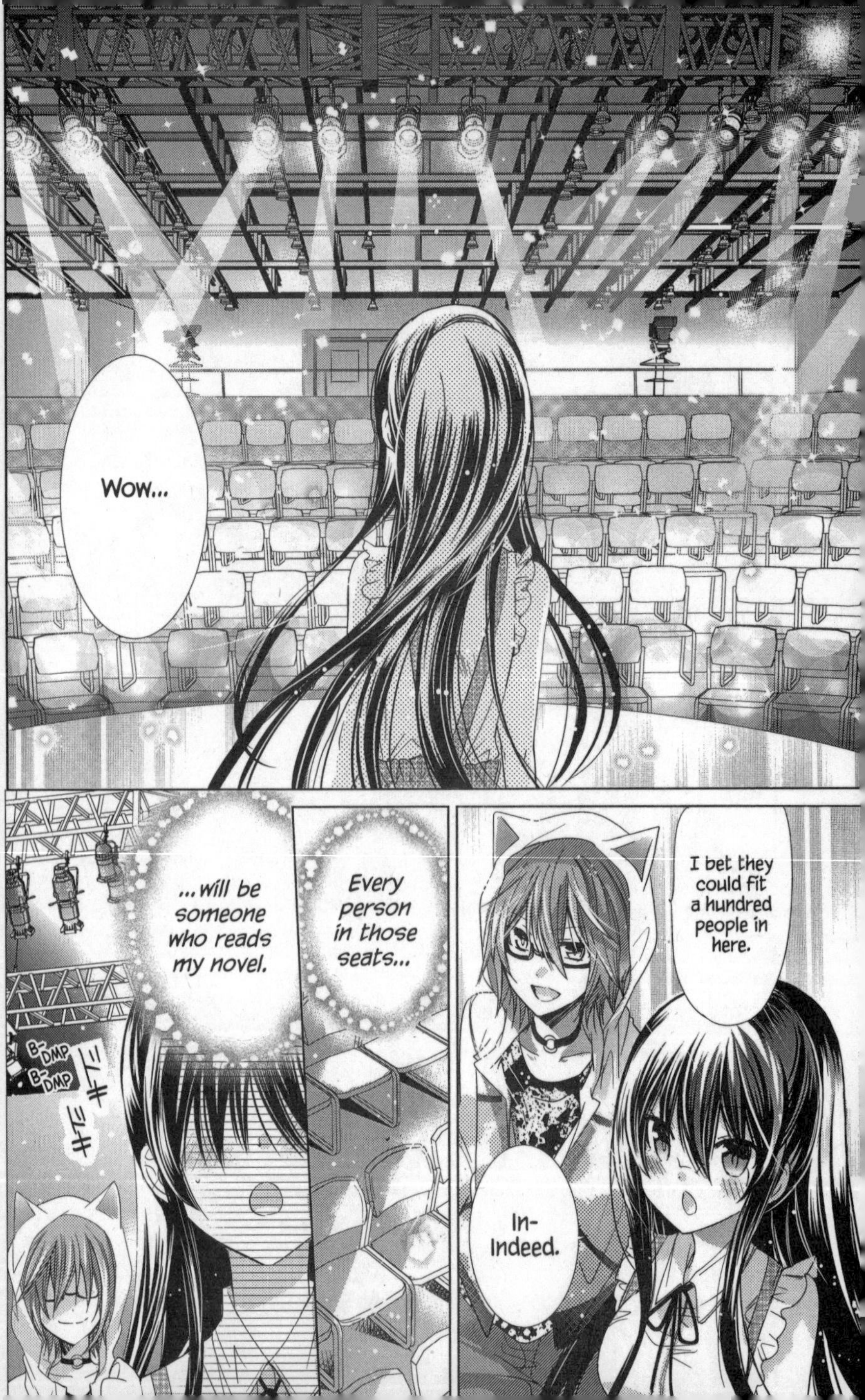
Wow...
I bet they could fit a hundred people in here.
In- Indeed.
Every person in those seats...
...will be someone who reads my novel.
B-DMP
B-DMP

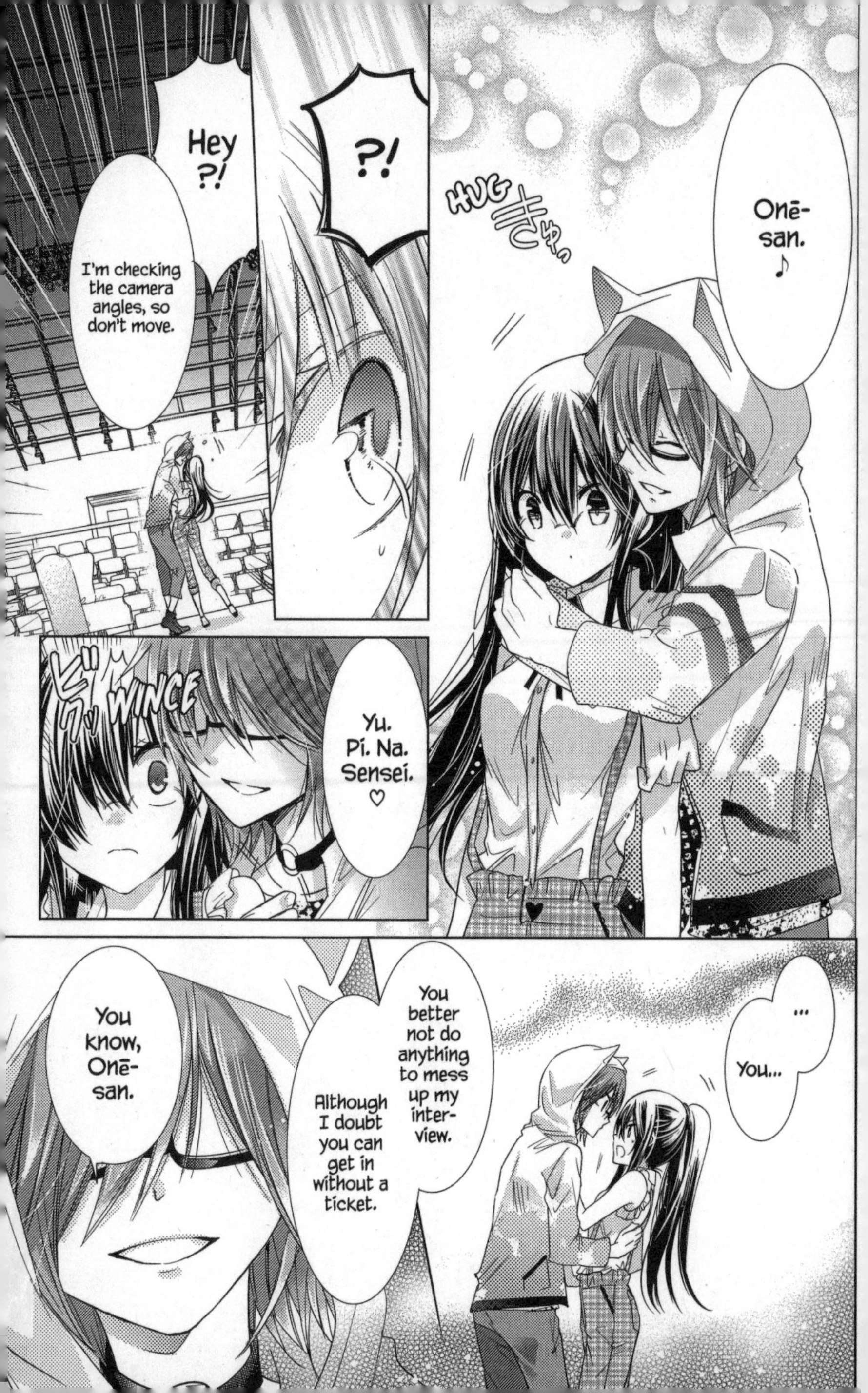
Onē-san. ♪
HUG きゅっ
?!
Hey ?!
I'm checking the camera angles, so don't move.
ビクッ WINCE
Yu. Pi. Na. Sensei. ♡
...
You...
You better not do anything to mess up my inter-view.
Although I doubt you can get in without a ticket.
You know, Onē-san.

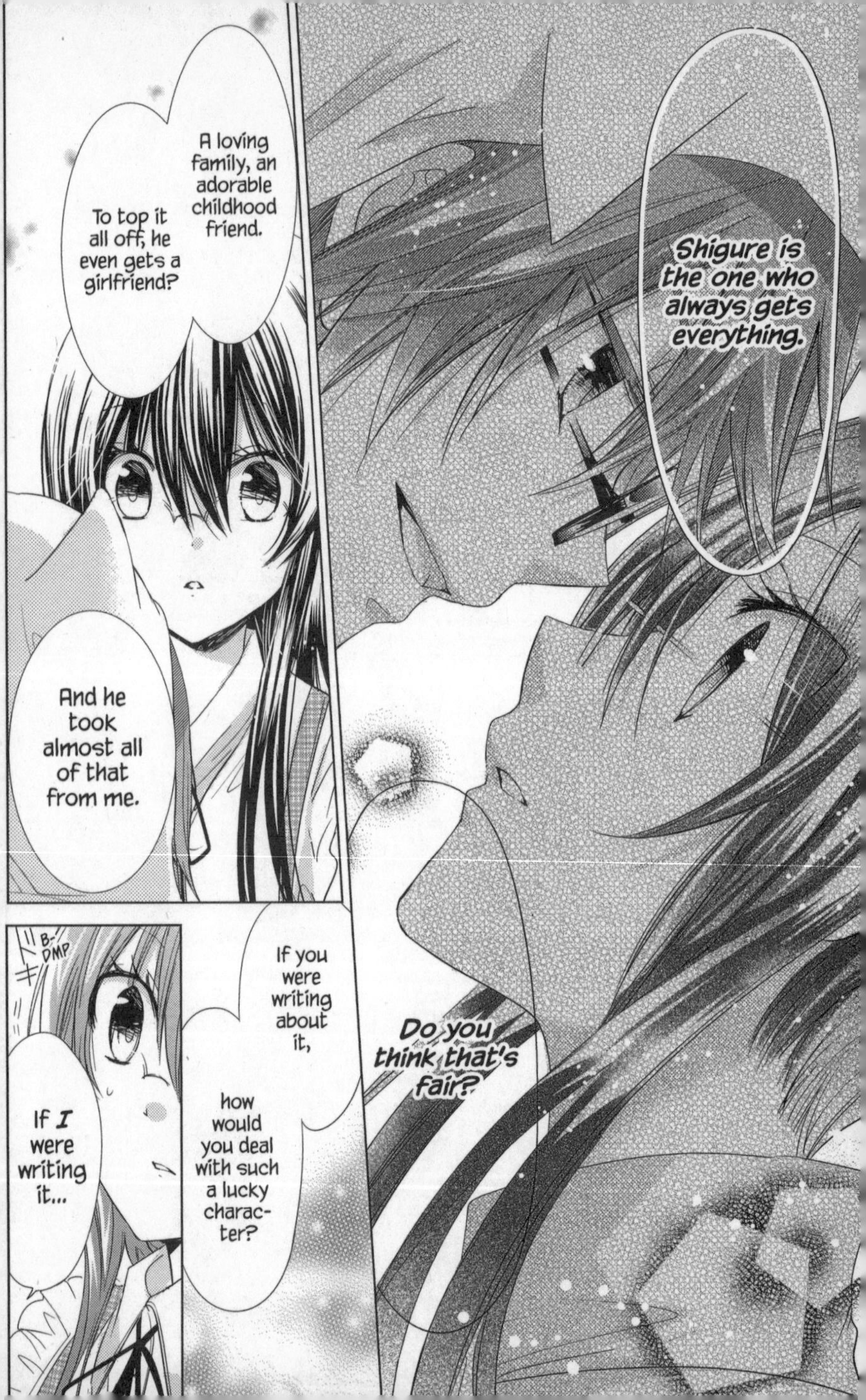
Shigure is the one who always gets everything.
Do you think that's fair?
A loving family, an adorable childhood friend.
To top it all off, he even gets a girlfriend?
And he took almost all of that from me.
If you were writing about it,
how would you deal with such a lucky character?
B-DMP
If *I* were writing it...

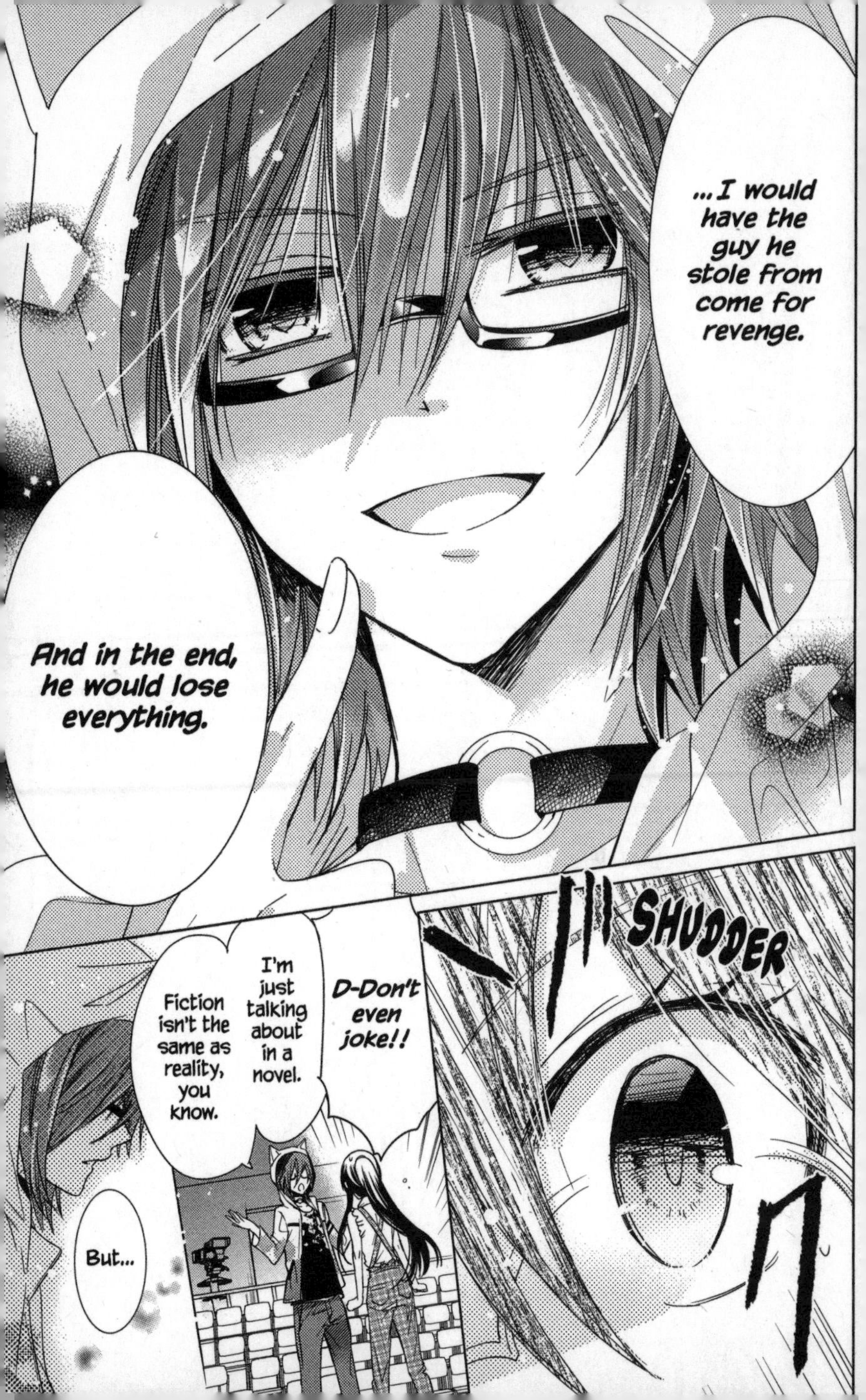

...I would have the guy he stole from come for revenge.
And in the end, he would lose everything.
SHUDDER
D-Don't even joke!!
I'm just talking about in a novel.
Fiction isn't the same as reality, you know.
But...

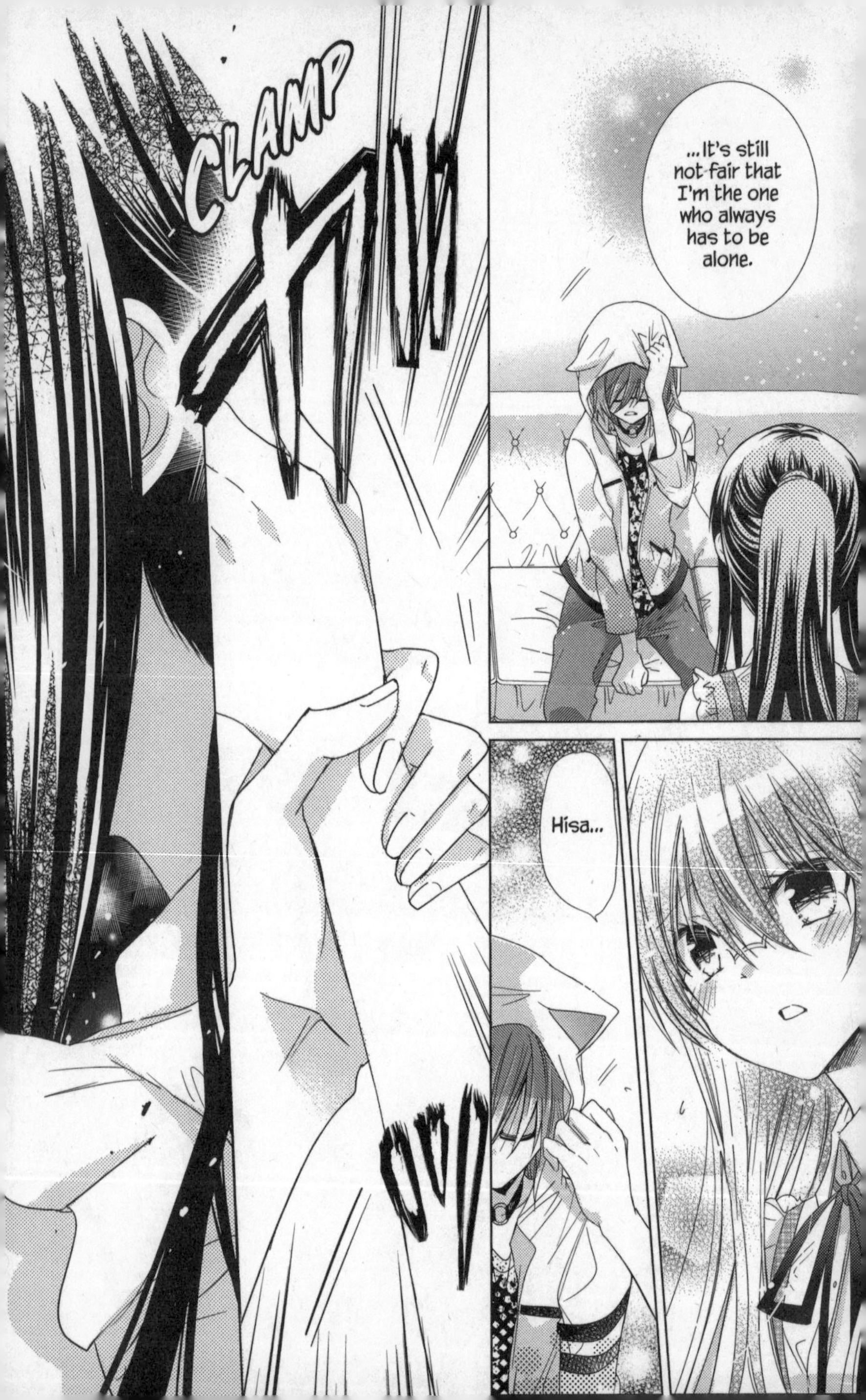
...It's still not fair that I'm the one who always has to be alone.
Hisa...
CLAMP

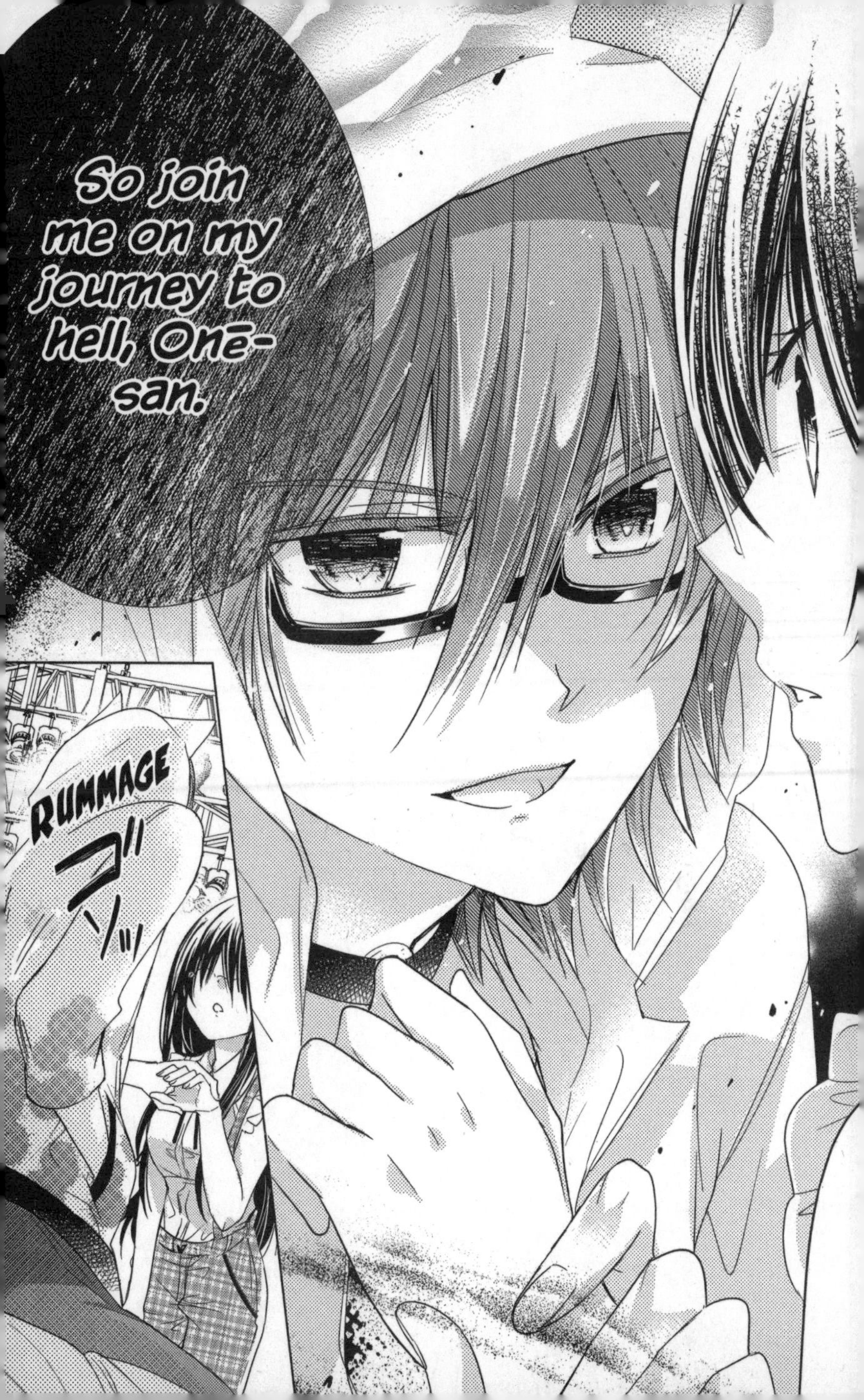
So join me on my journey to hell, Onē-san.
RUMMAGE
ゴソッ

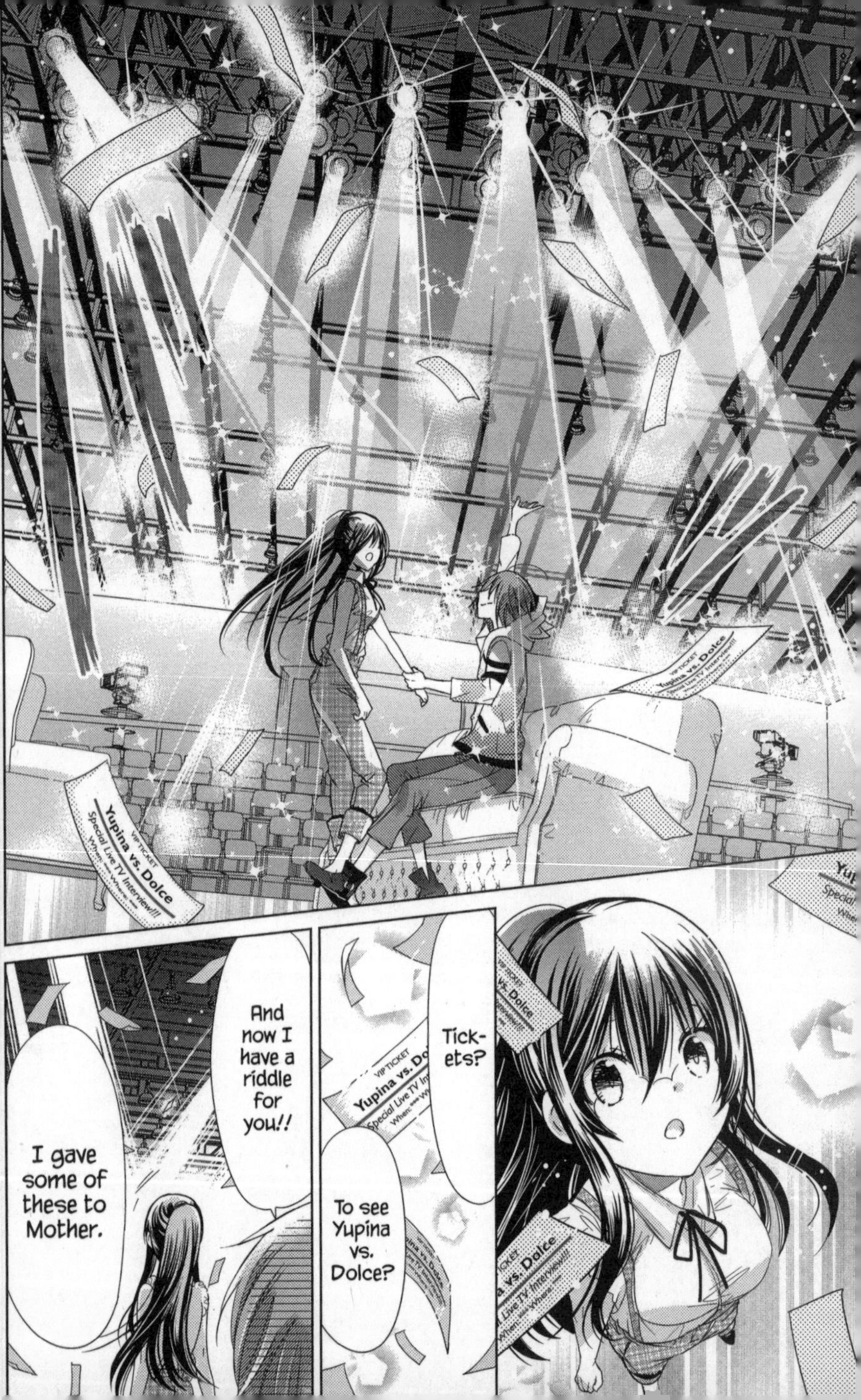
VIP TICKET
Yupina vs. Dolce
Special Live TV Interview!!!
Tick-ets?
To see Yupina vs. Dolce?
And now I have a riddle for you!!
I gave some of these to Mother.

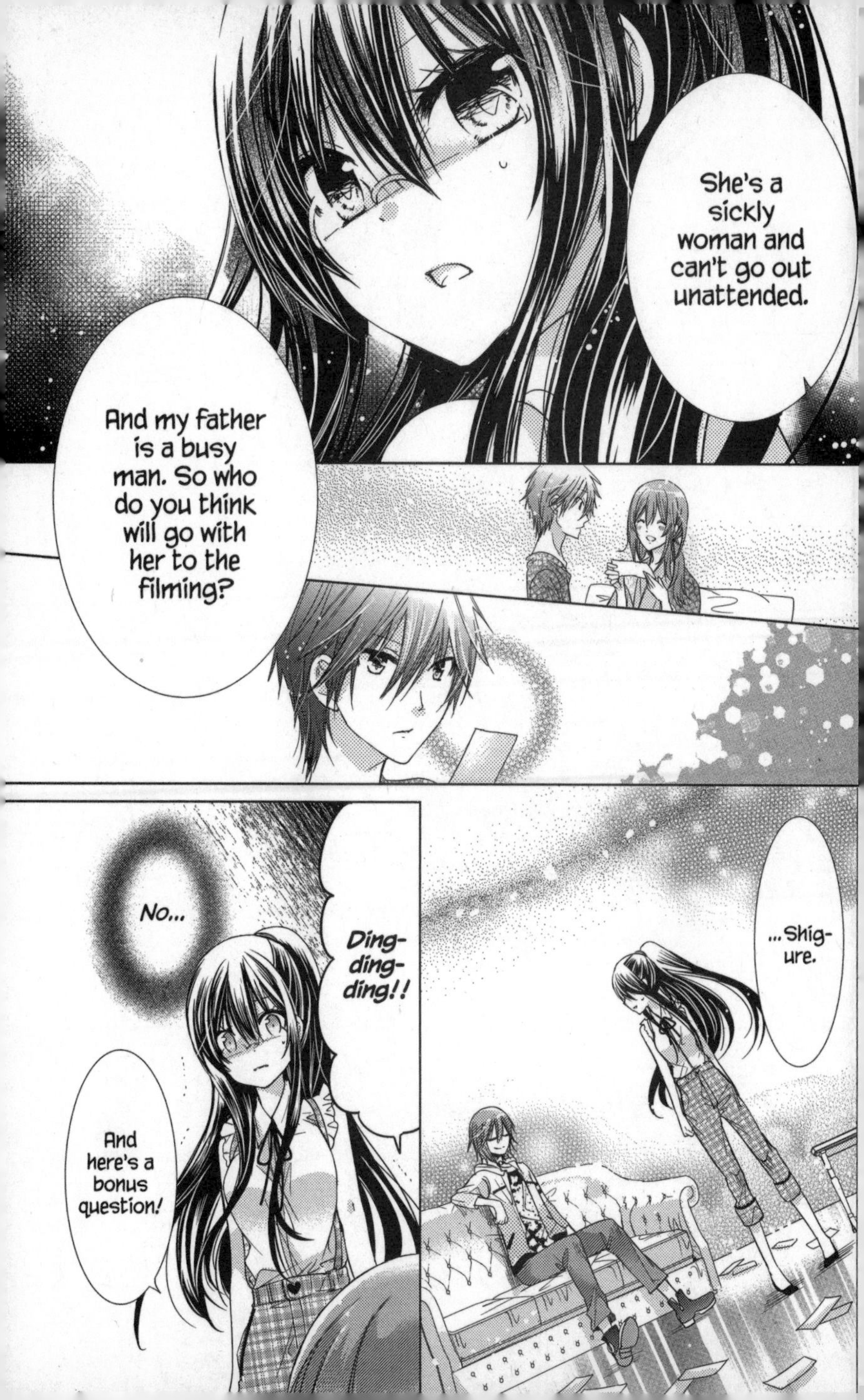
She's a sickly woman and can't go out unattended.
And my father is a busy man. So who do you think will go with her to the filming?
...Shig-ure.
Ding-ding-ding!!
No...
And here's a bonus question!

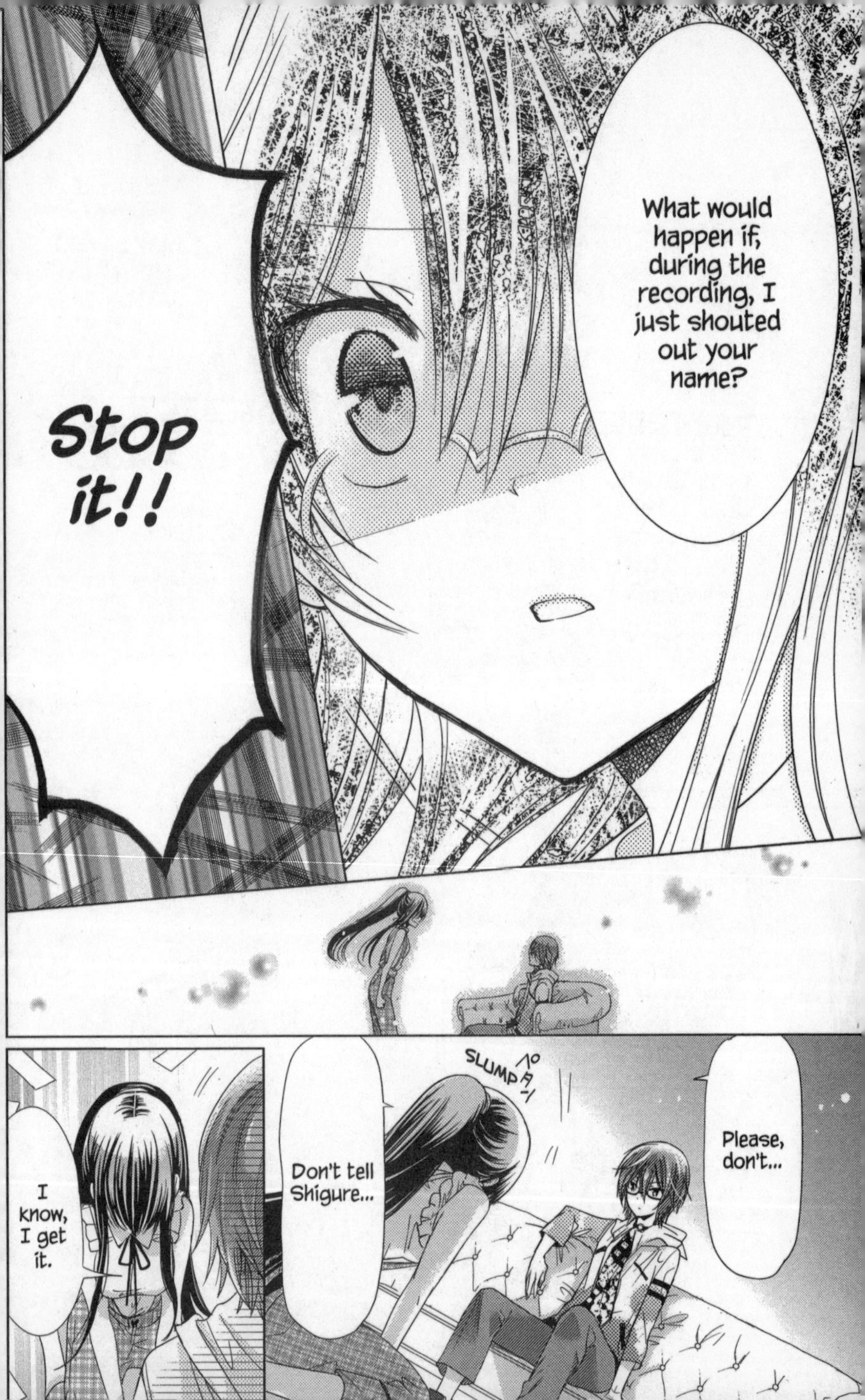
What would happen if, during the recording, I just shouted out your name?
Stop it!!
Please, don't...
SLUMP
Don't tell Shigure...
I know, I get it.

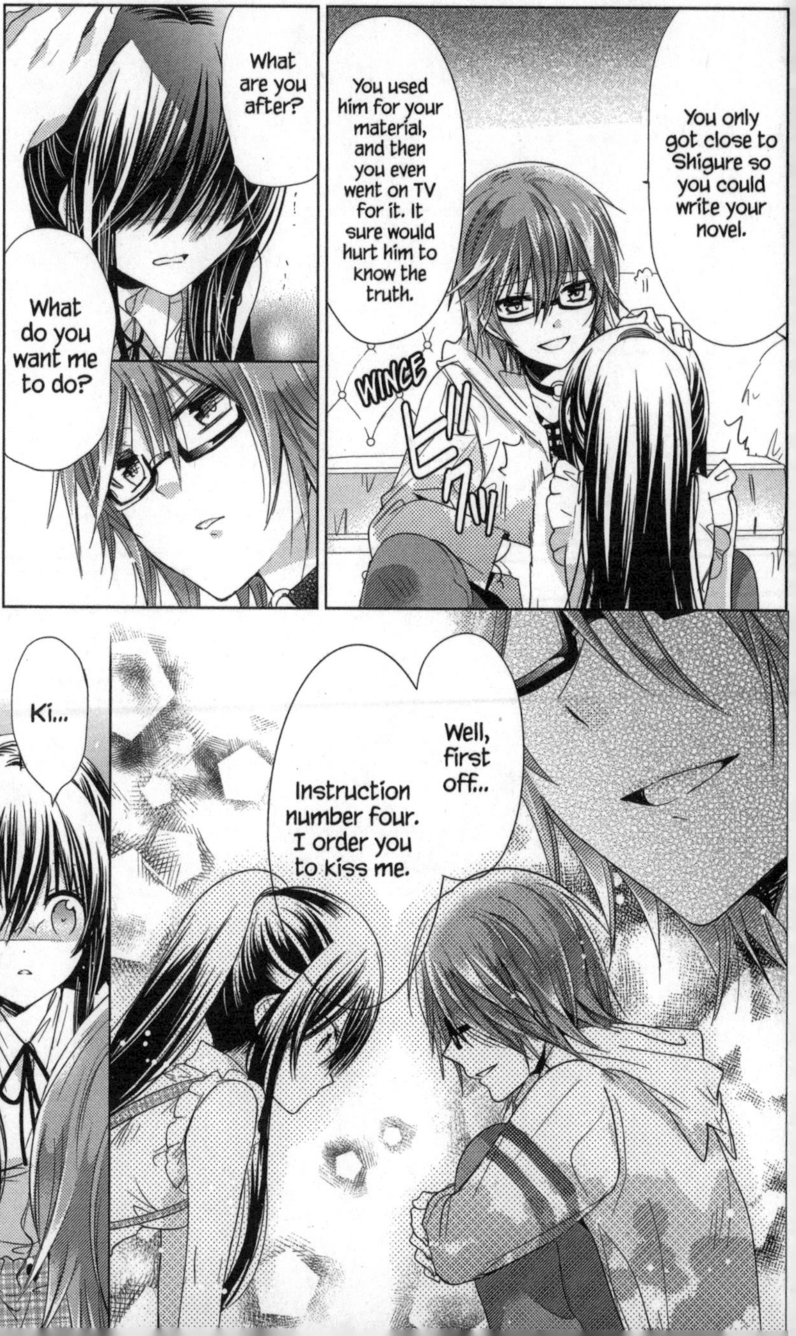
You only got close to Shigure so you could write your novel.
You used him for your material, and then you even went on TV for it. It sure would hurt him to know the truth.
WINCE
What are you after?
What do you want me to do?
Well, first off...
Instruction number four. I order you to kiss me.
Ki...

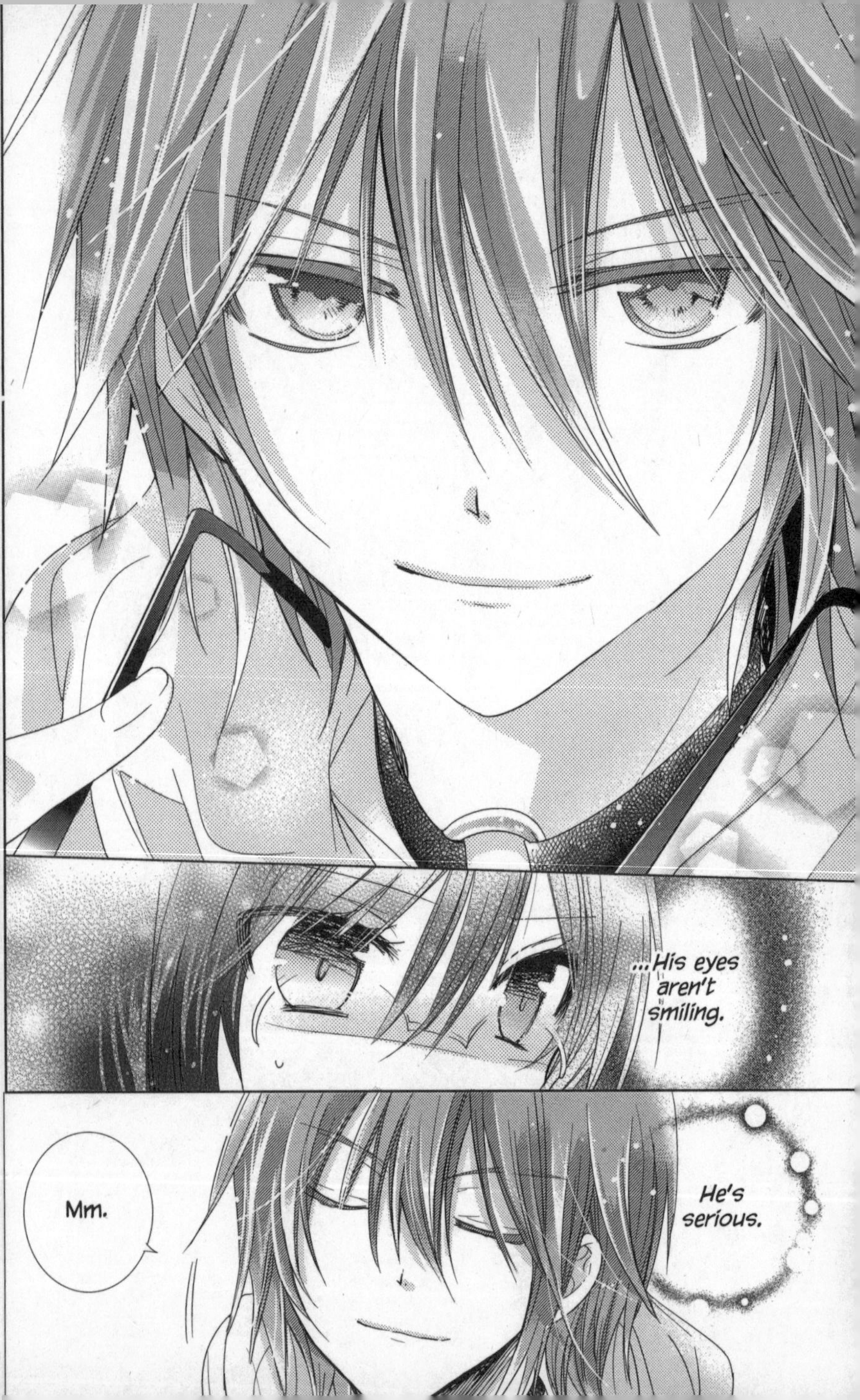
...His eyes aren't smiling.
He's serious.
Mm.

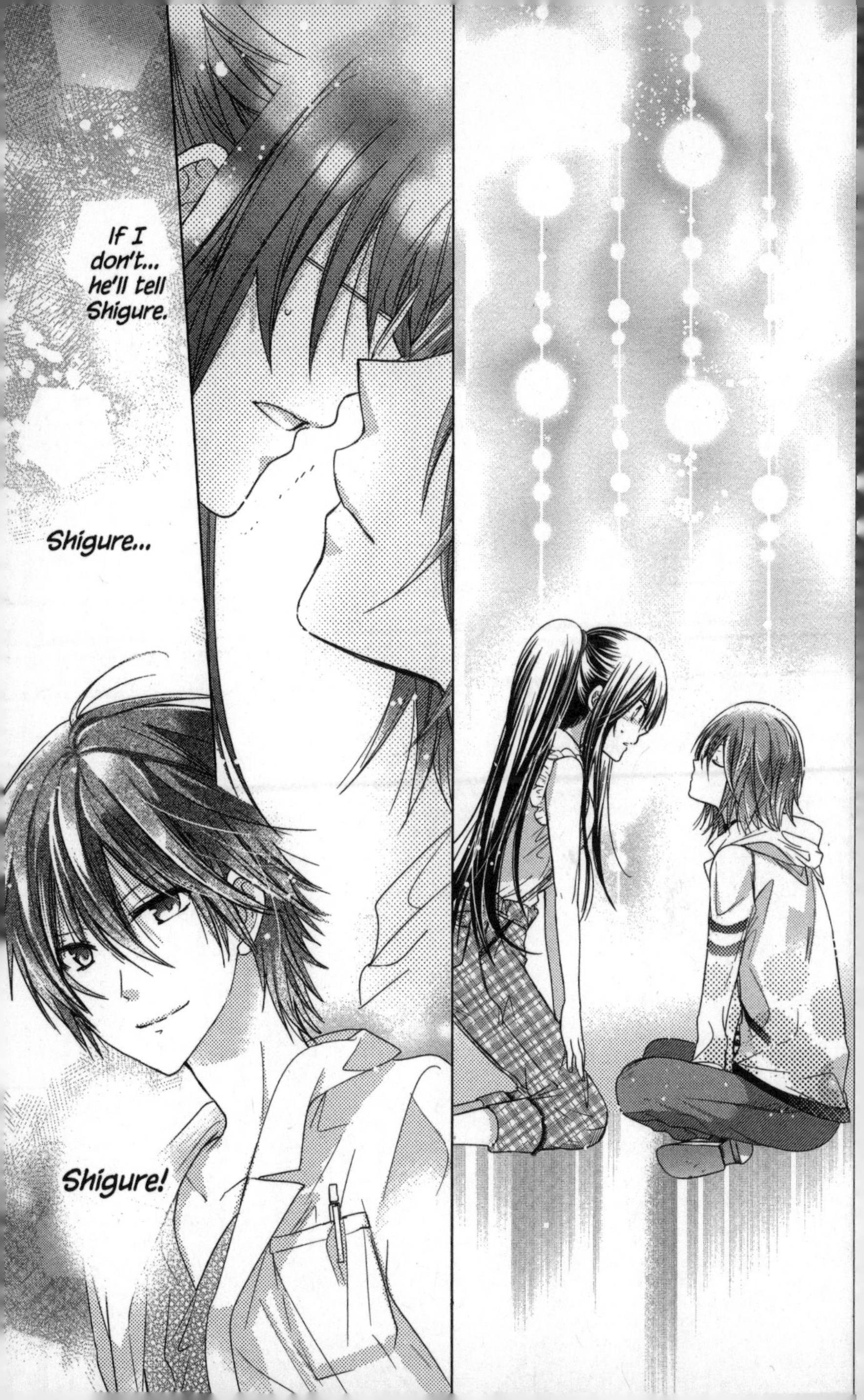
If I don't... he'll tell Shigure.
Shigure...
Shigure!

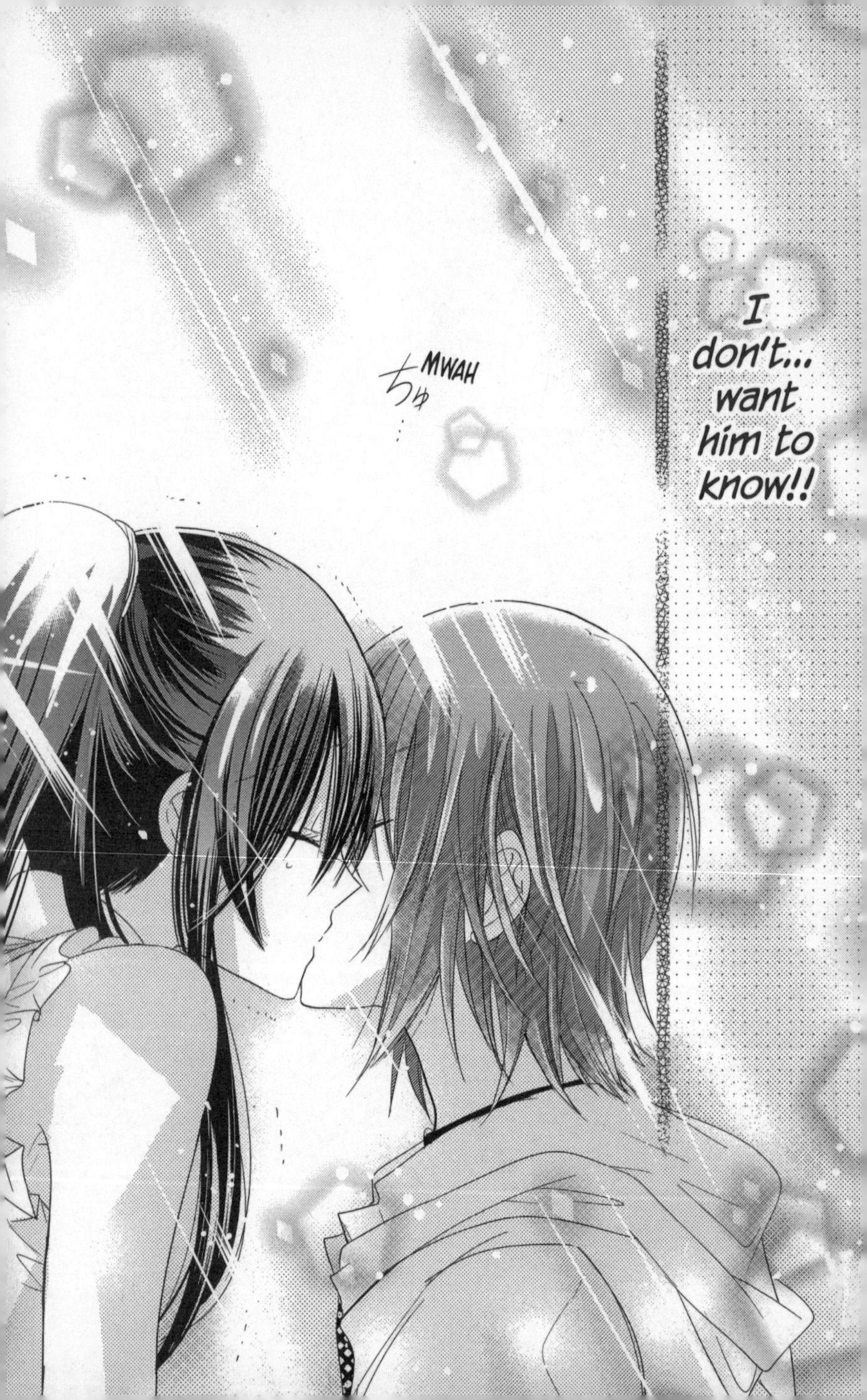
I don't... want him to know!!
ちゅ MWAH

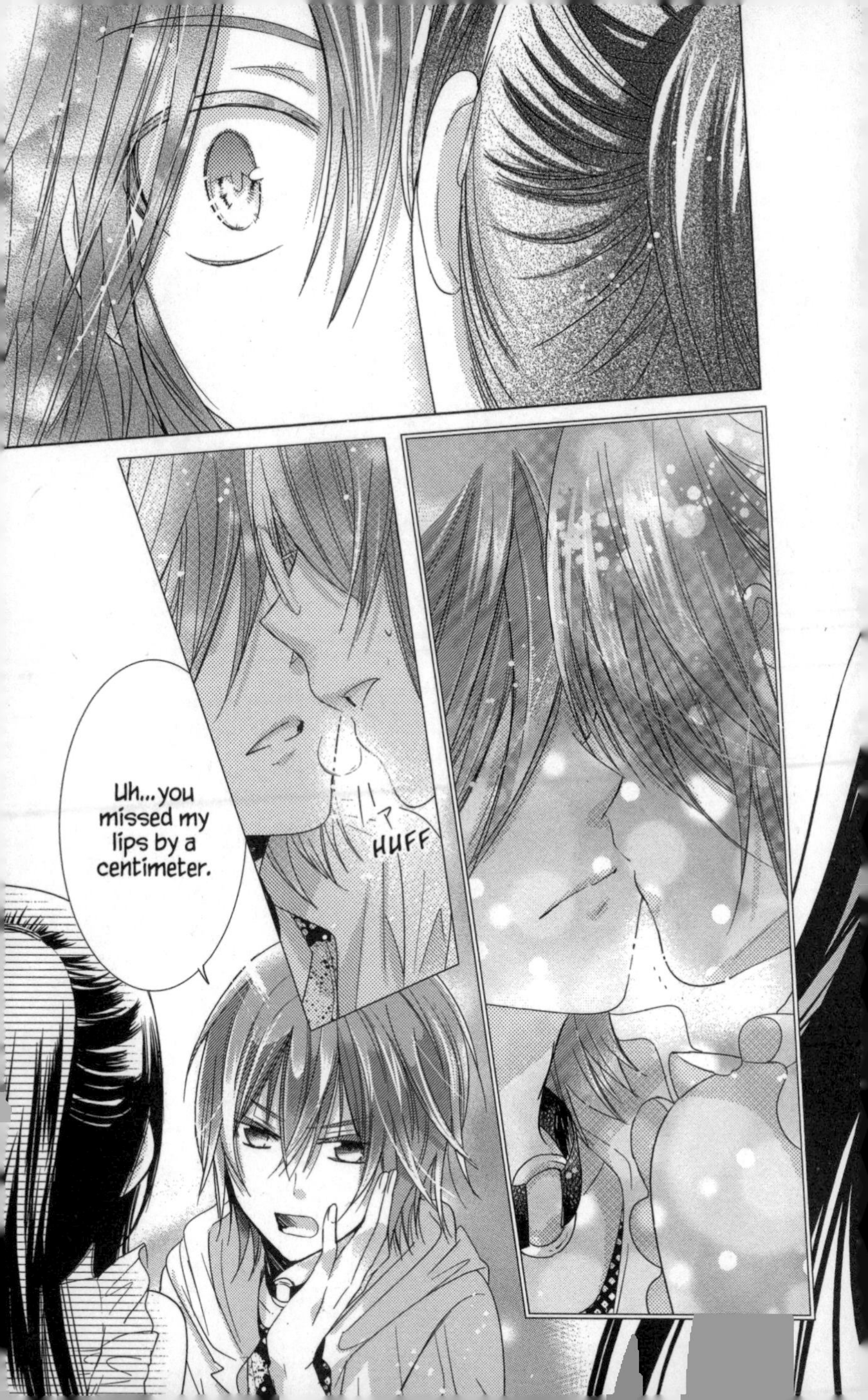
HUFF
Uh...you missed my lips by a centimeter.

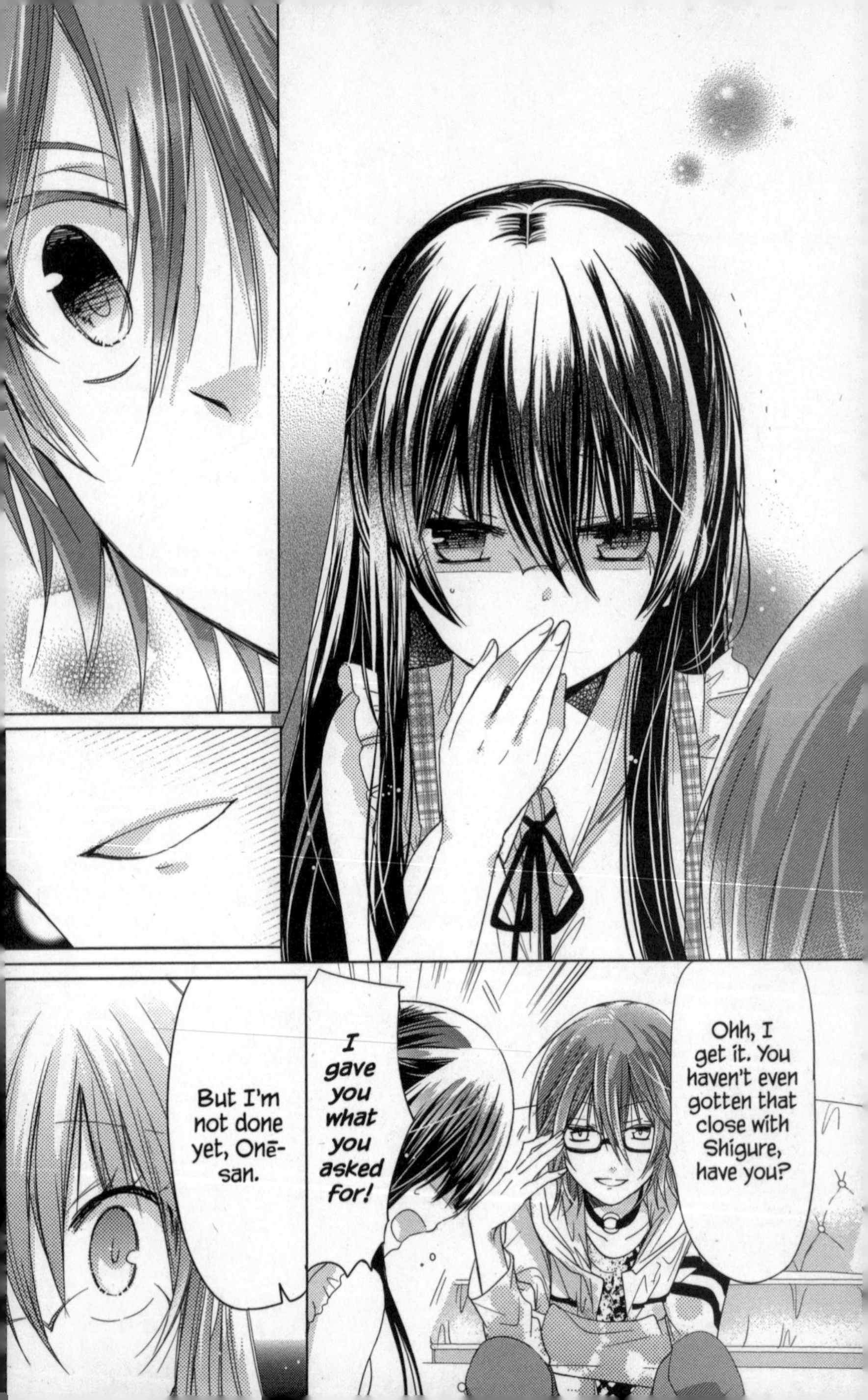
Ohh, I get it. You haven't even gotten that close with Shigure, have you?
I gave you what you asked for!
But I'm not done yet, Onē-san.

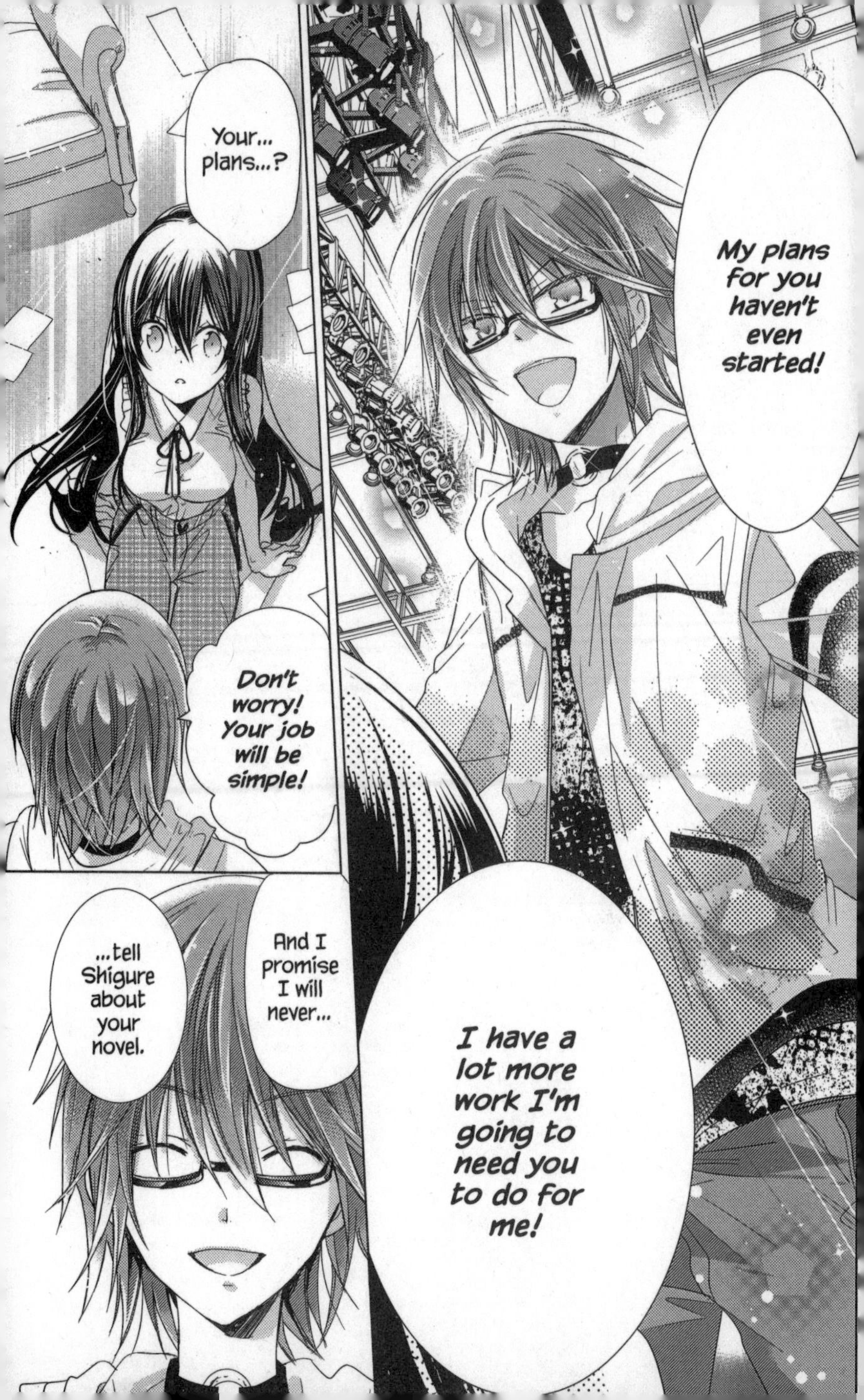
My plans for you haven't even started!
I have a lot more work I'm going to need you to do for me!
Your... plans...?
Don't worry! Your job will be simple!
And I promise I will never...
...tell Shigure about your novel.

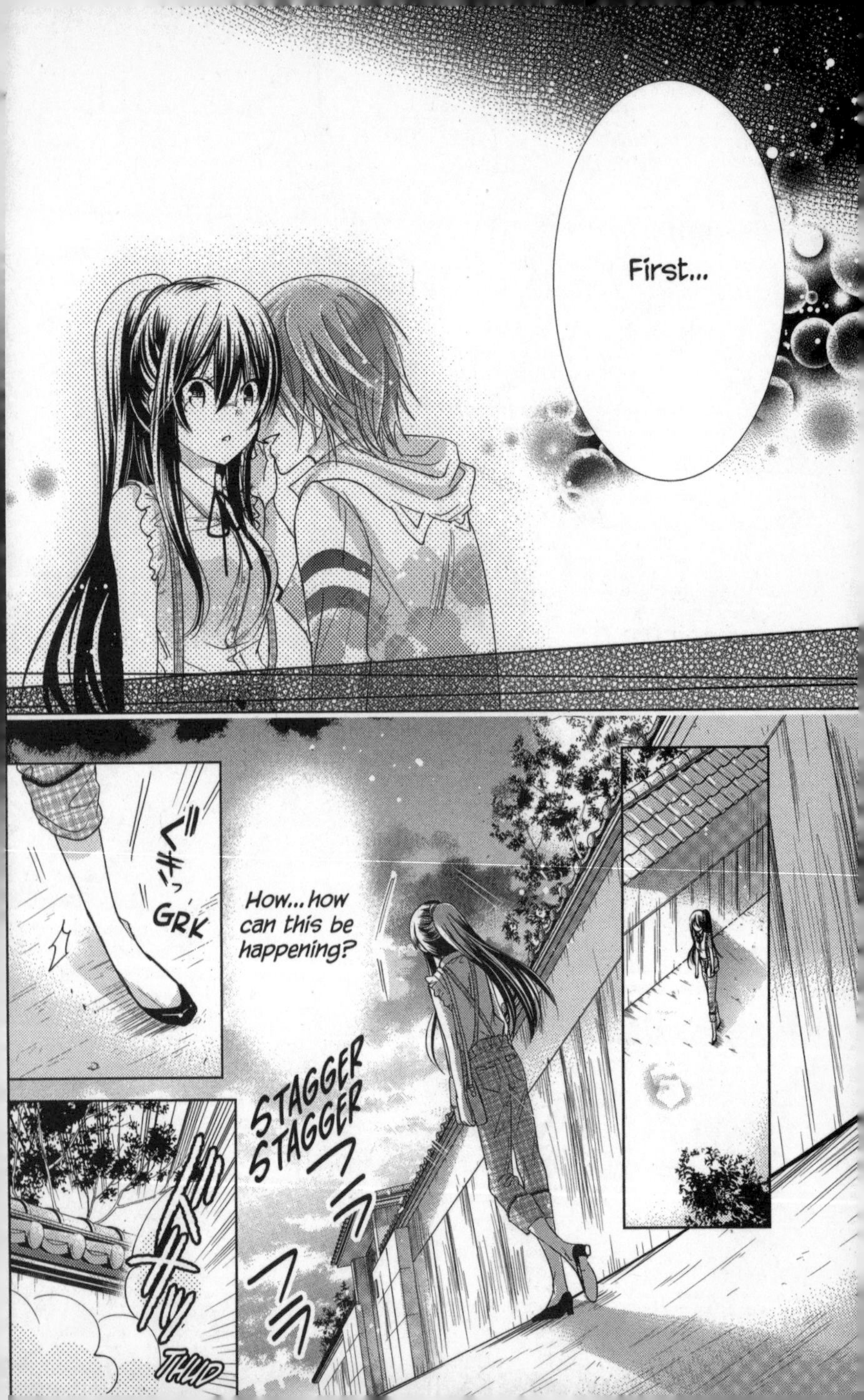
First...
How...how can this be happening?
STAGGER STAGGER
GRK
THUD

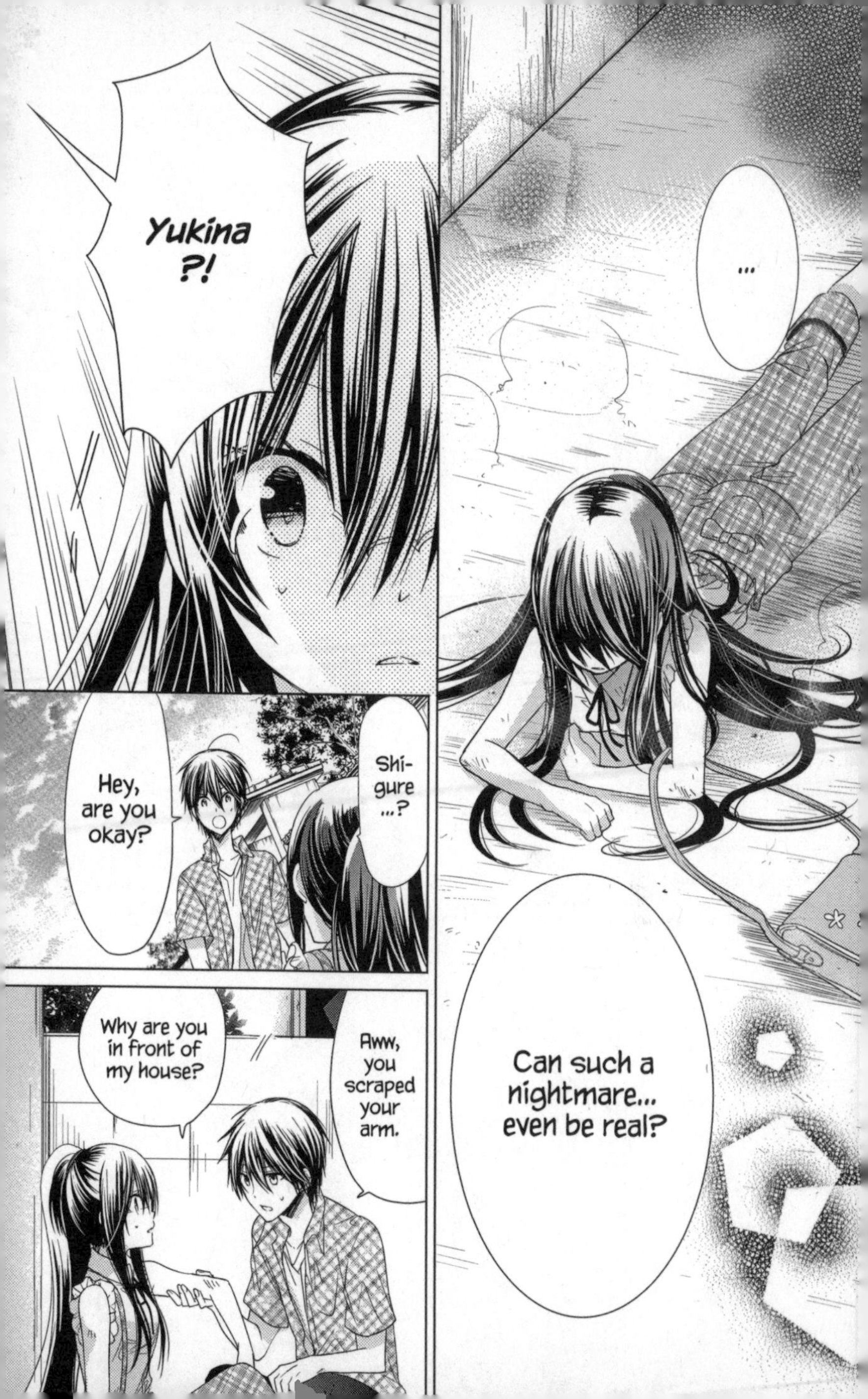
...
Can such a nightmare... even be real?
Yukina ?!
Shi-gure ...?
Hey, are you okay?
Aww, you scraped your arm.
Why are you in front of my house?

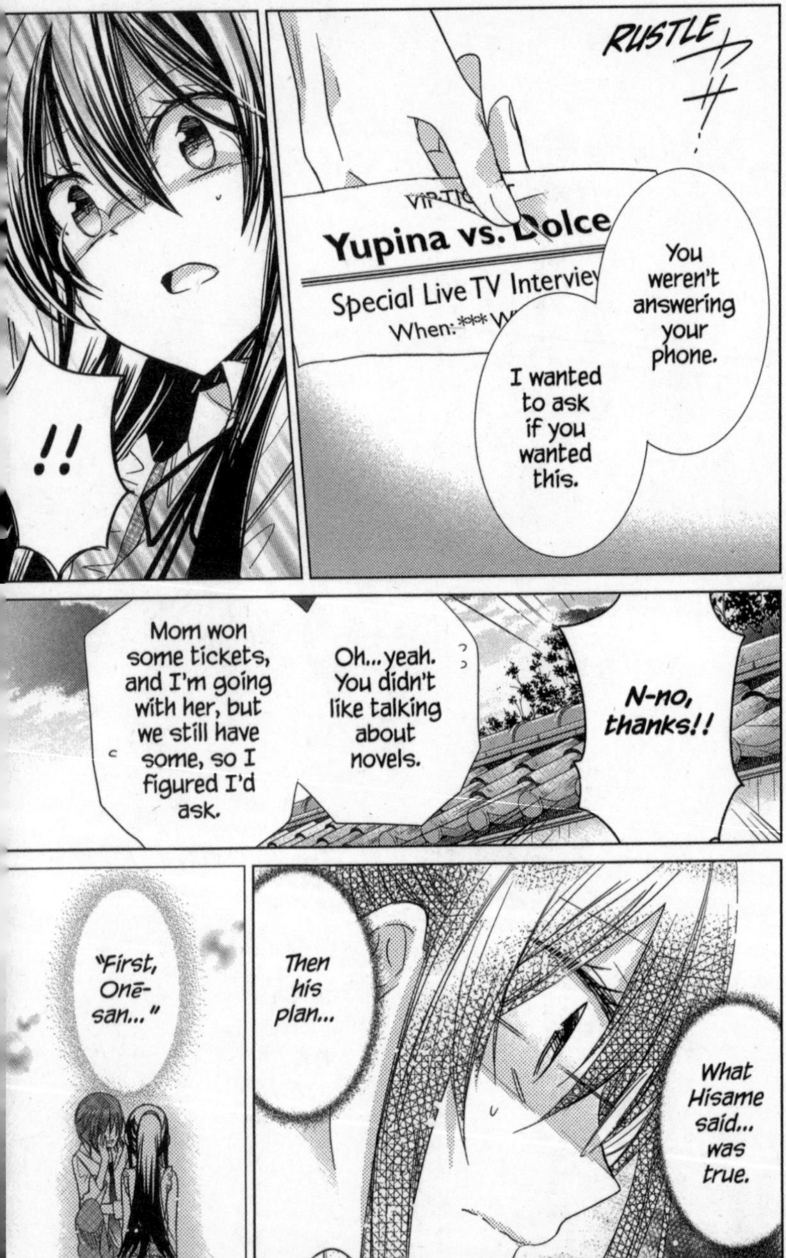
RUSTLE
VIPTIC
Yupina vs. Dolce
Special Live TV Intervie
When: *** W
You weren't answering your phone.
I wanted to ask if you wanted this.
!!
N-no, thanks!!
Oh...yeah. You didn't like talking about novels.
Mom won some tickets, and I'm going with her, but we still have some, so I figured I'd ask.
What Hisame said... was true.
Then his plan...
"First, Onē-san..."

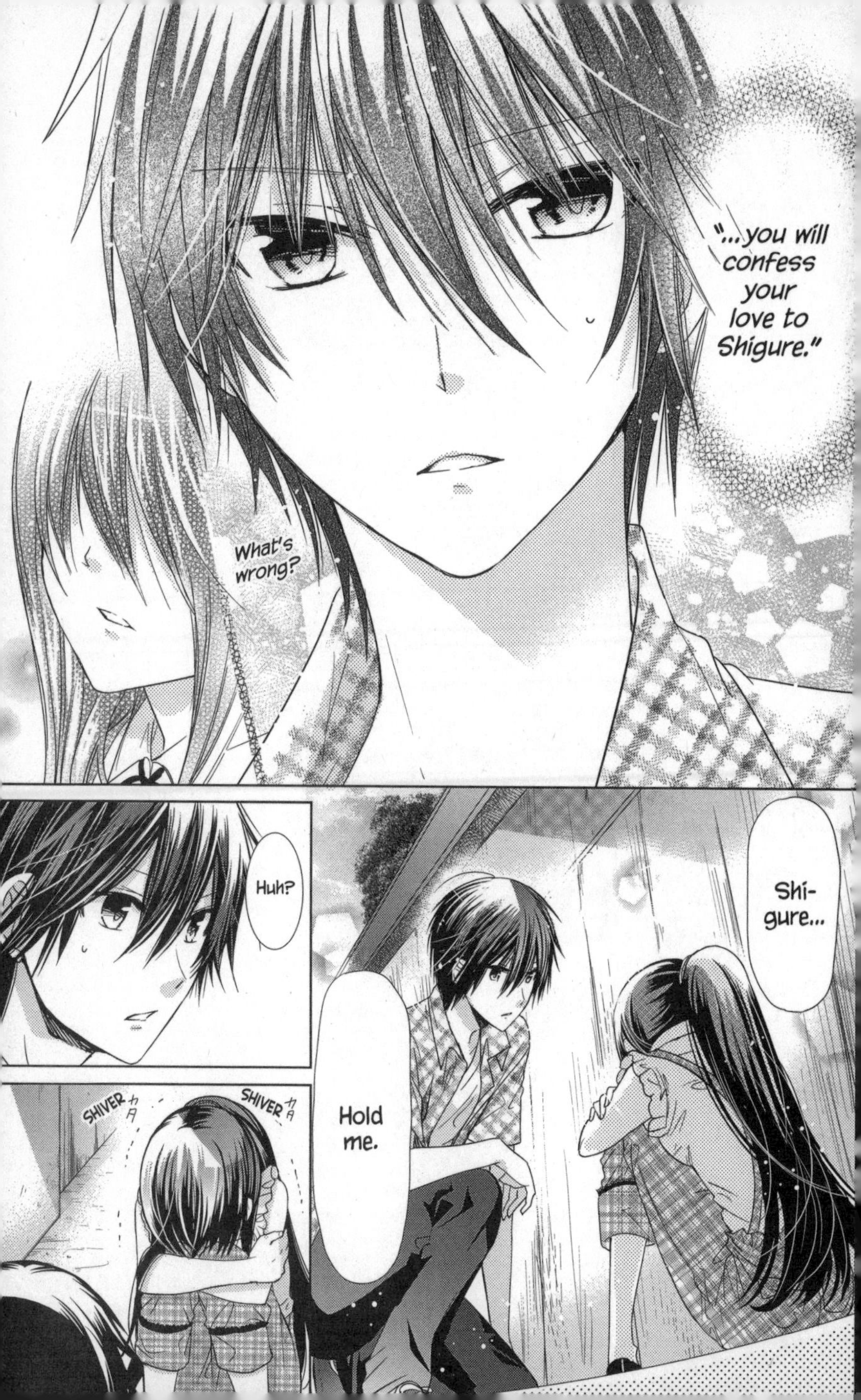
"...you will confess your love to Shigure."
What's wrong?
Shi-gure...
Hold me.
Huh?
SHIVER
SHIVER

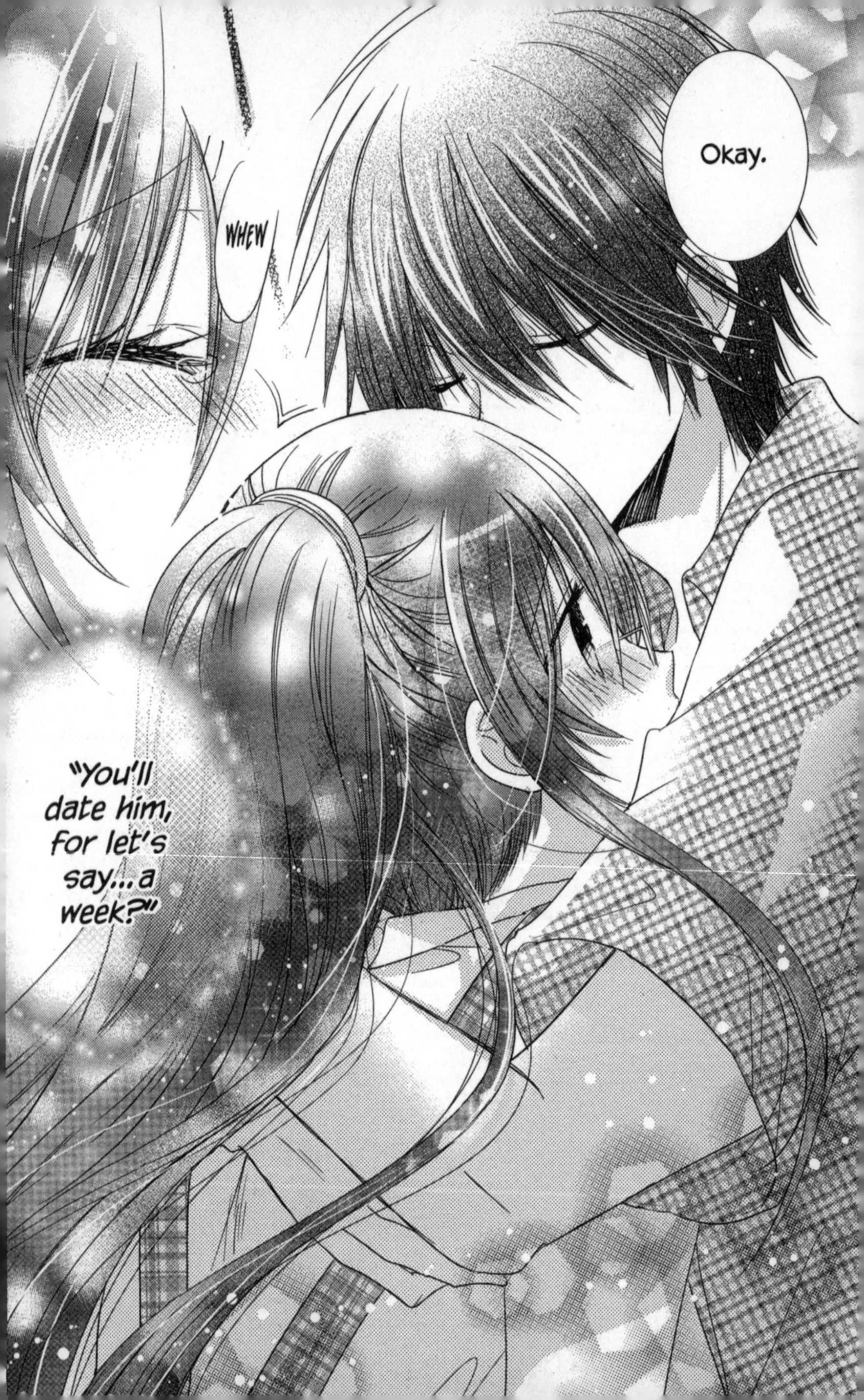
Okay.
WHEW
"You'll date him, for let's say... a week?"

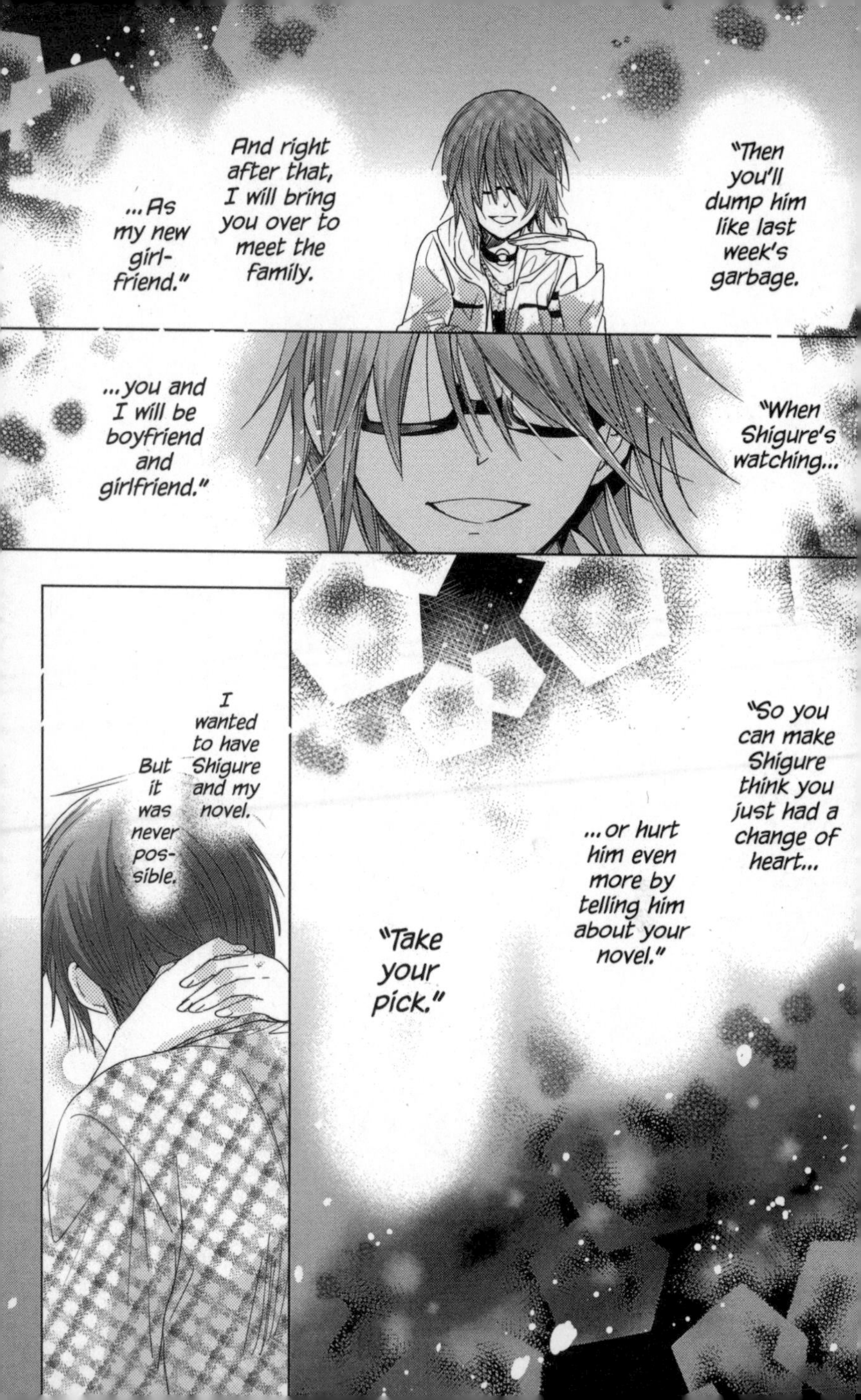
"Then you'll dump him like last week's garbage.
And right after that, I will bring you over to meet the family.
...As my new girl-friend."
"When Shigure's watching...
...you and I will be boyfriend and girlfriend."
"So you can make Shigure think you just had a change of heart...
...or hurt him even more by telling him about your novel."
"Take your pick."
I wanted to have Shigure and my novel.
But it was never possible.

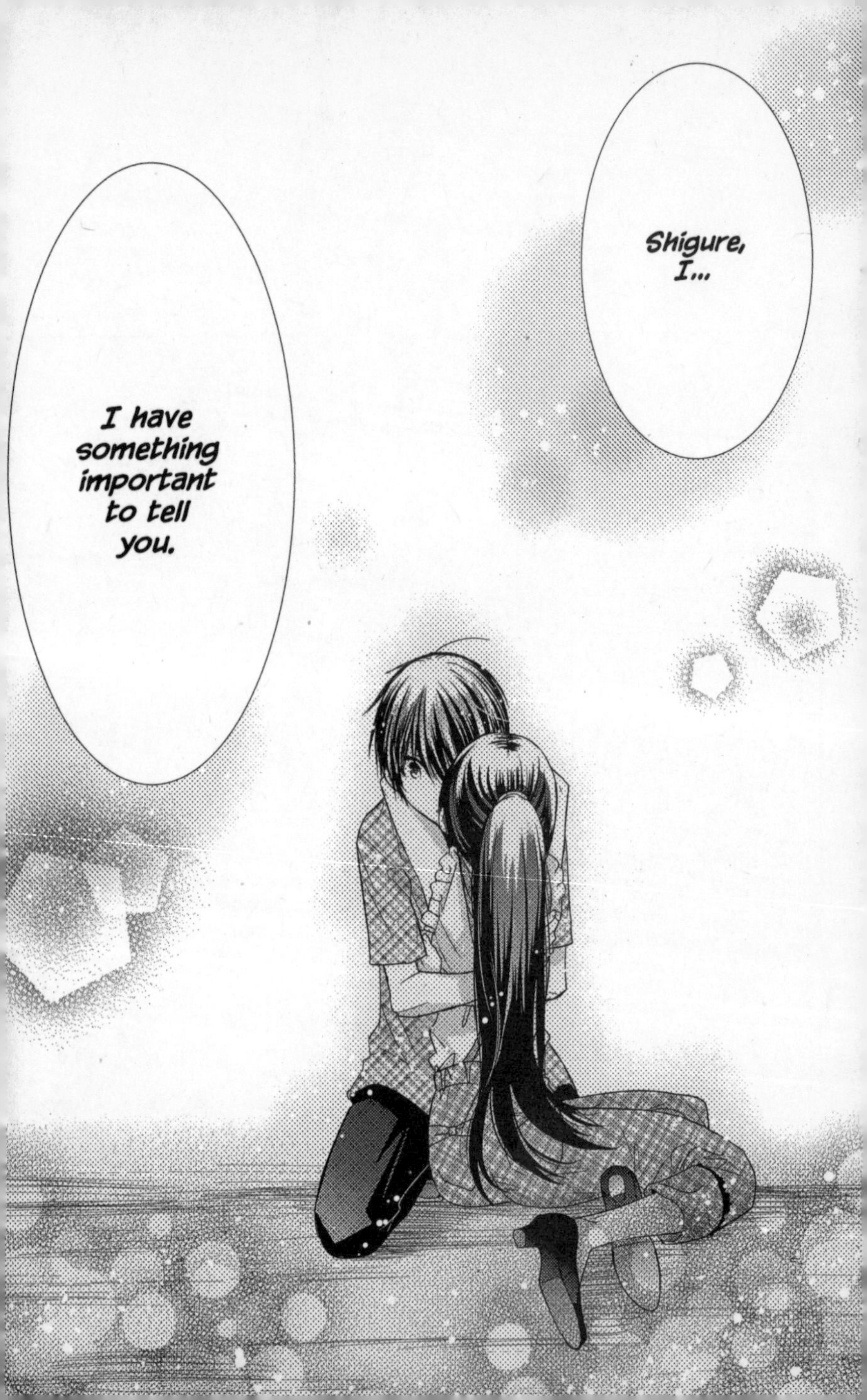
Shigure, I...
I have something important to tell you.

Mission 70
The Heart's Voice
Missions of Love

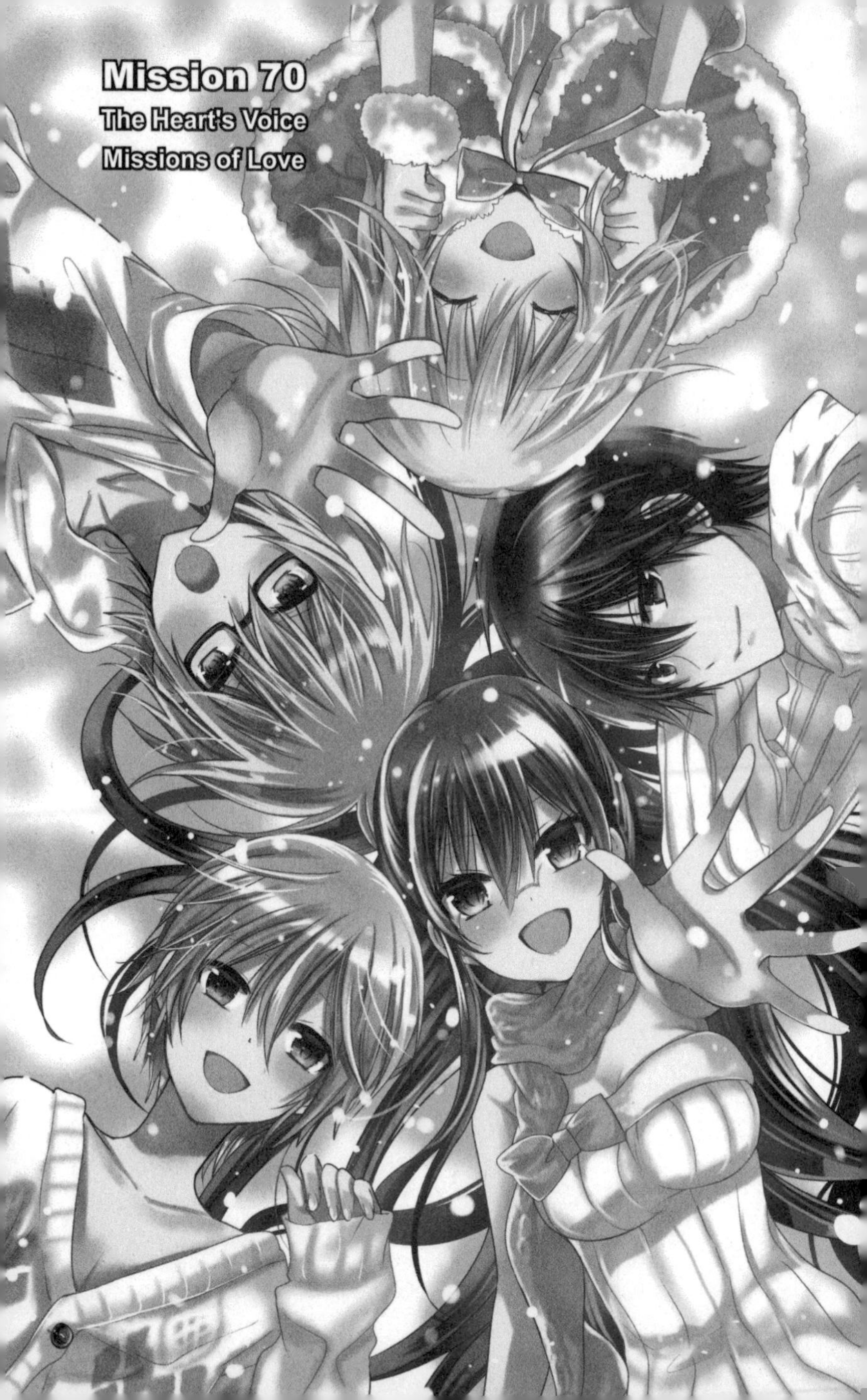

Missions of Love

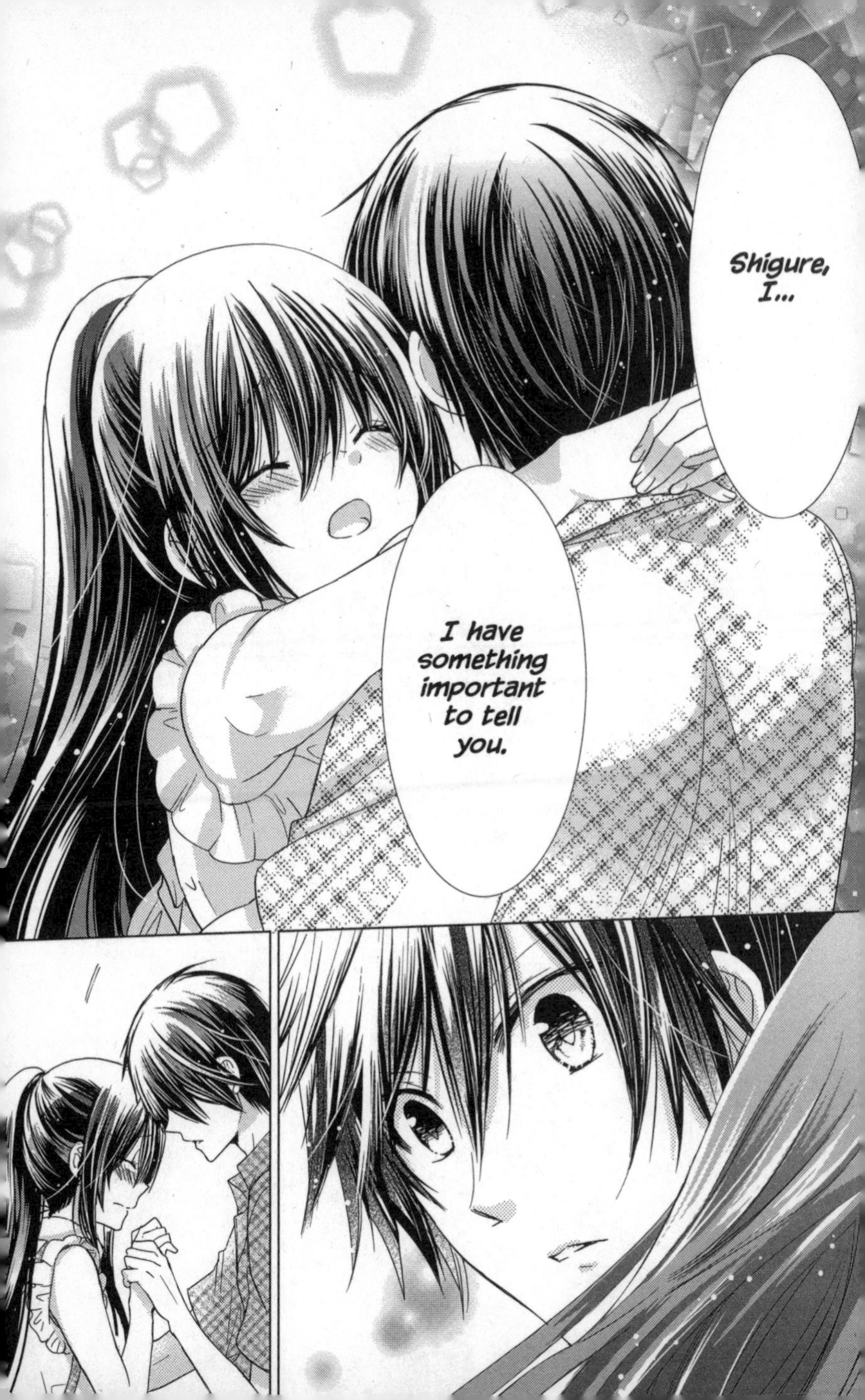
Shigure, I...
I have something important to tell you.

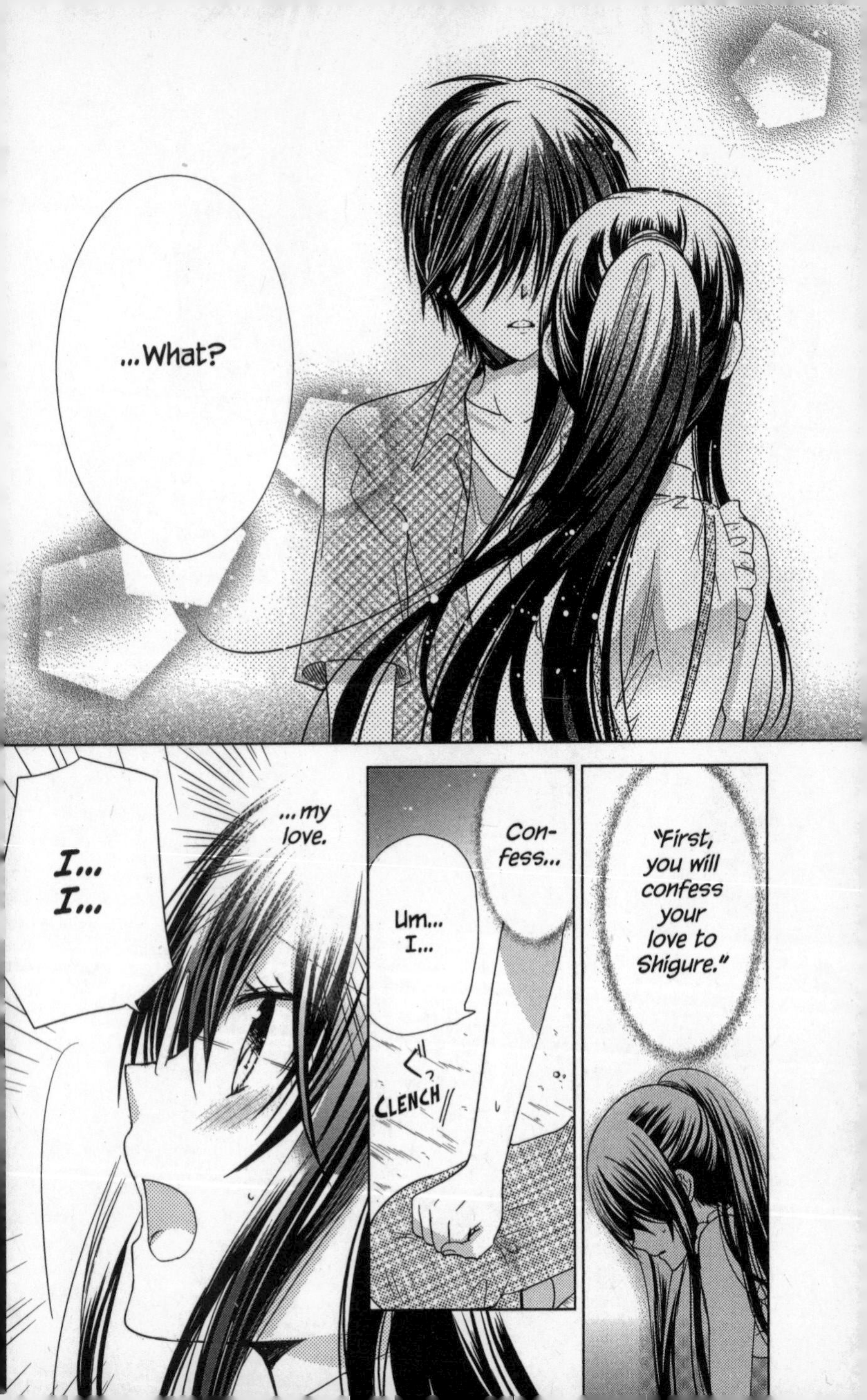
...What?
"First, you will confess your love to Shigure."
Con-fess...
Um... I...
CLENCH
I... I...
...my love.

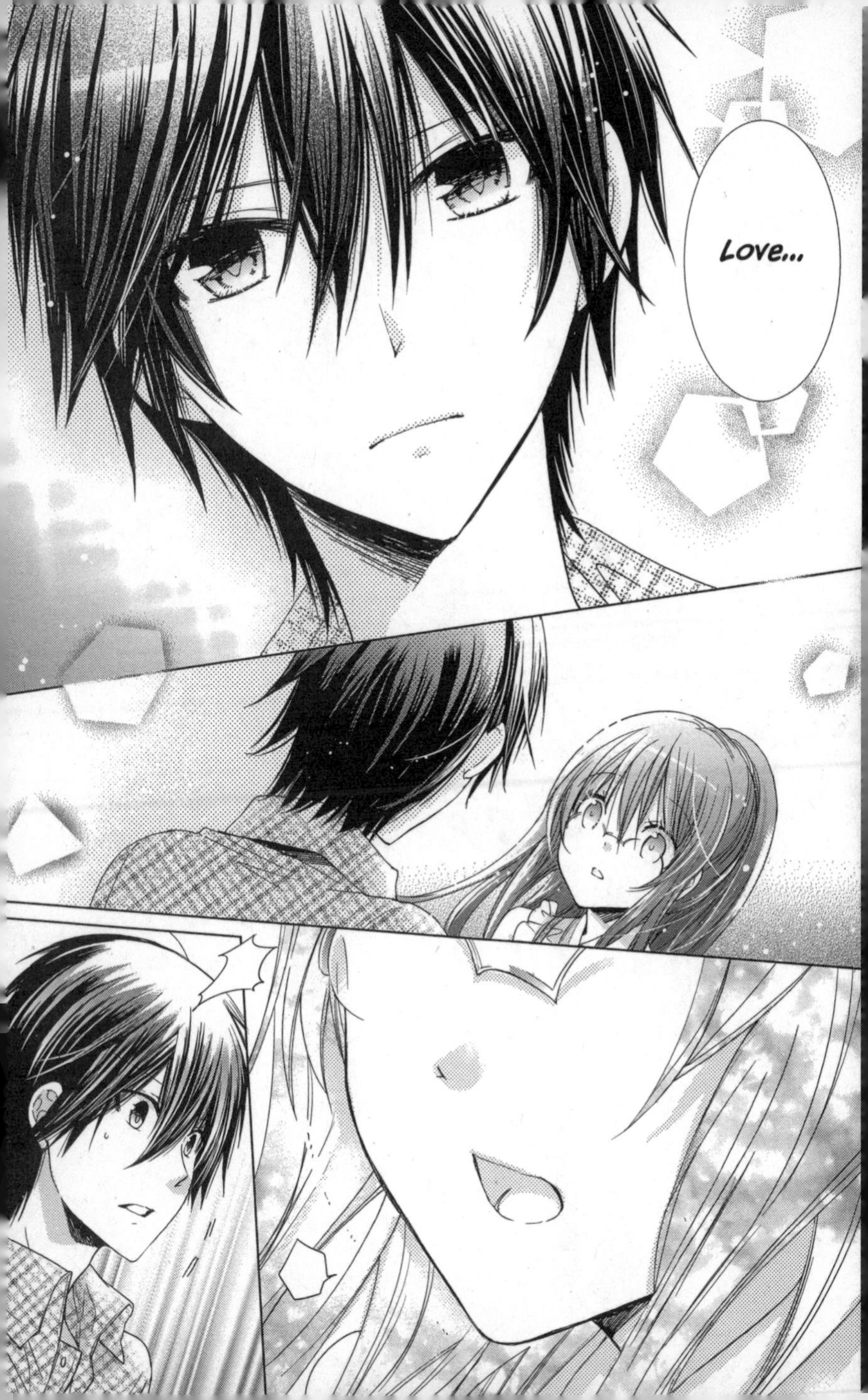
Love...

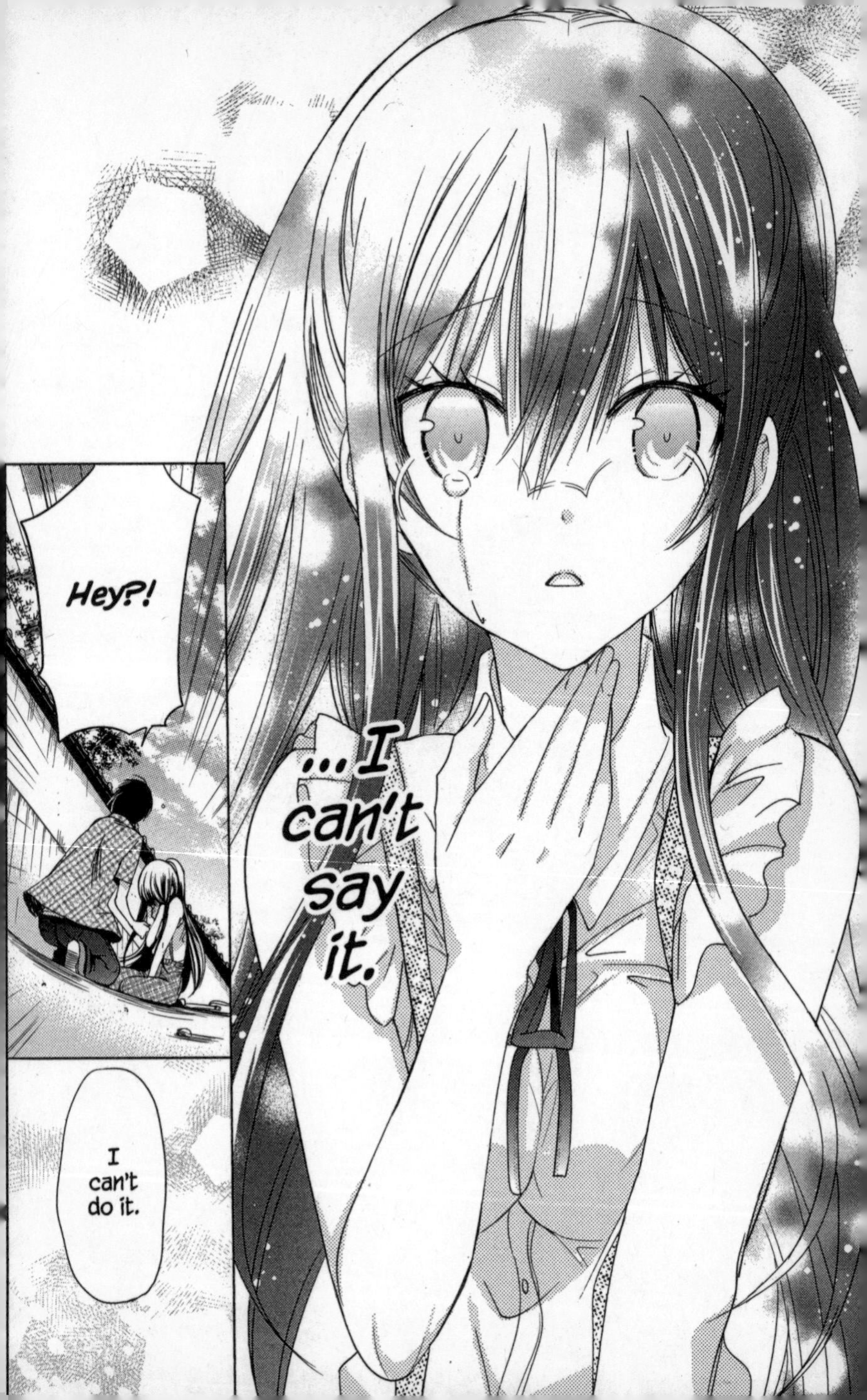
...I can't say it.
Hey?!
I can't do it.

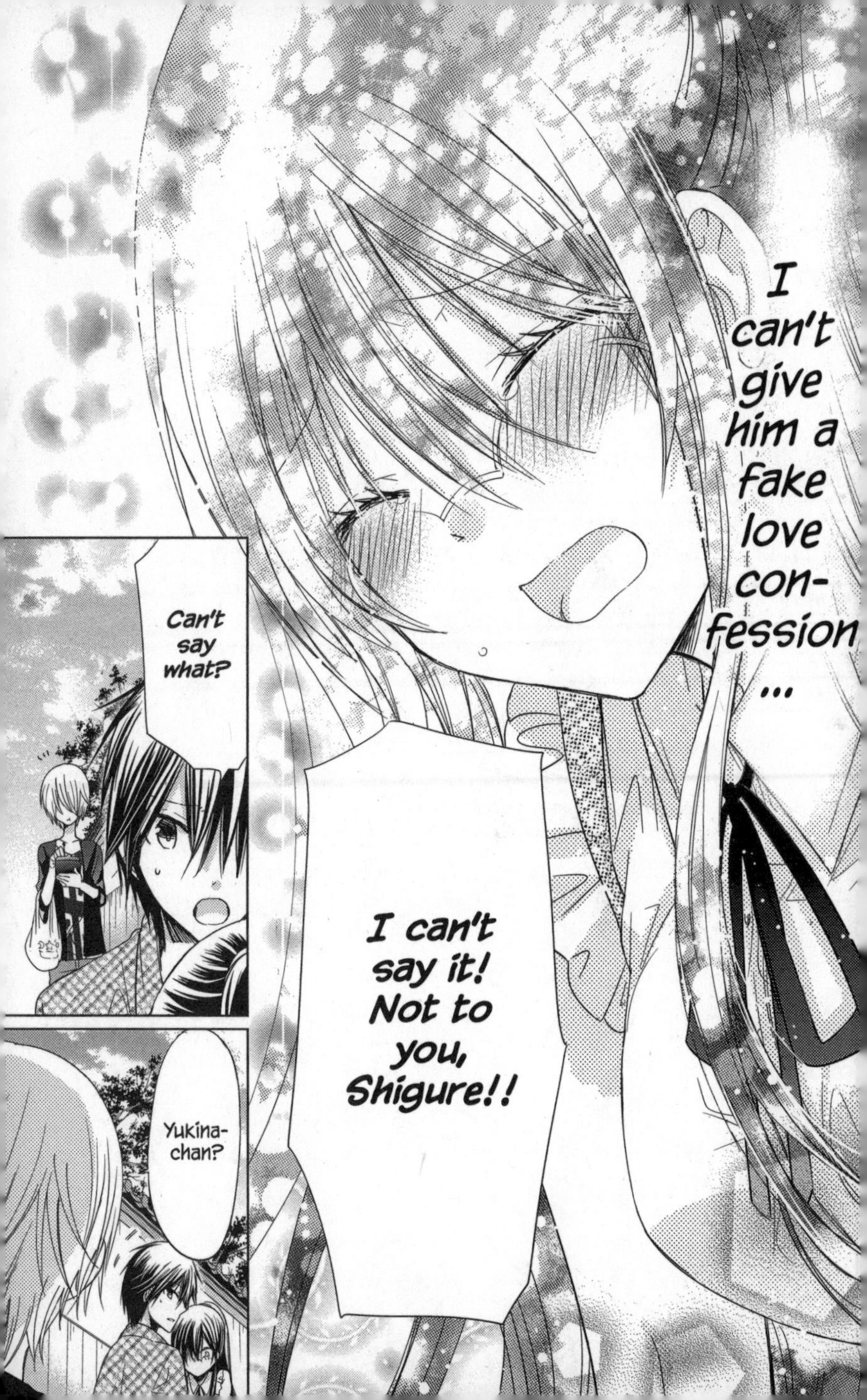

I can't give him a fake love confession...
I can't say it! Not to you, Shigure!!
Can't say what?
Yukina-chan?

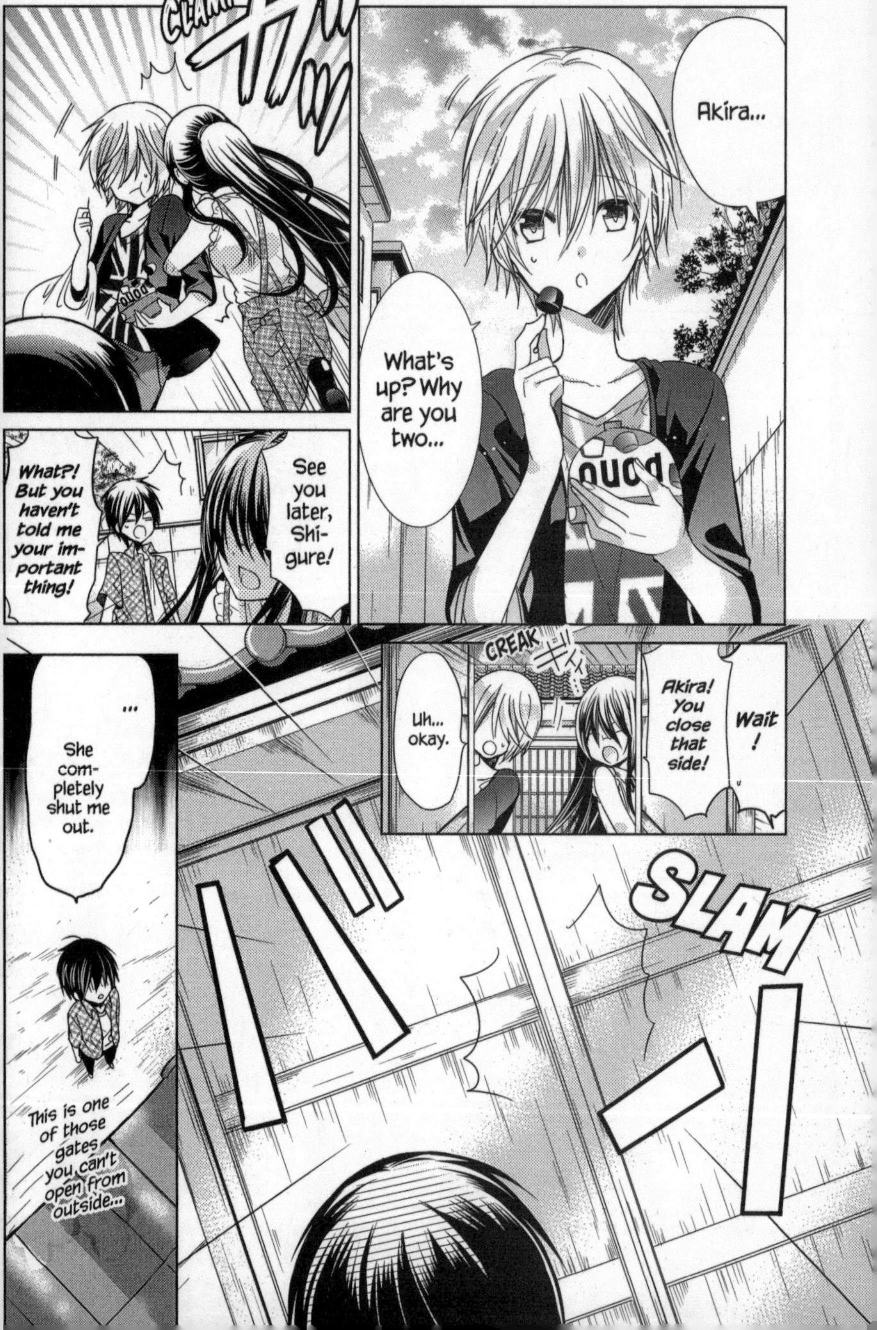
Akira...
What's up? Why are you two...
CLAMP
See you later, Shigure!
What?! But you haven't told me your important thing!
Wait!
Akira! You close that side!
CREAK
Uh... okay.
SLAM
...
She completely shut me out.
This is one of those gates you can't open from outside...

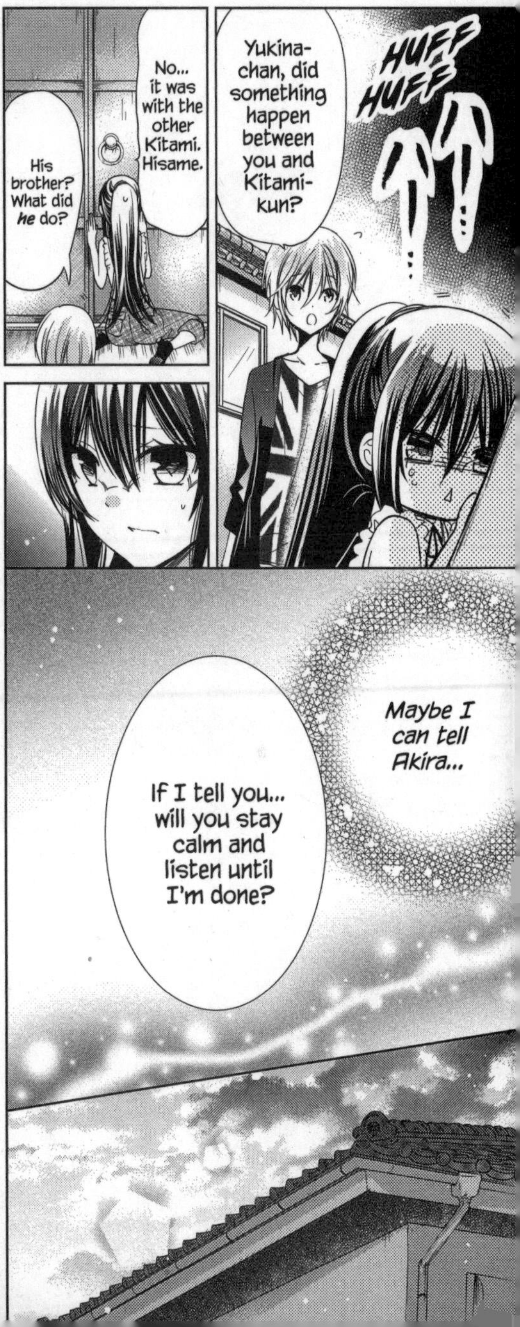
HUFF HUFF
Yukina-chan, did something happen between you and Kitami-kun?
No... it was with the other Kitami. Hisame.
His brother? What did he do?
Maybe I can tell Akira...
If I tell you... will you stay calm and listen until I'm done?

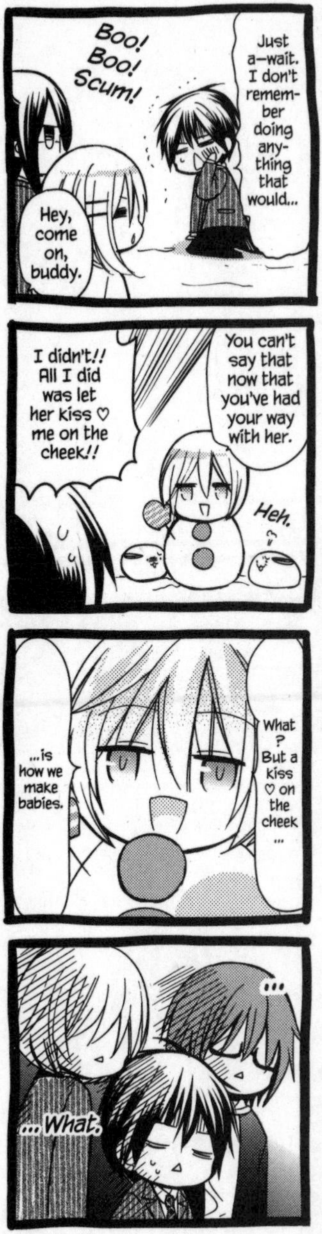
Just a—wait. I don't remember doing anything that would...
Boo! Boo! Scum!
Hey, come on, buddy.
You can't say that now that you've had your way with her.
I didn't!! All I did was let her kiss ♡ me on the cheek!!
Heh.
What? But a kiss ♡ on the cheek...
...is how we make babies.
...
...What.

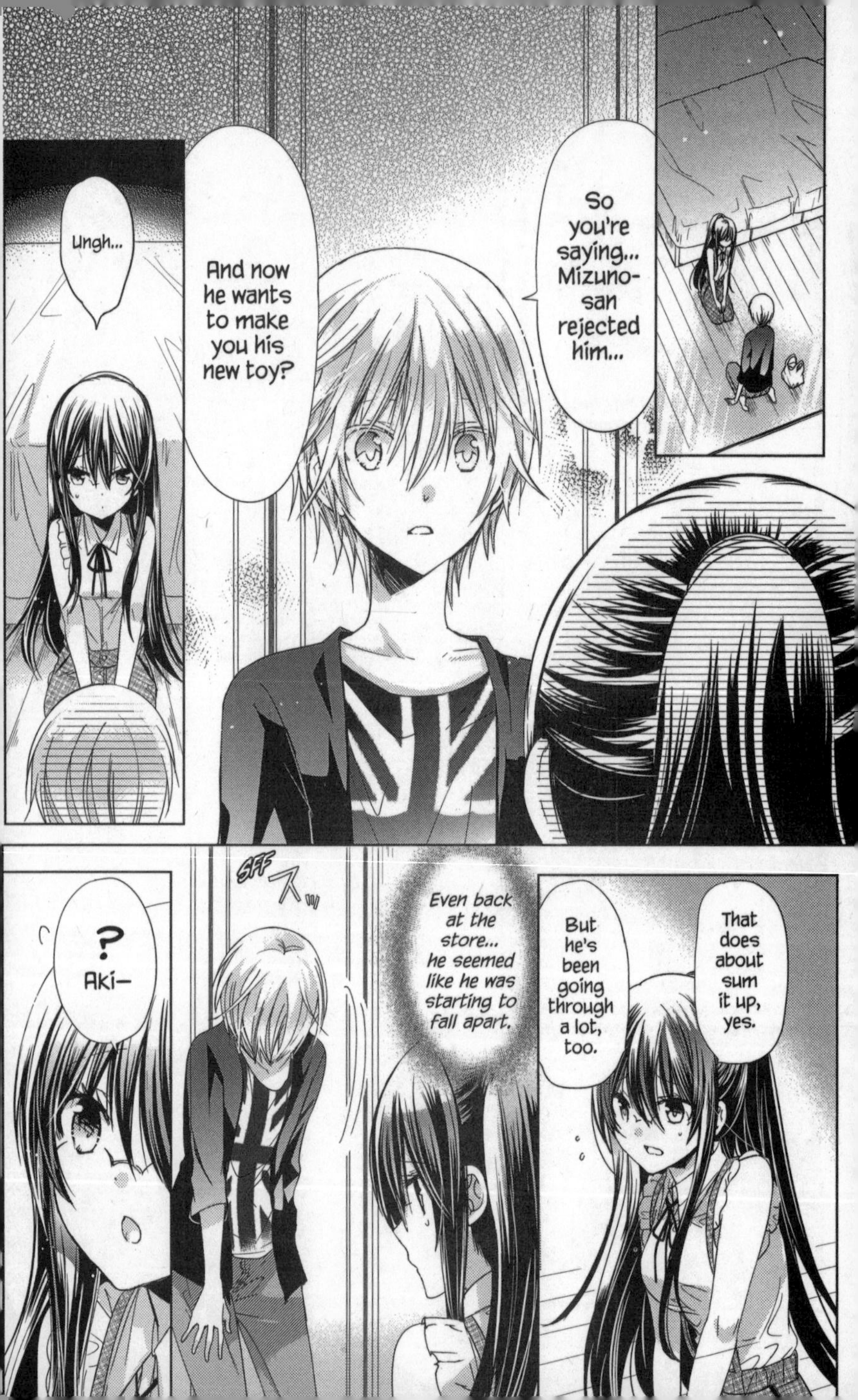
So you're saying... Mizuno-san rejected him...
And now he wants to make you his new toy?
Ungh...
That does about sum it up, yes.
But he's been going through a lot, too.
Even back at the store... he seemed like he was starting to fall apart.
SFF
ス
? Aki-

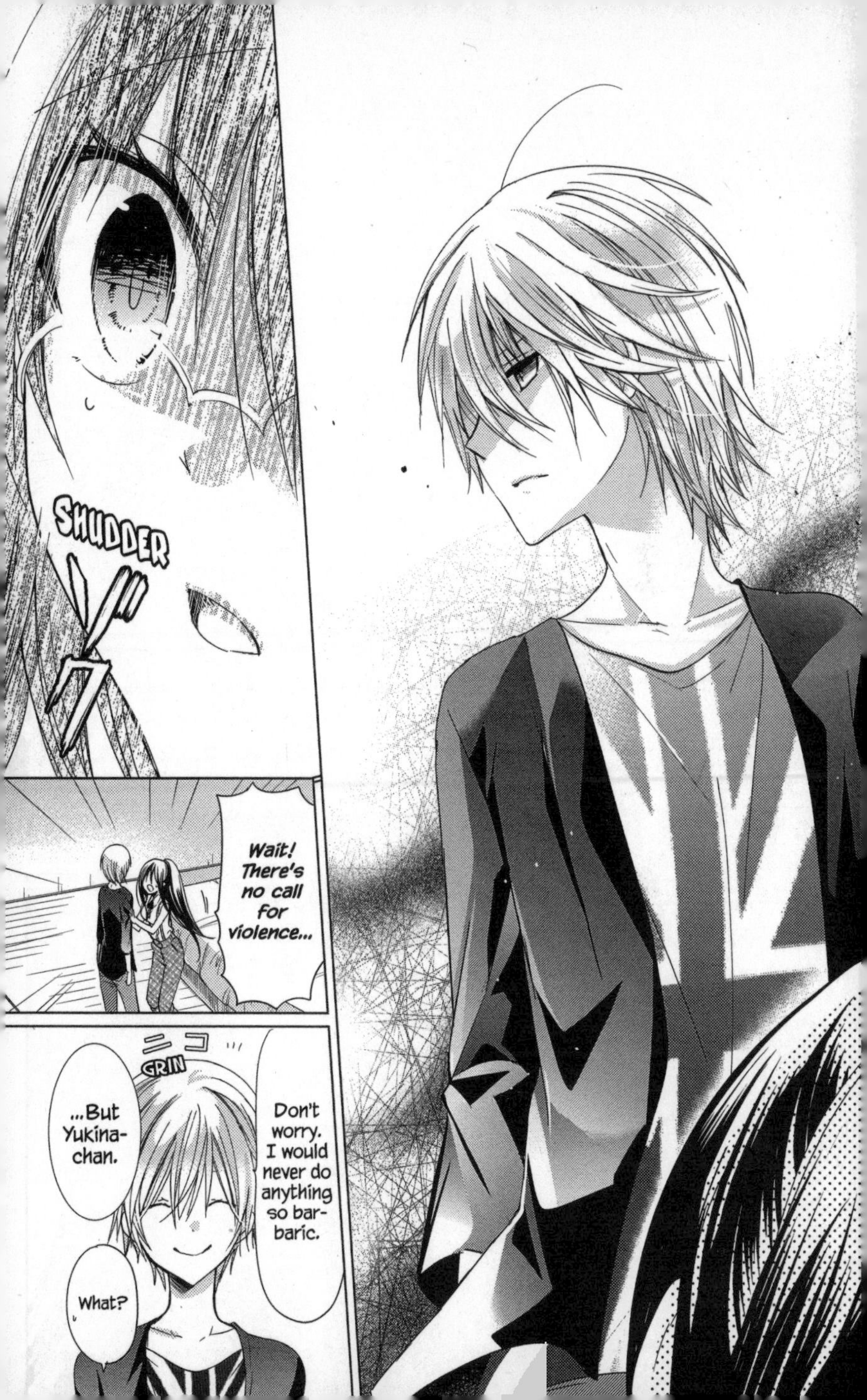
SHUDDER
Wait! There's no call for violence...
Don't worry. I would never do anything so barbaric.
ニコ
GRIN
...But Yukina-chan.
What?

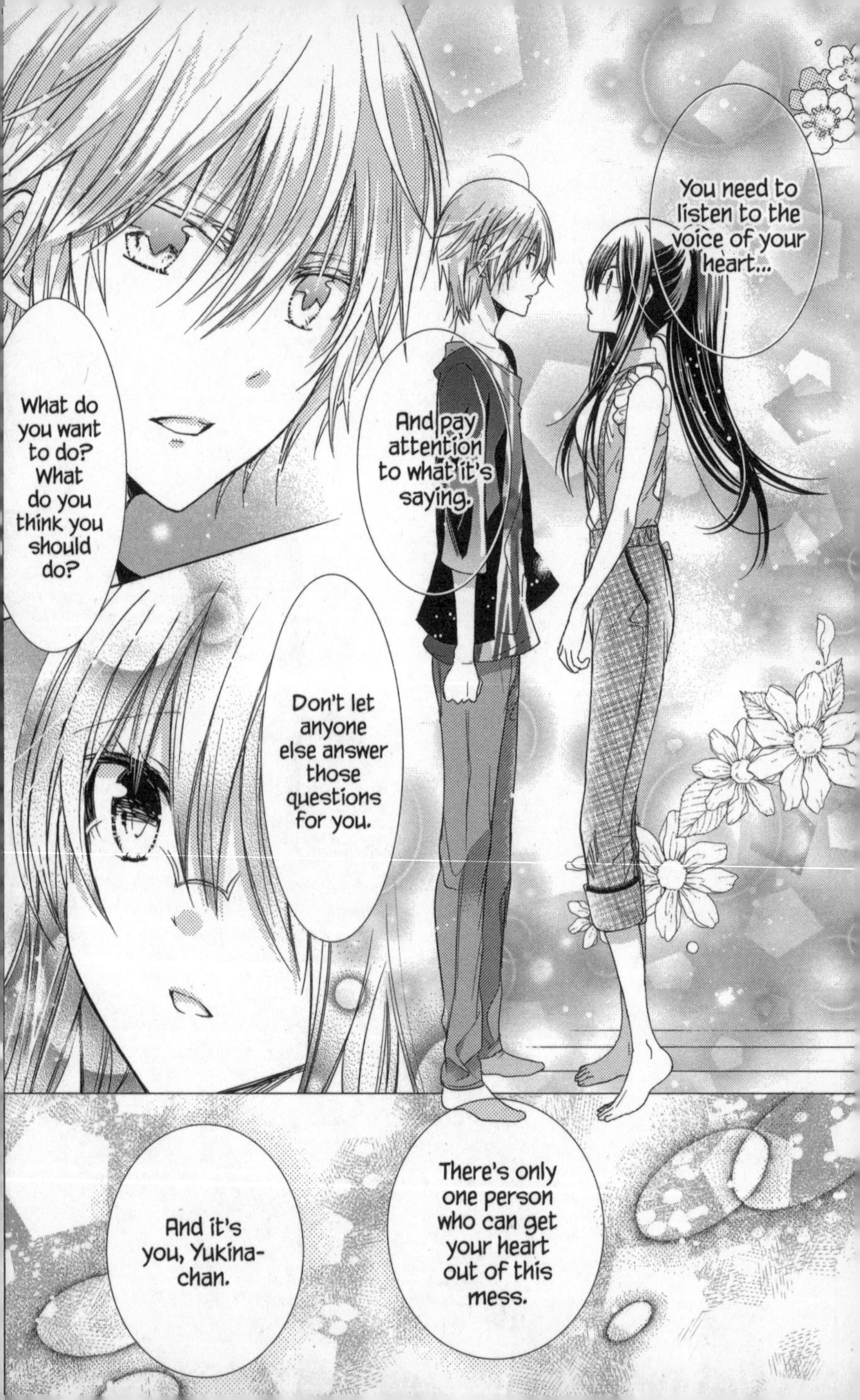
You need to listen to the voice of your heart...
And pay attention to what it's saying.
What do you want to do? What do you think you should do?
Don't let anyone else answer those questions for you.
There's only one person who can get your heart out of this mess.
And it's you, Yukina-chan.

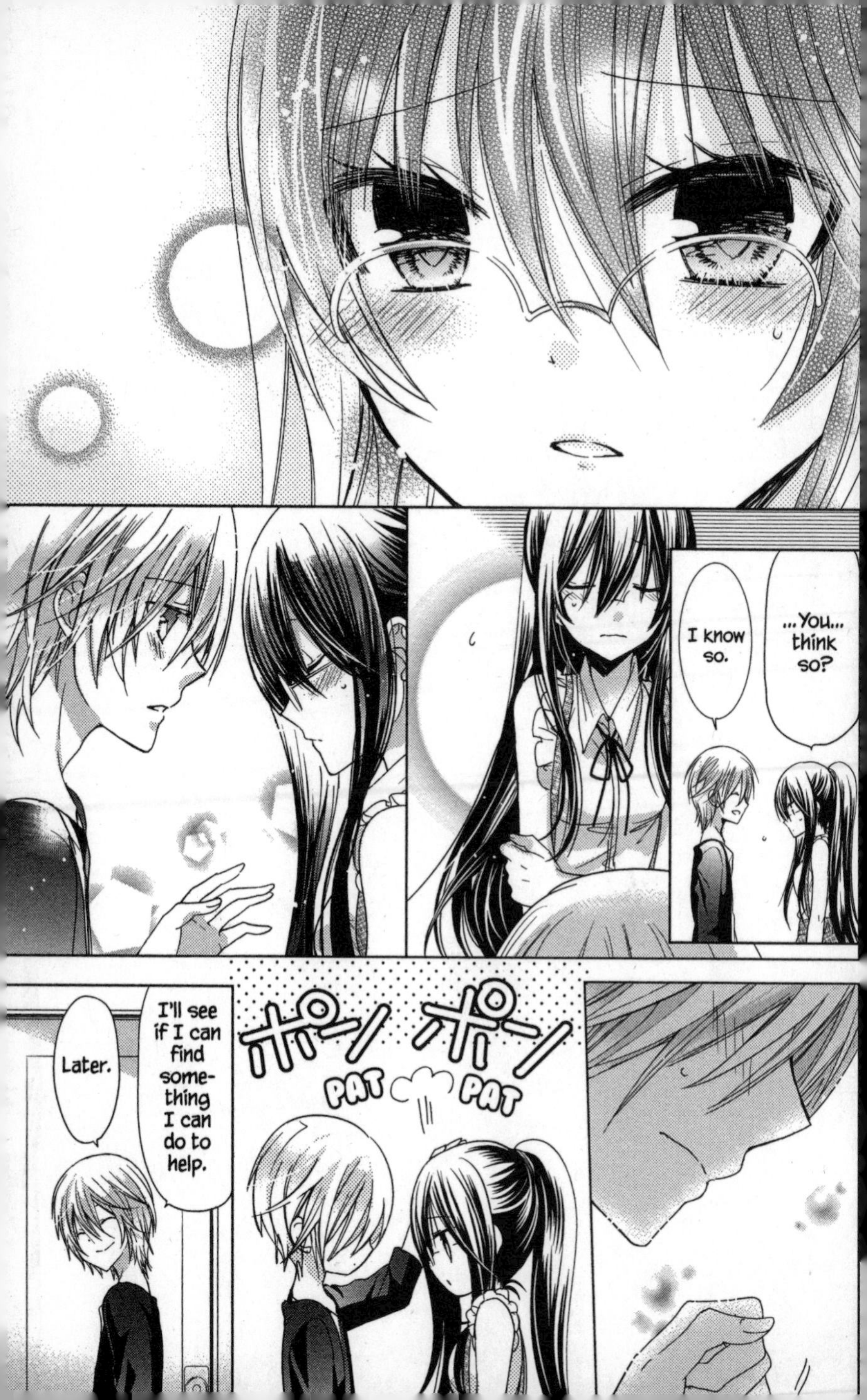
...You... think so?
I know so.
PAT PAT
I'll see if I can find some-thing I can do to help.
Later.

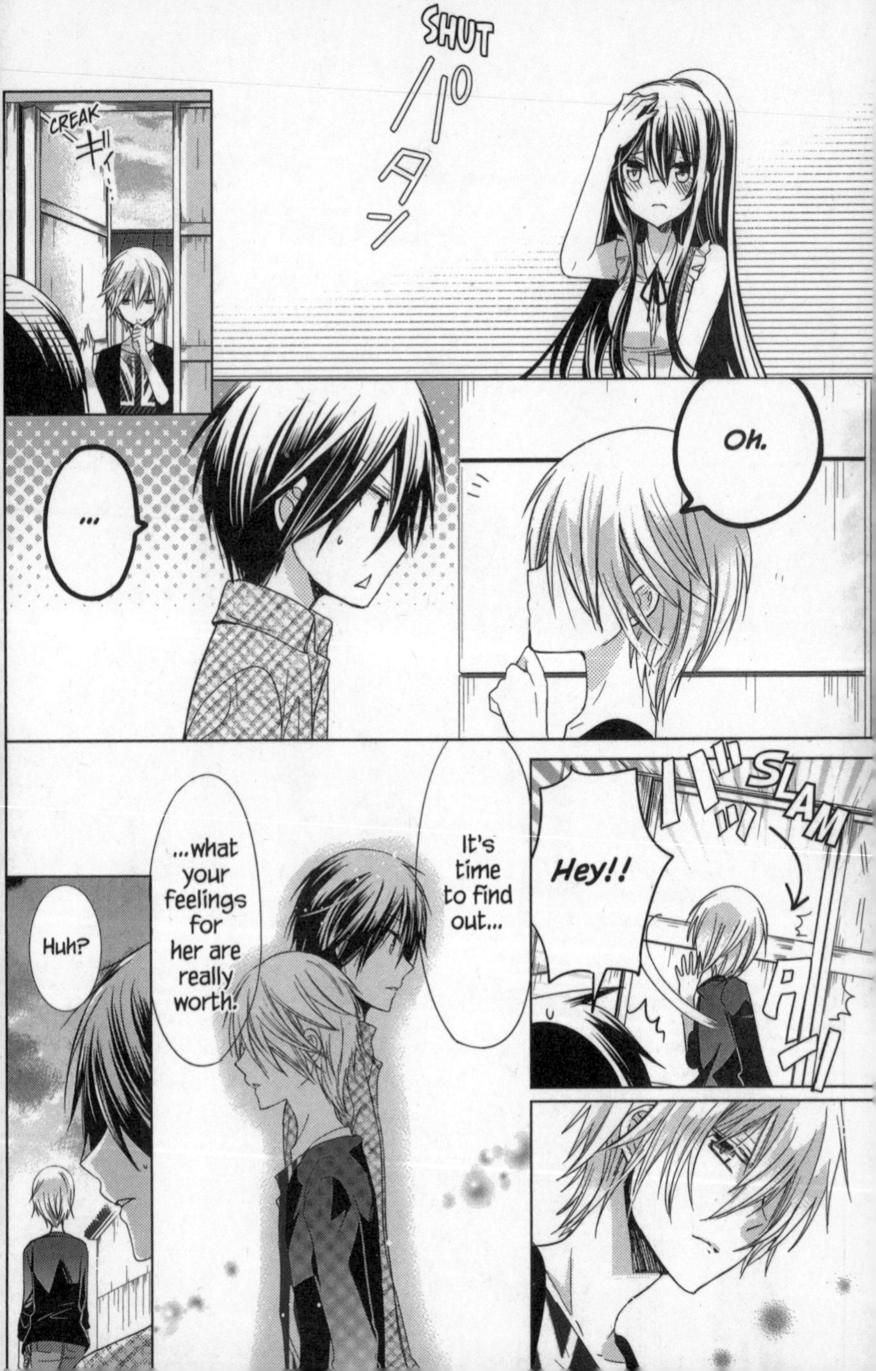
SHUT
パタン
CREAK
ギィ…
Oh.
...
SLAM
Hey!!
It's time to find out...
...what your feelings for her are really worth.
Huh?

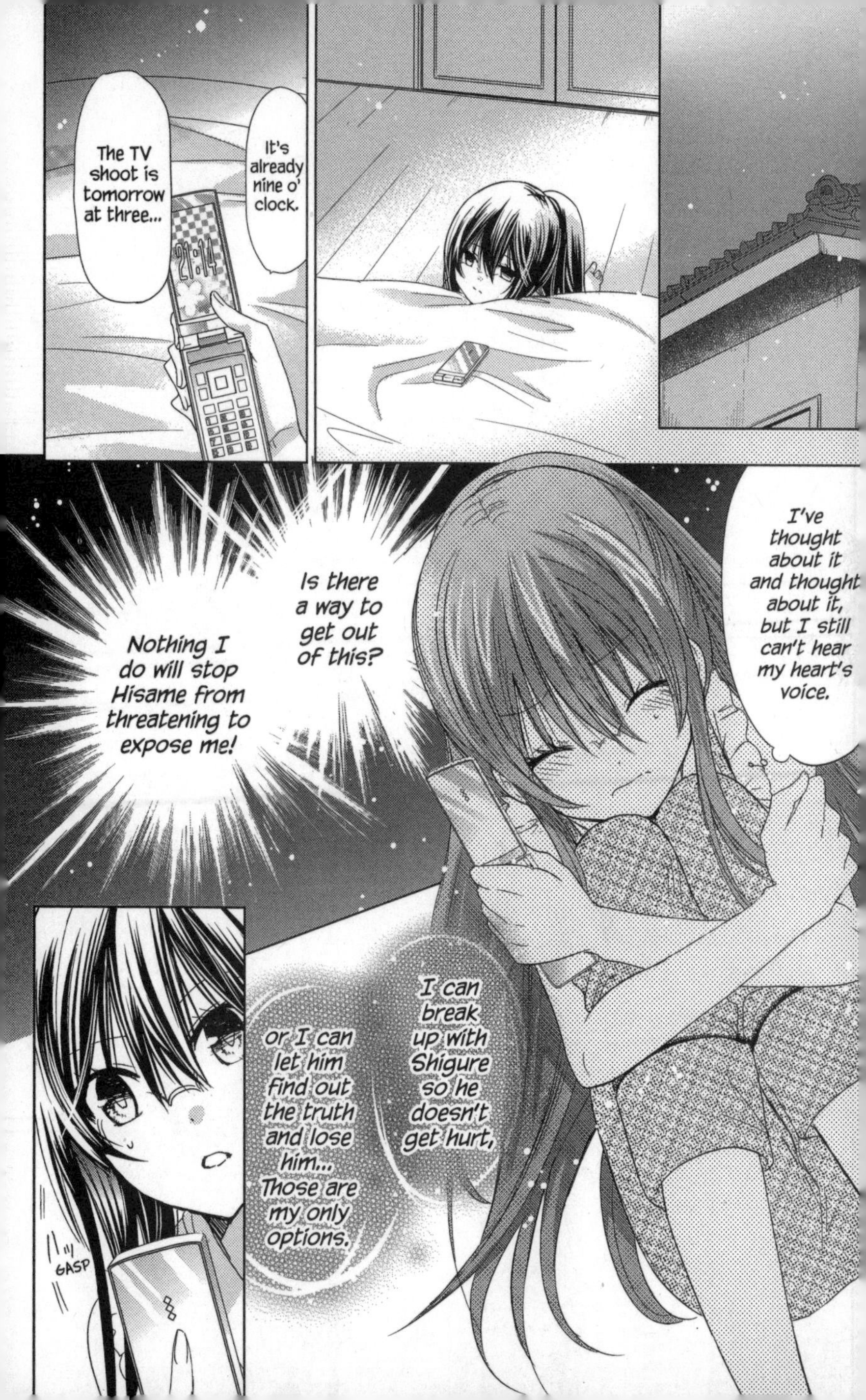

It's already nine o' clock.
The TV shoot is tomorrow at three...
21:14
I've thought about it and thought about it, but I still can't hear my heart's voice.
Is there a way to get out of this?
Nothing I do will stop Hisame from threatening to expose me!
I can break up with Shigure so he doesn't get hurt,
or I can let him find out the truth and lose him... Those are my only options.
GASP

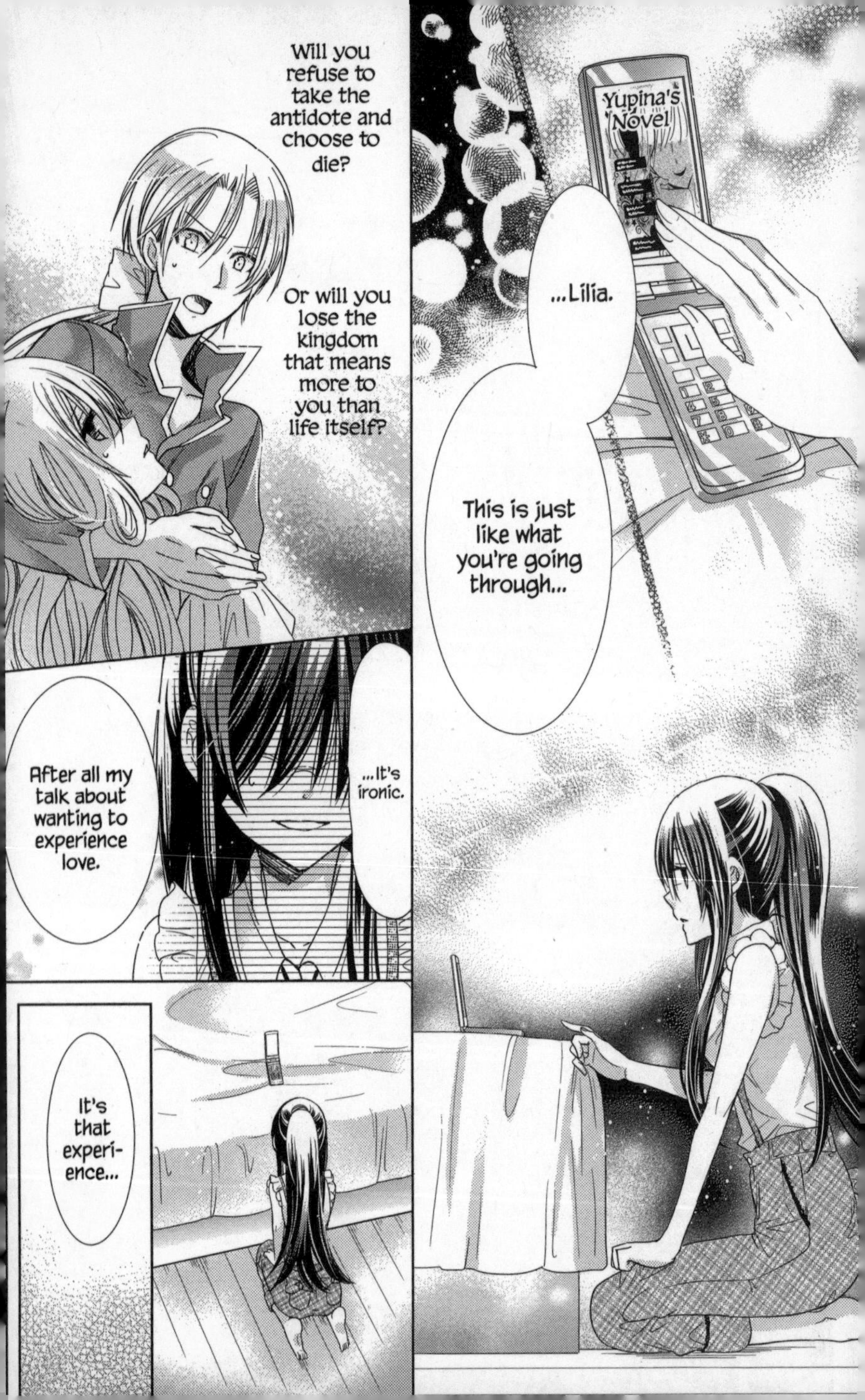
Yupina's Novel
...Lilia.
This is just like what you're going through...
Will you refuse to take the antidote and choose to die?
Or will you lose the kingdom that means more to you than life itself?
...It's ironic.
After all my talk about wanting to experience love.
It's that experience...

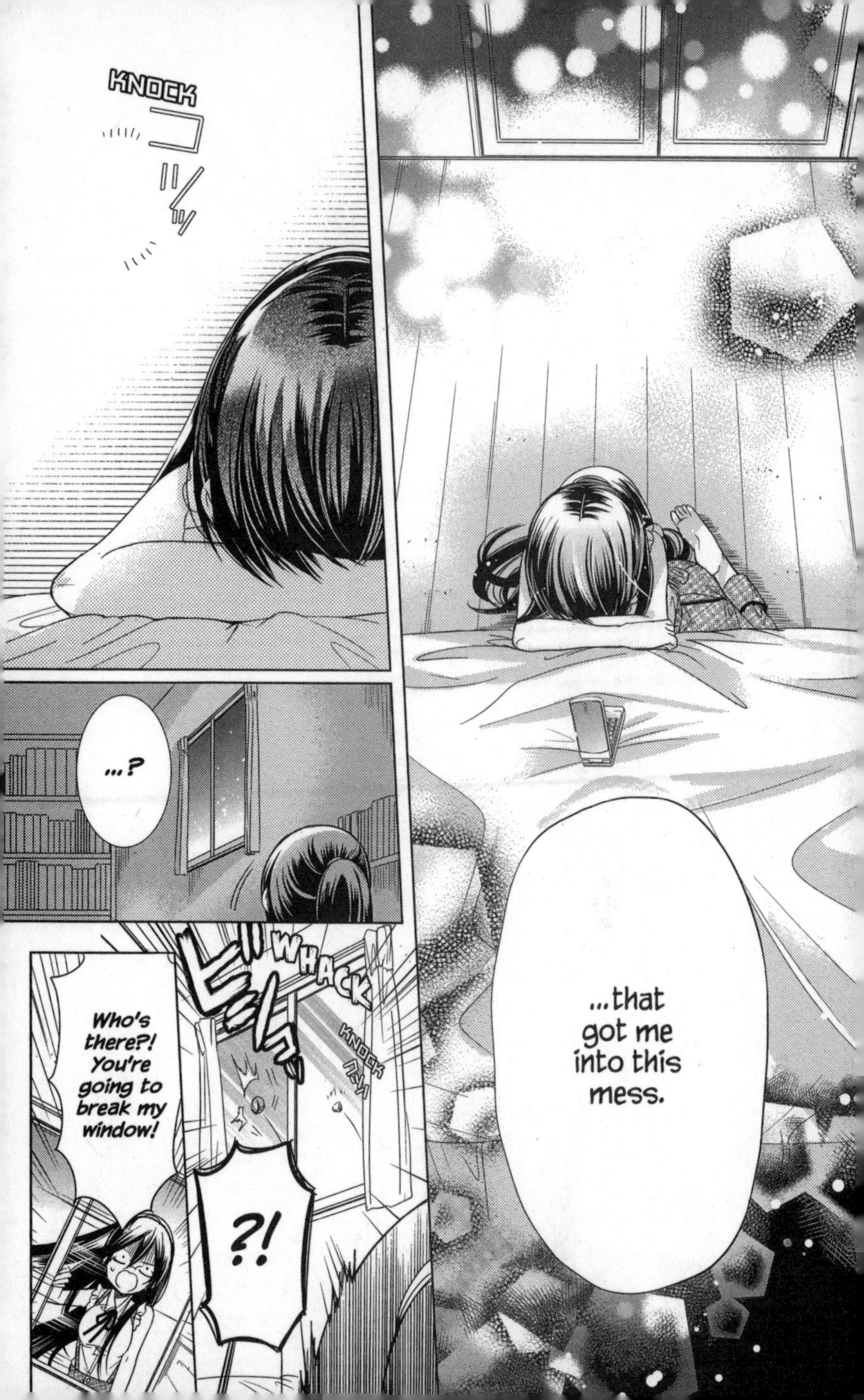
...that got me into this mess.
KNOCK
...?
WHACK
KNOCK
Who's there?! You're going to break my window!
?!

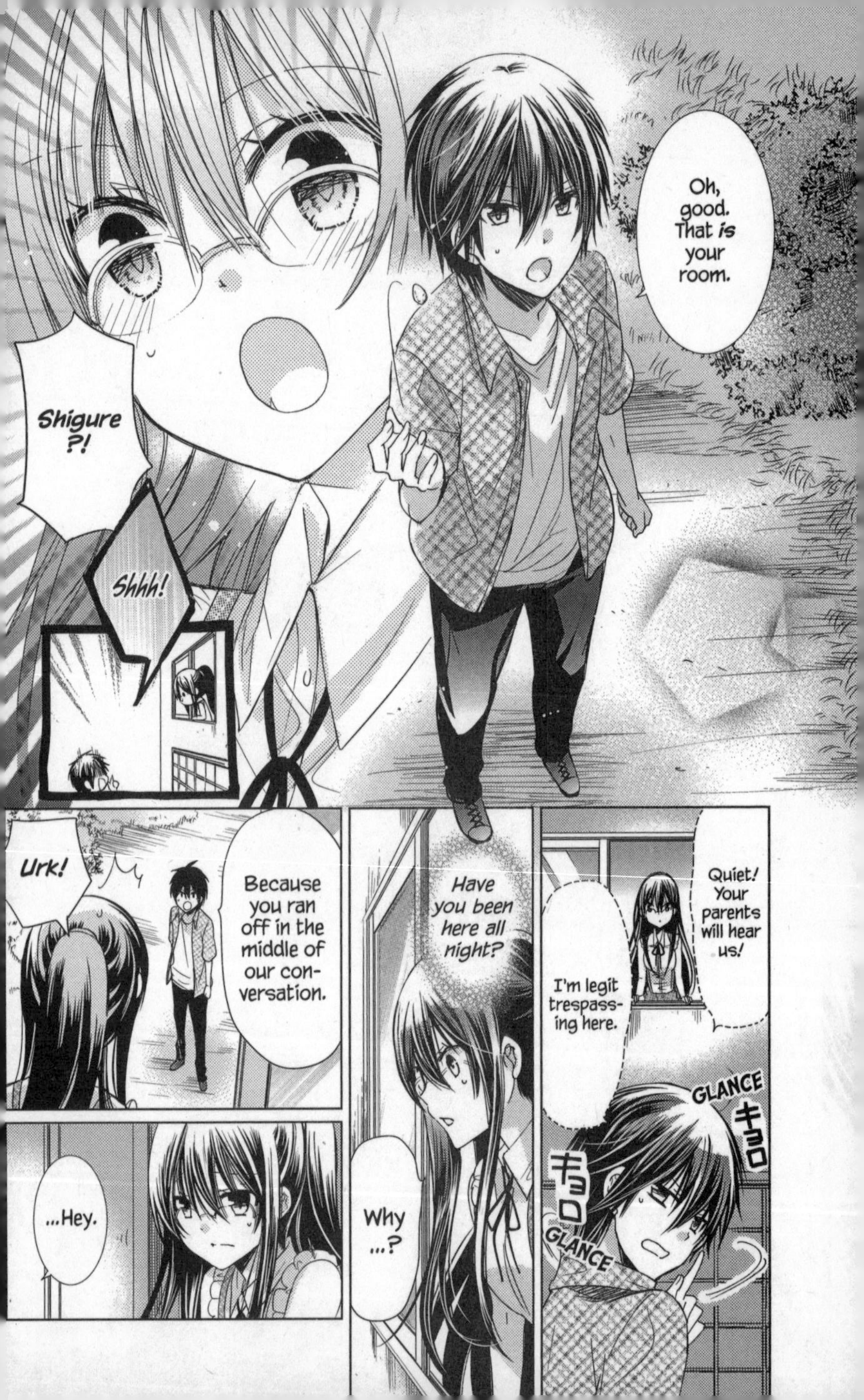
Oh, good. That *is* your room.
Shigure ?!
Shhh!
Quiet! Your parents will hear us!
I'm legit trespassing here.
GLANCE
キョロ
キョロ
GLANCE
Have you been here all night?
Why ...?
Because you ran off in the middle of our conversation.
Urk!
...Hey.

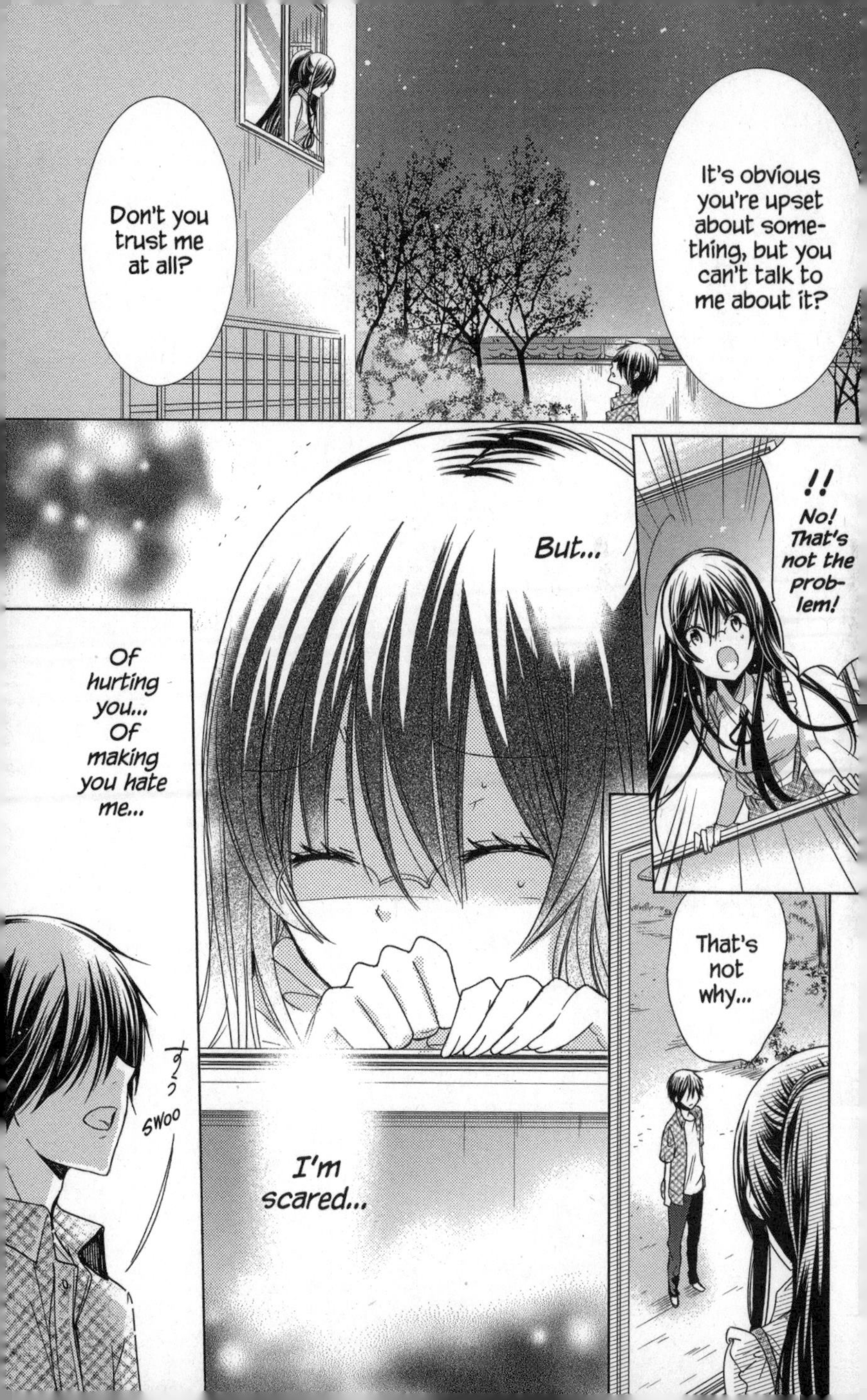
It's obvious you're upset about some-thing, but you can't talk to me about it?
Don't you trust me at all?
!!
No! That's not the prob-lem!
That's not why...
But...
Of hurting you... Of making you hate me...
I'm scared...
すっ
SWOO

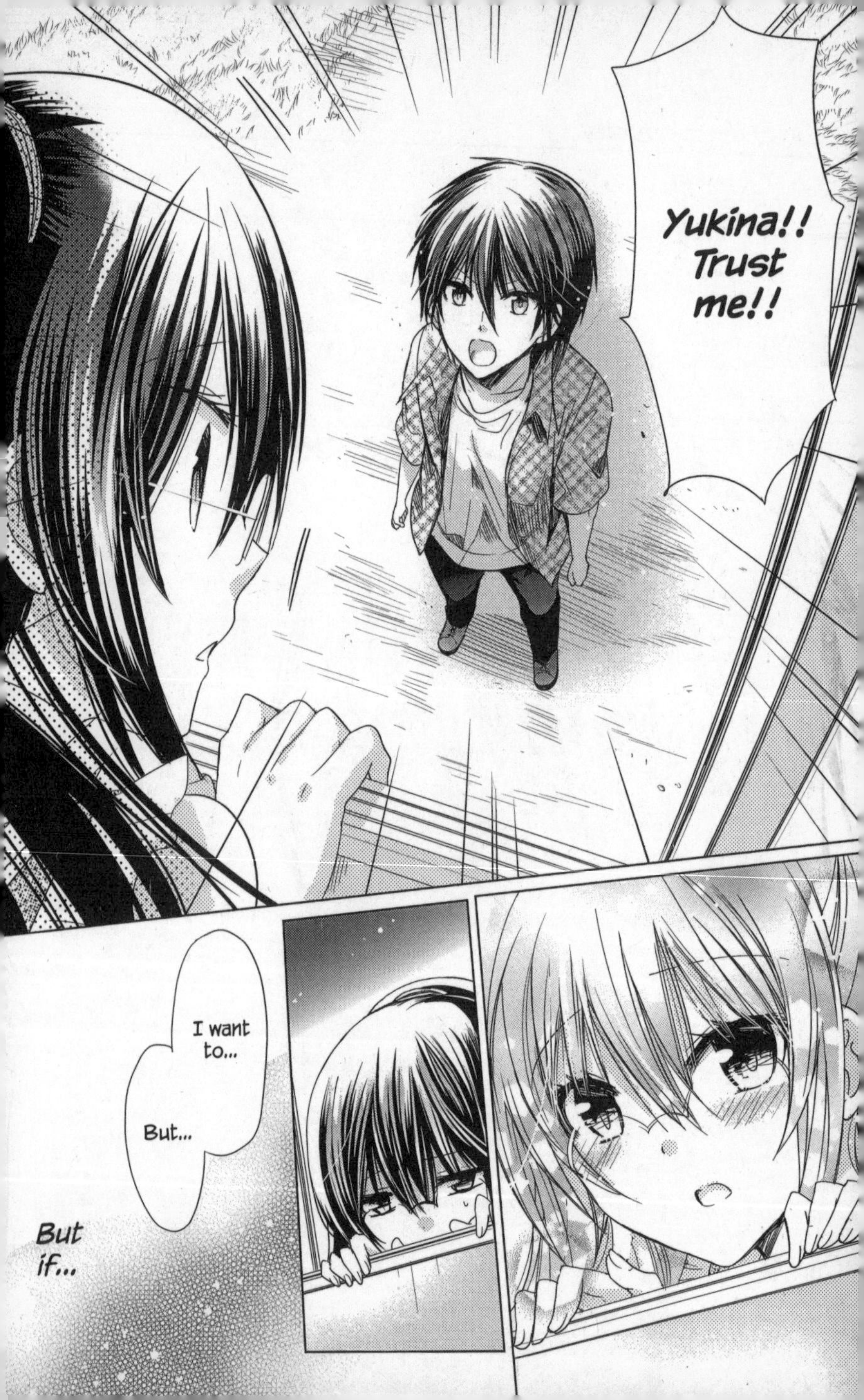
Yukina!! Trust me!!
I want to...
But...
But if...

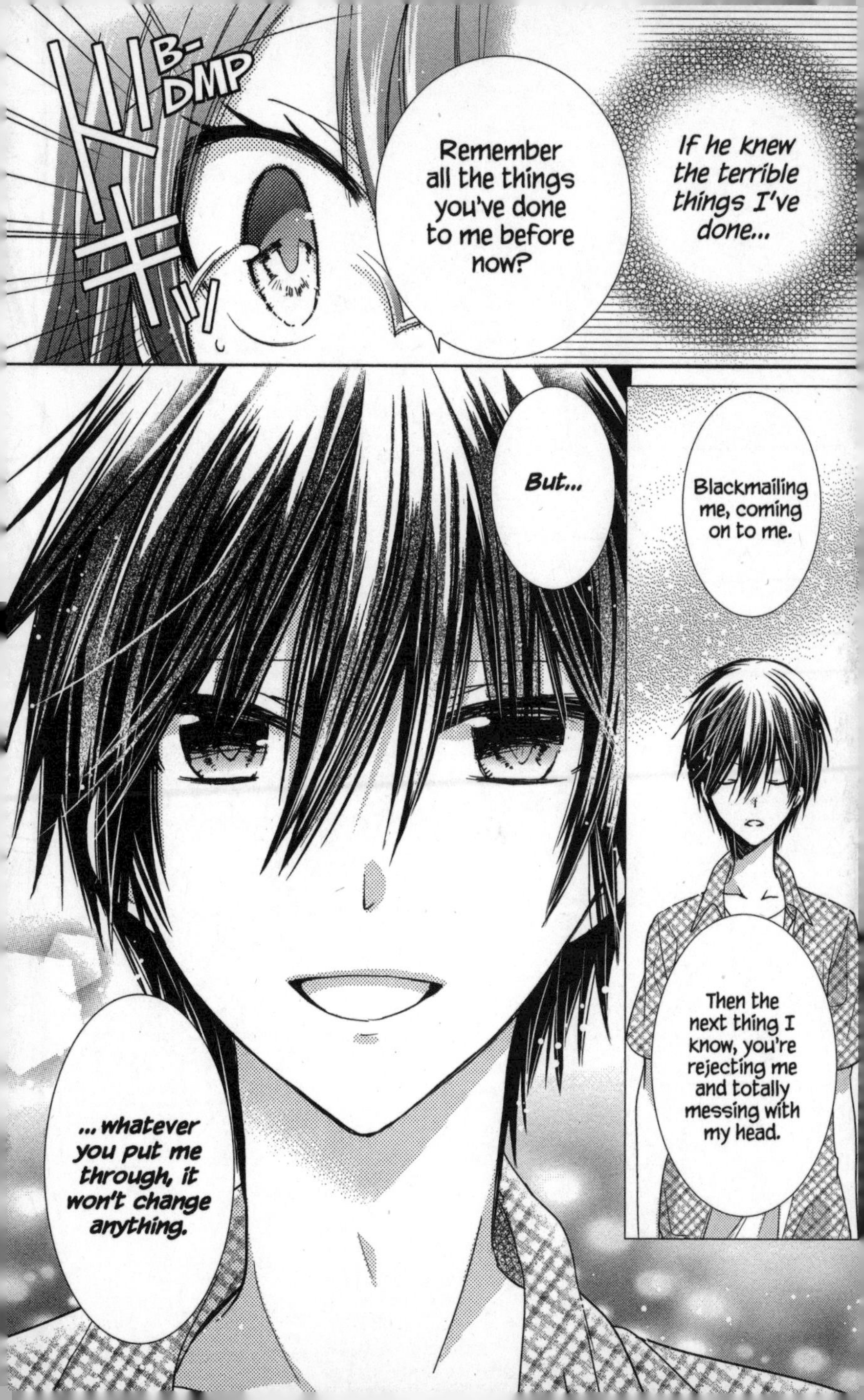
If he knew the terrible things I've done...
Remember all the things you've done to me before now?
B-DMP
Blackmailing me, coming on to me.
Then the next thing I know, you're rejecting me and totally messing with my head.
But...
...whatever you put me through, it won't change anything.

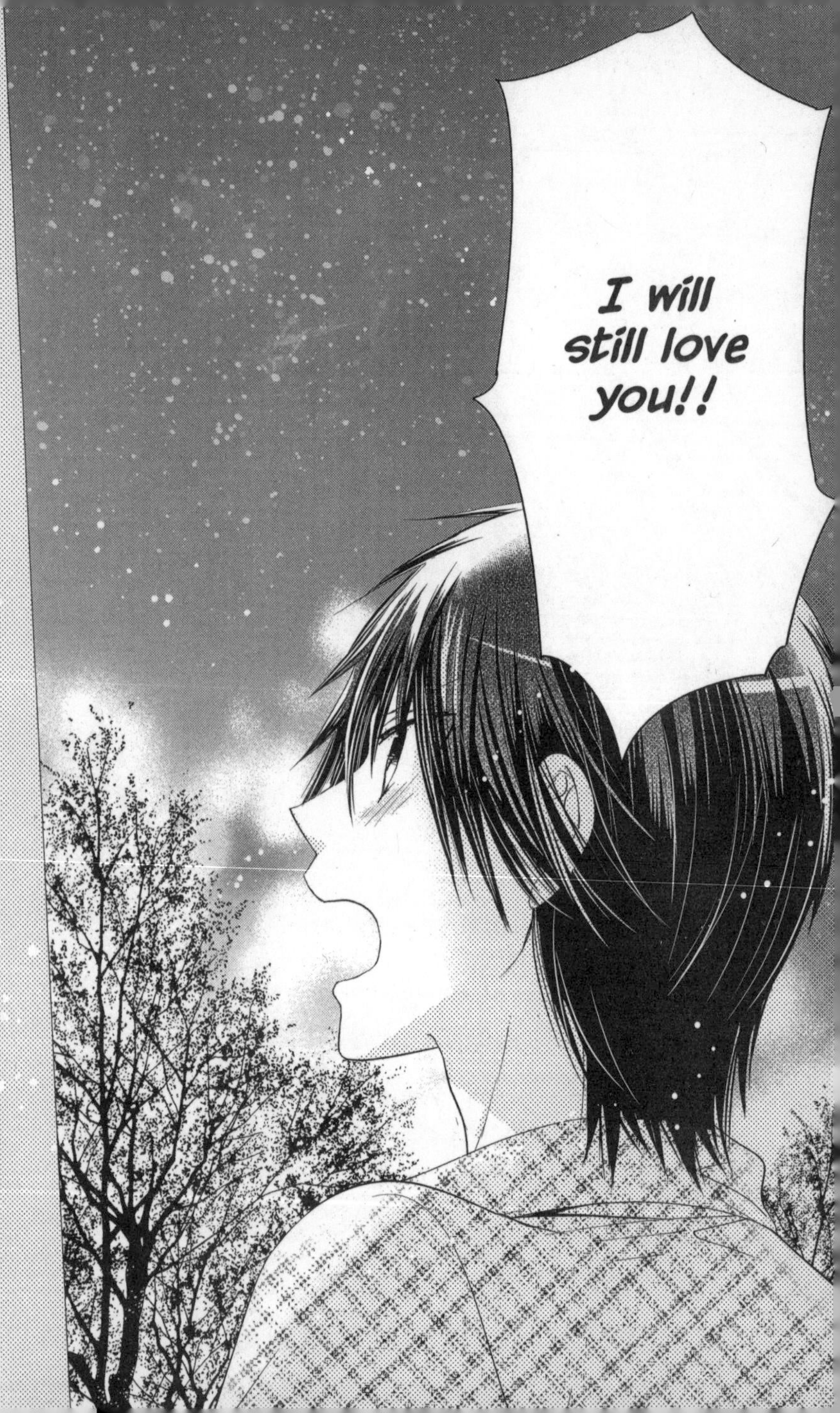
I will still love you!!

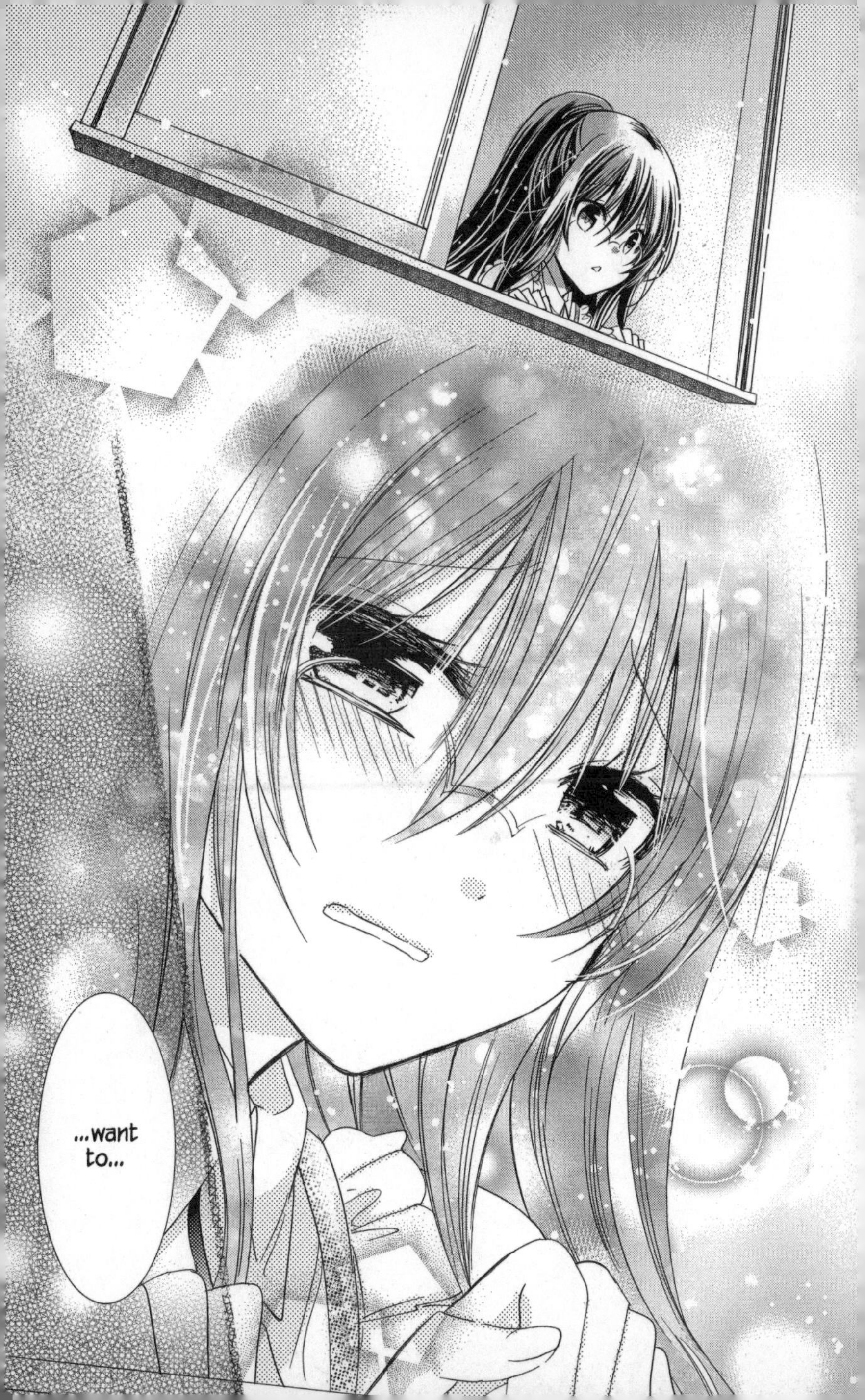
...want to...

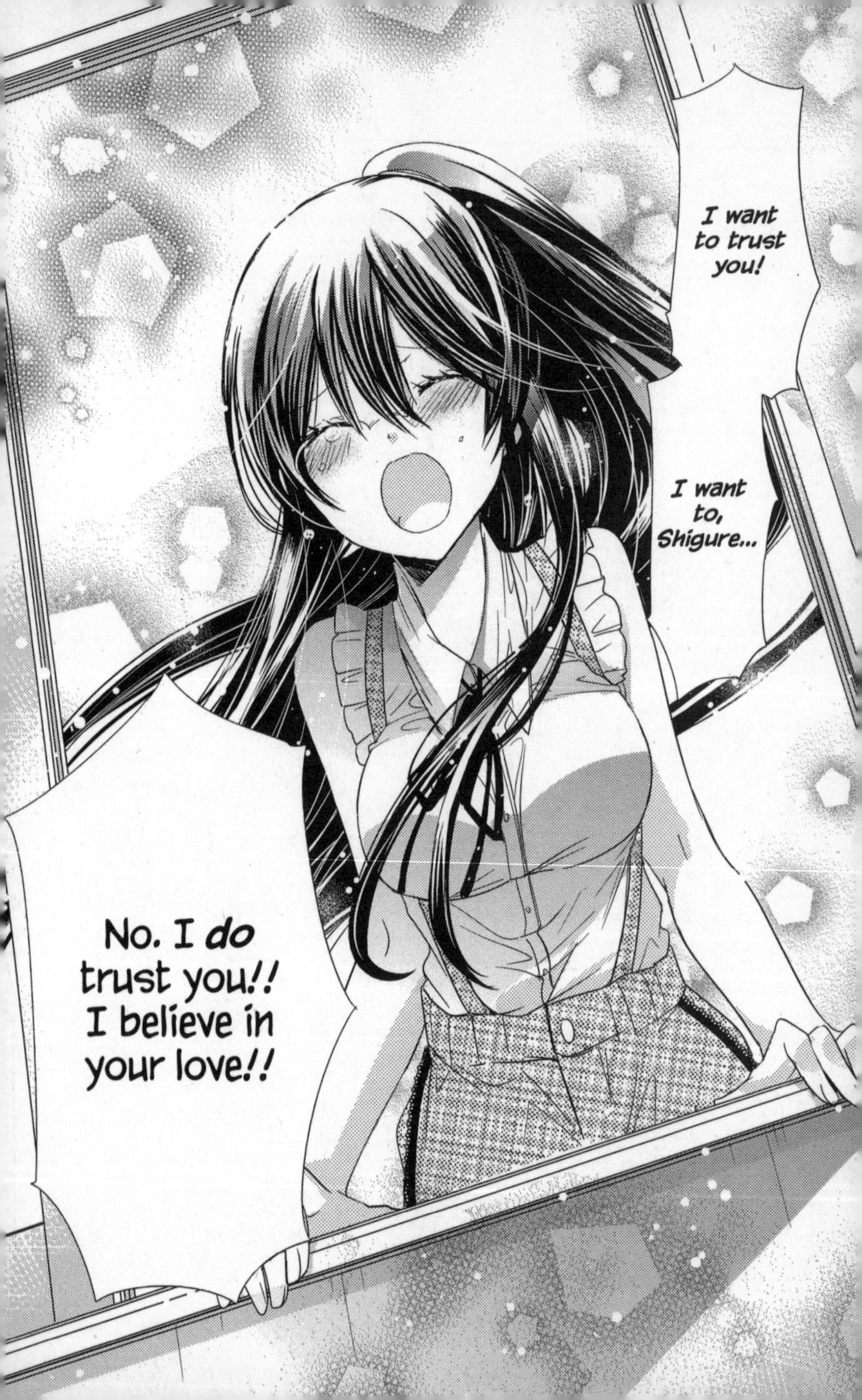
I want to trust you!
I want to, Shigure...
No. I *do* trust you!! I believe in your love!!

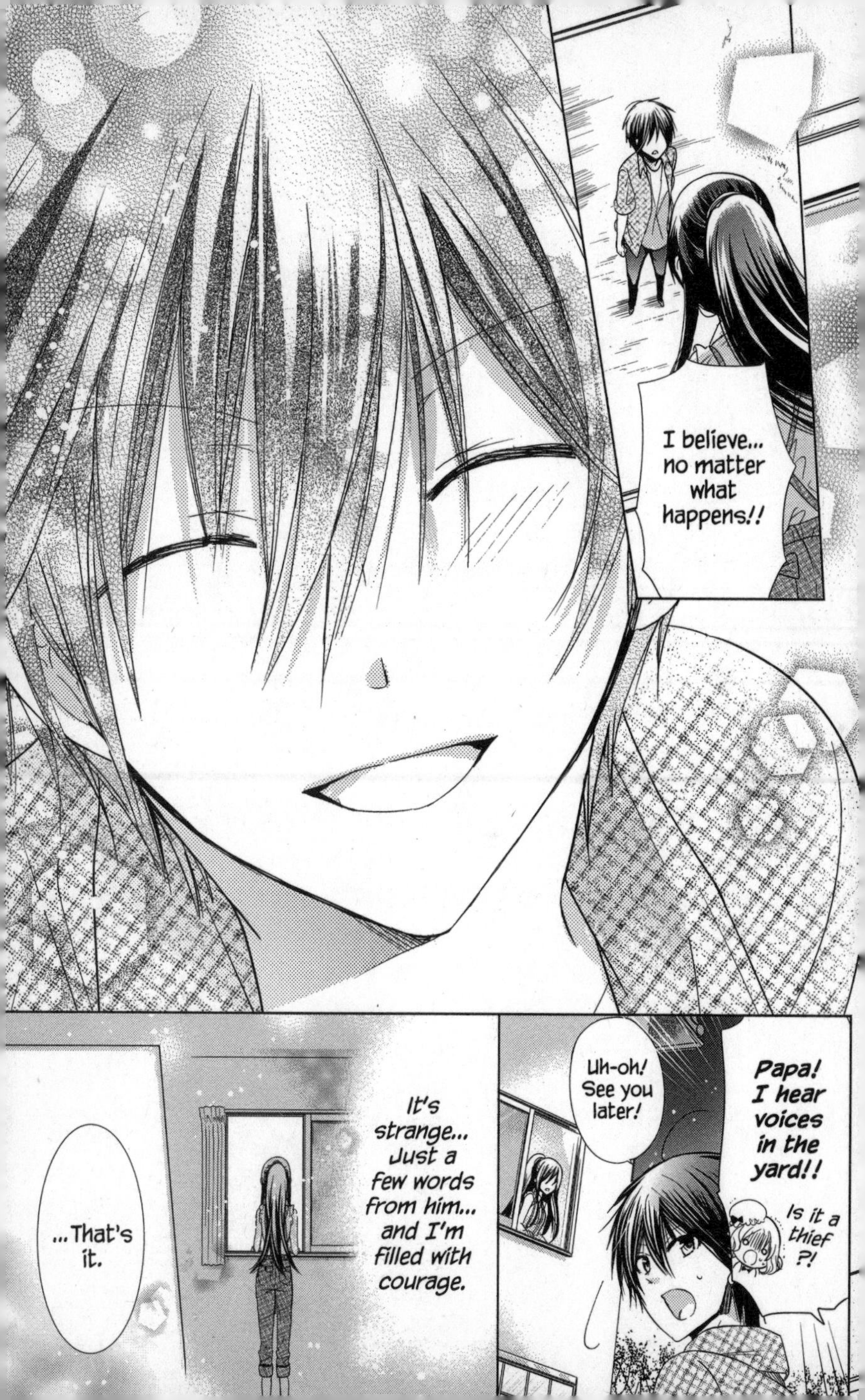
I believe... no matter what happens!!
Papa! I hear voices in the yard!!
Is it a thief ?!
Uh-oh! See you later!
It's strange... Just a few words from him... and I'm filled with courage.
...That's it.

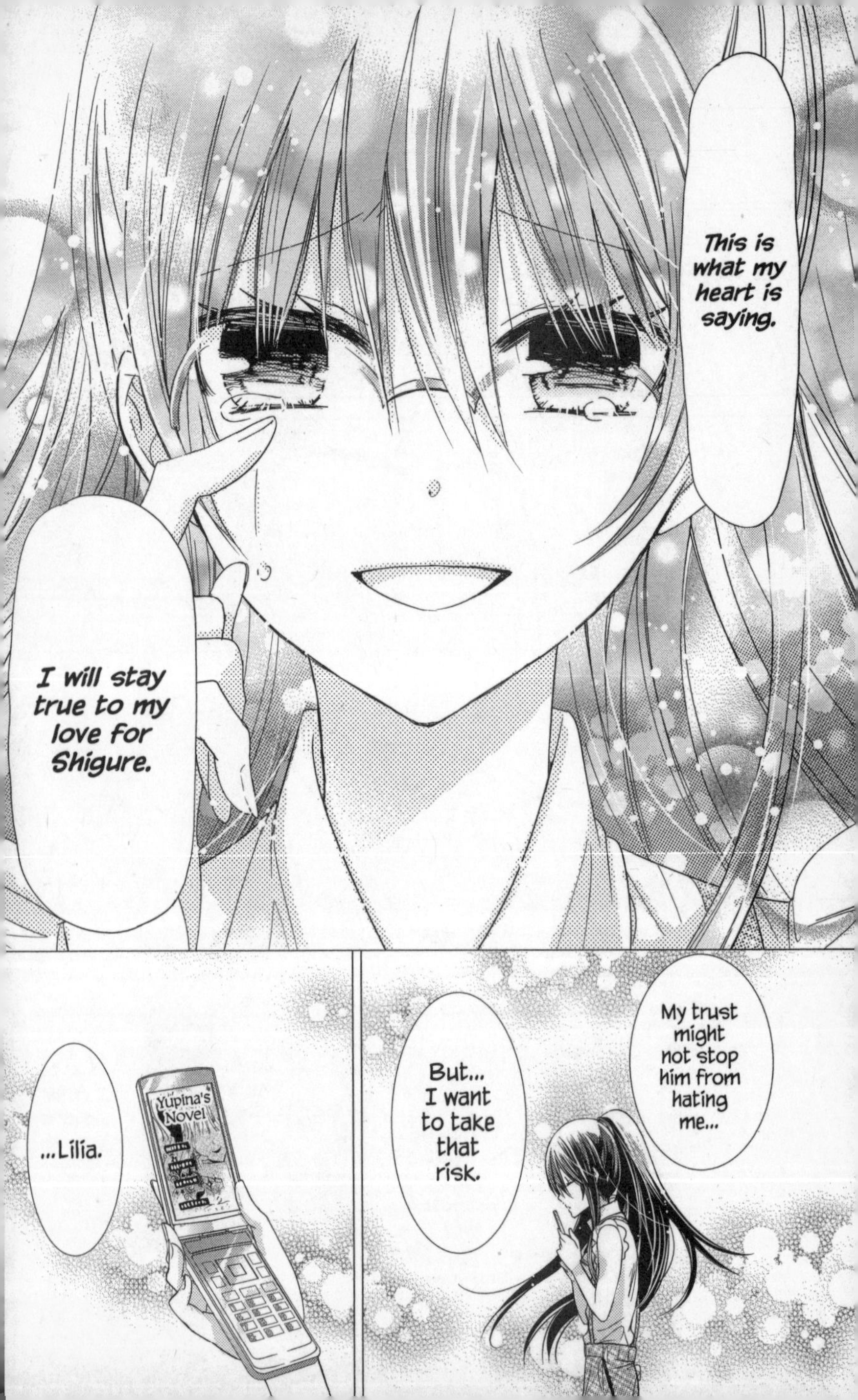
This is what my heart is saying.
I will stay true to my love for Shigure.
My trust might not stop him from hating me...
But... I want to take that risk.
Yupina's Novel
...Lilia.

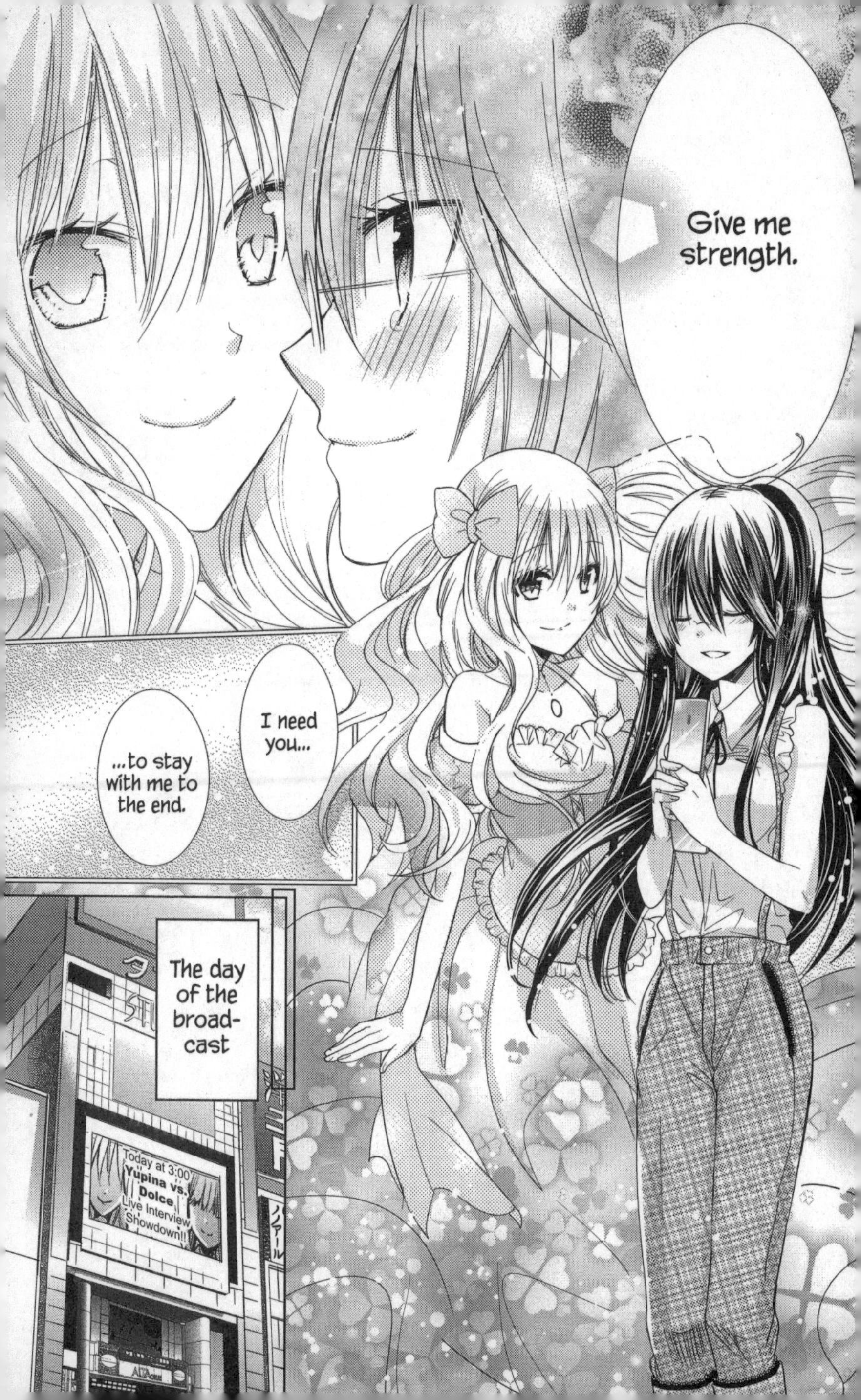
Give me strength.
I need you...
...to stay with me to the end.
The day of the broad-cast
Today at 3:00 Yupina vs. Dolce Live Interview Showdown!!

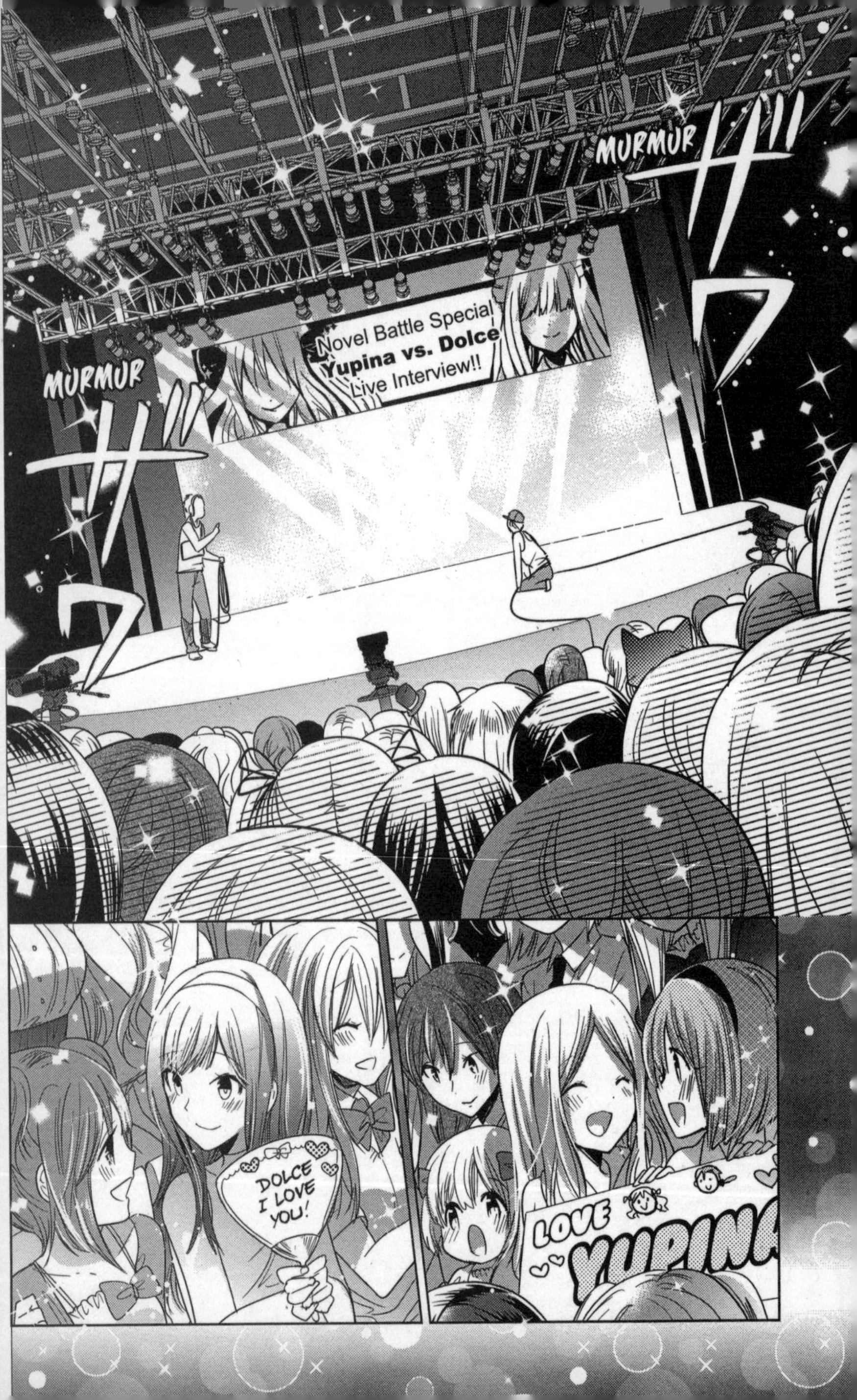
MURMUR
ザワ
Novel Battle Special
Yupina vs. Dolce
Live Interview!!
MURMUR
ザワ
LOVE
YUPINA
DOLCE
I LOVE
YOU!

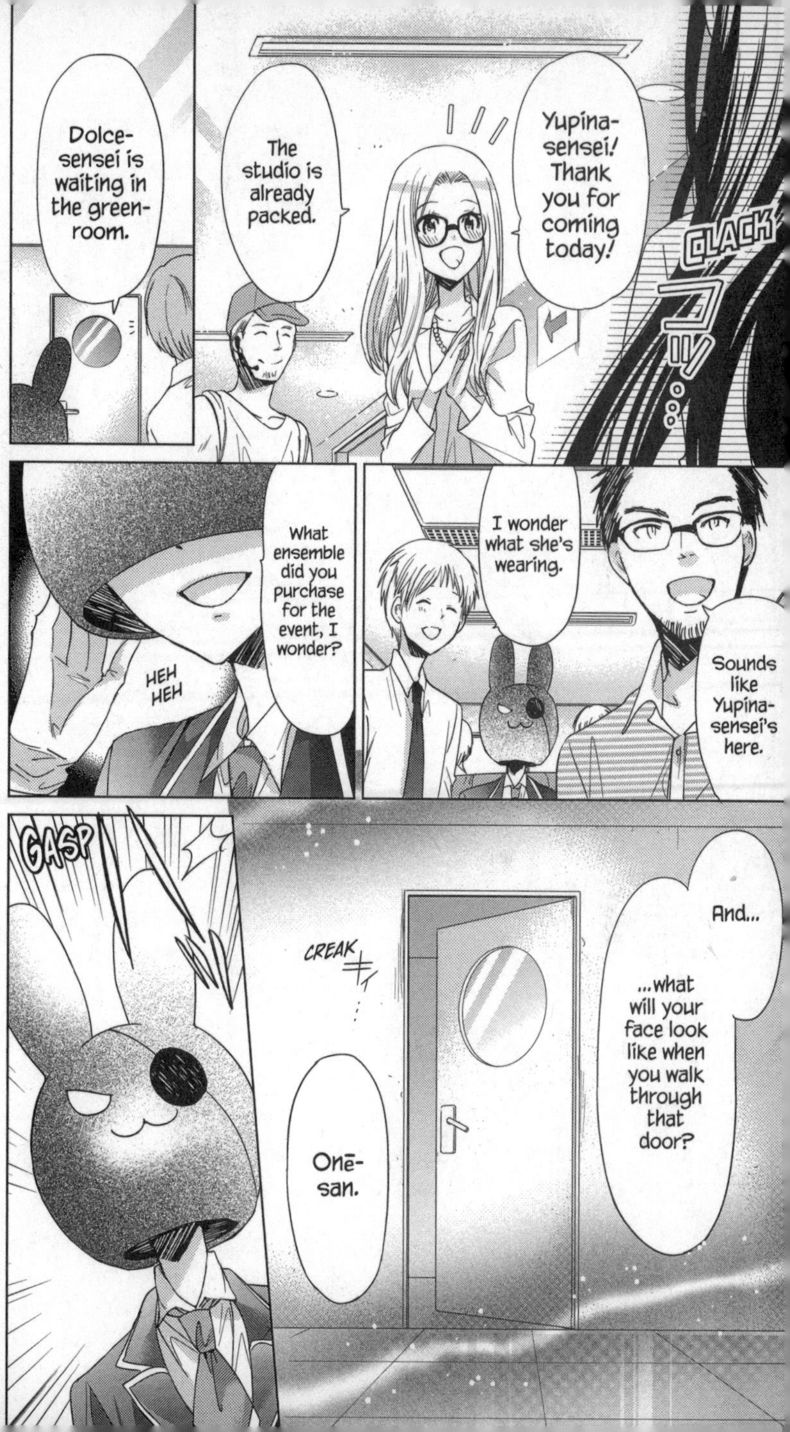
CLACK
Yupina-sensei! Thank you for coming today!
The studio is already packed.
Dolce-sensei is waiting in the green-room.
Sounds like Yupina-sensei's here.
I wonder what she's wearing.
What ensemble did you purchase for the event, I wonder?
HEH HEH
And...
...what will your face look like when you walk through that door?
CREAK
Onē-san.
GASP

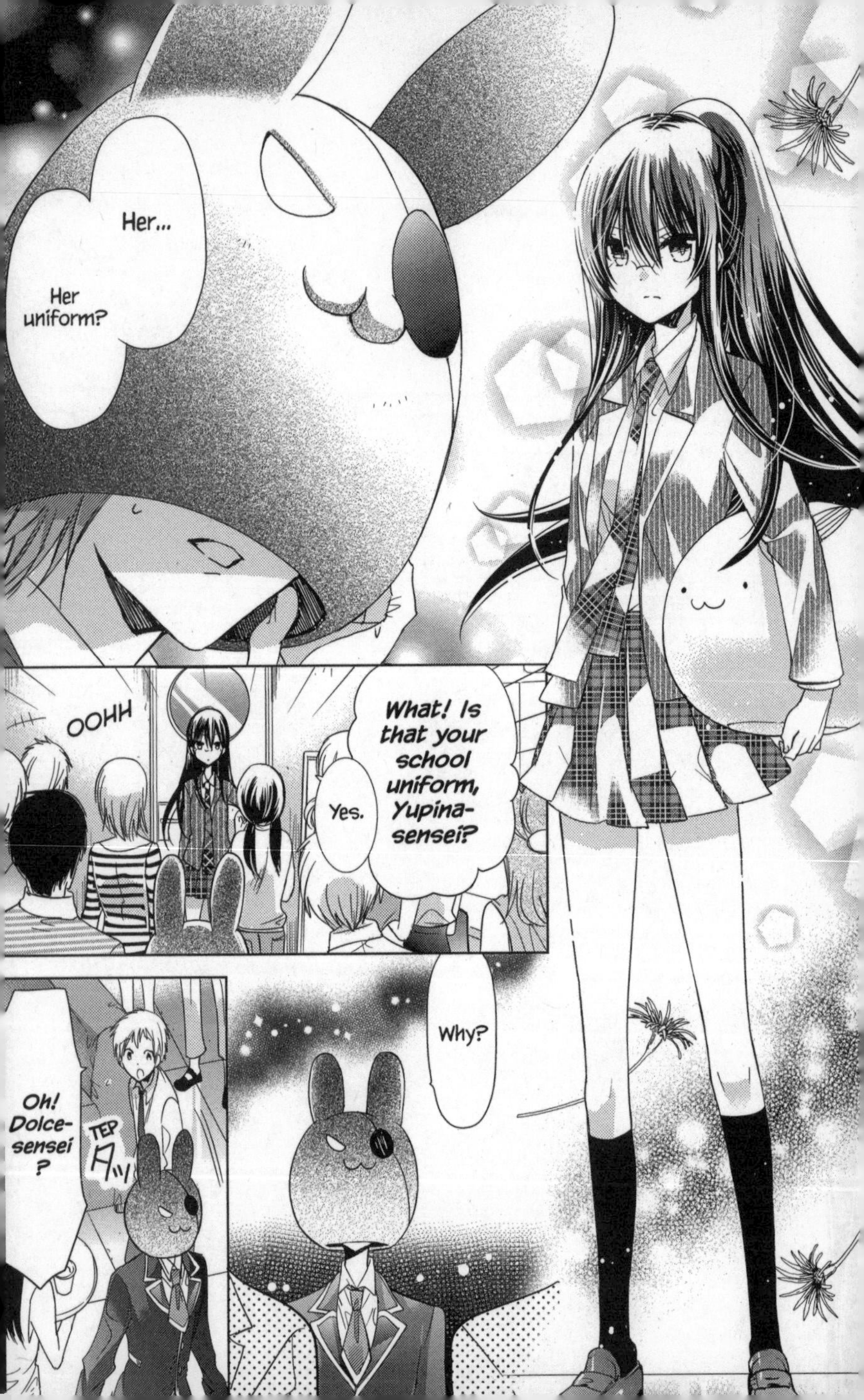
Her...
Her uniform?
What! Is that your school uniform, Yupina-sensei?
Yes.
OOHH
Why?
Oh! Dolce-sensei?
TEP

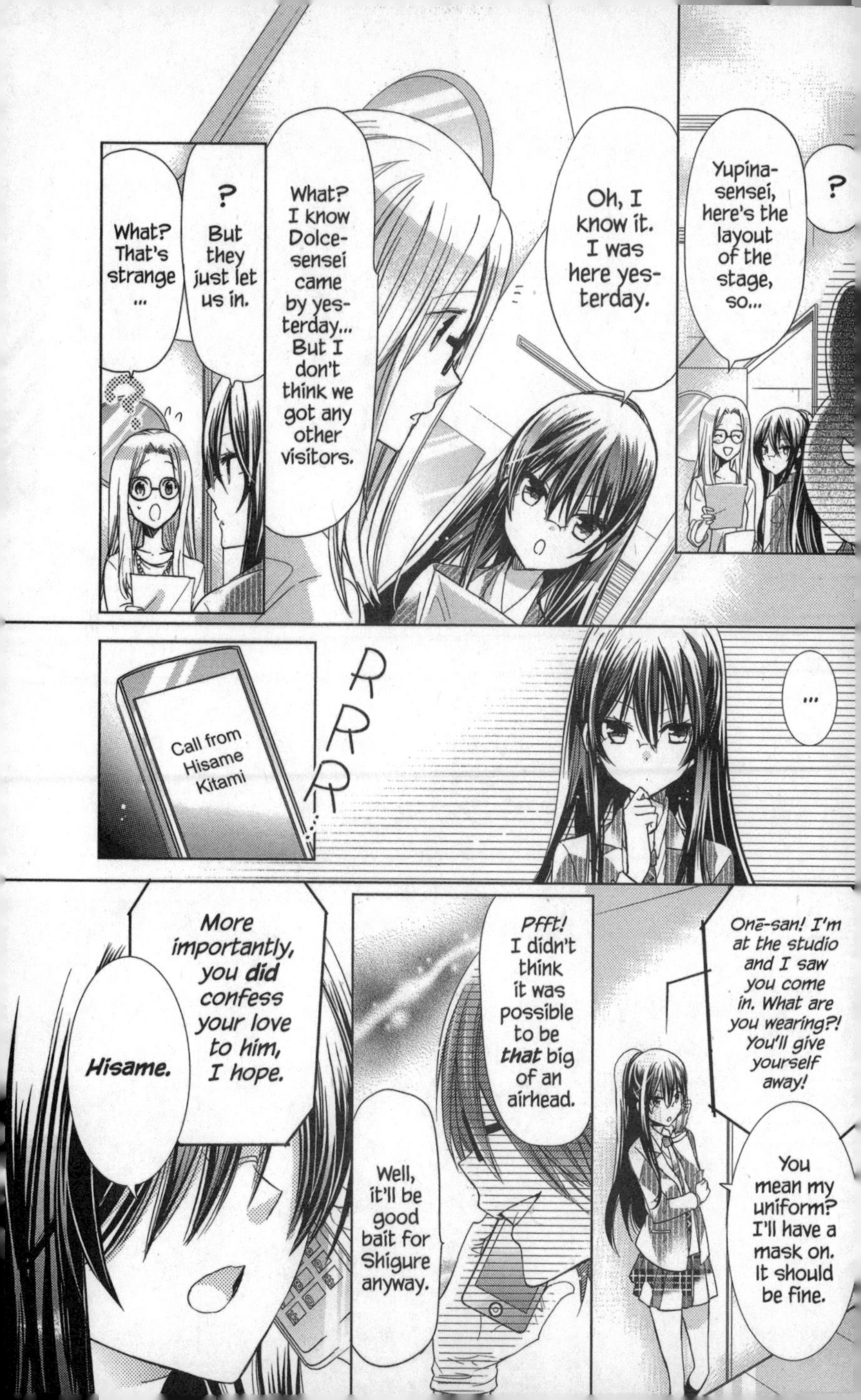
?
Yupina-sensei, here's the layout of the stage, so...
Oh, I know it. I was here yesterday.
What? I know Dolce-sensei came by yesterday... But I don't think we got any other visitors.
? But they just let us in.
What? That's strange ...
...
RRR
Call from Hisame Kitami
One-san! I'm at the studio and I saw you come in. What are you wearing?! You'll give yourself away!
You mean my uniform? I'll have a mask on. It should be fine.
Pfft! I didn't think it was possible to be *that* big of an airhead.
Well, it'll be good bait for Shigure anyway.
More importantly, you **did** confess your love to him, I hope.
Hisame.

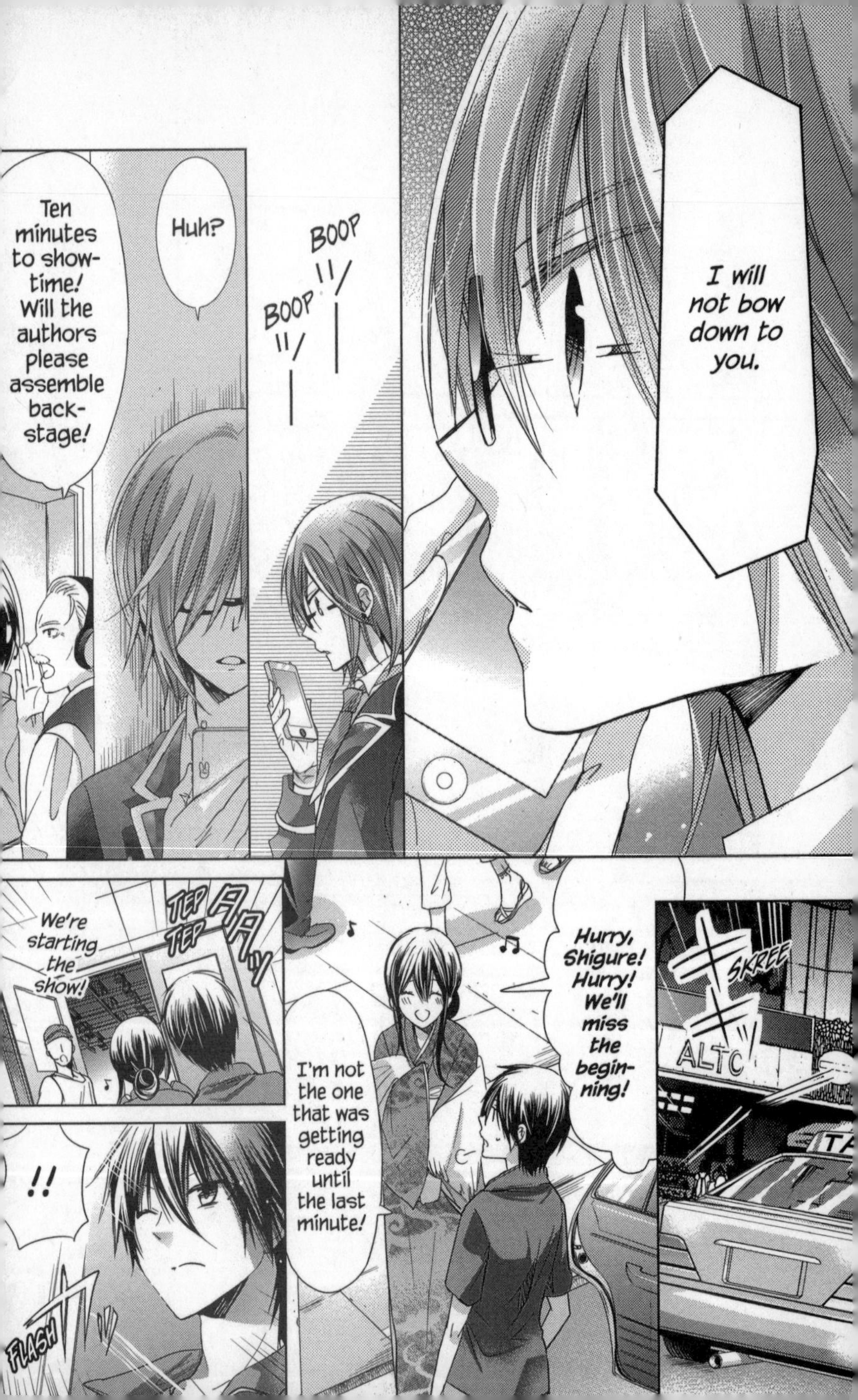
I will not bow down to you.
BOOP BOOP
Huh?
Ten minutes to show-time! Will the authors please assemble back-stage!
SKREE
ALTC
Hurry, Shigure! Hurry! We'll miss the begin-ning!
I'm not the one that was getting ready until the last minute!
TEP TEP
We're starting the show!
!!
FLASH

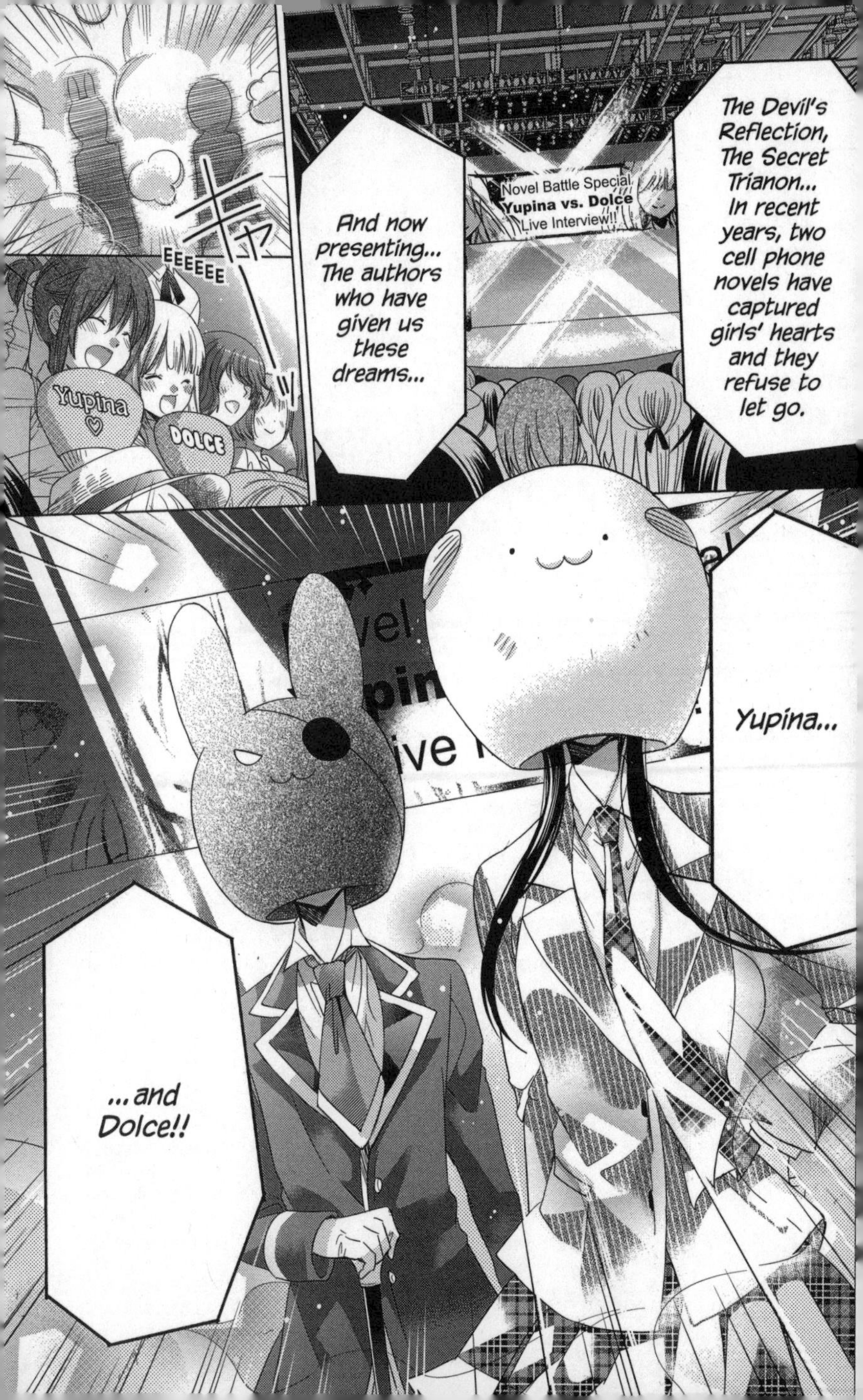

The Devil's Reflection, The Secret Trianon... In recent years, two cell phone novels have captured girls' hearts and they refuse to let go.
Novel Battle Special
Yupina vs. Dolce
Live Interview!!
And now presenting... The authors who have given us these dreams...
キャ
EEEEEE
Yupina ♡
DOLCE
Yupina...
...and Dolce!!

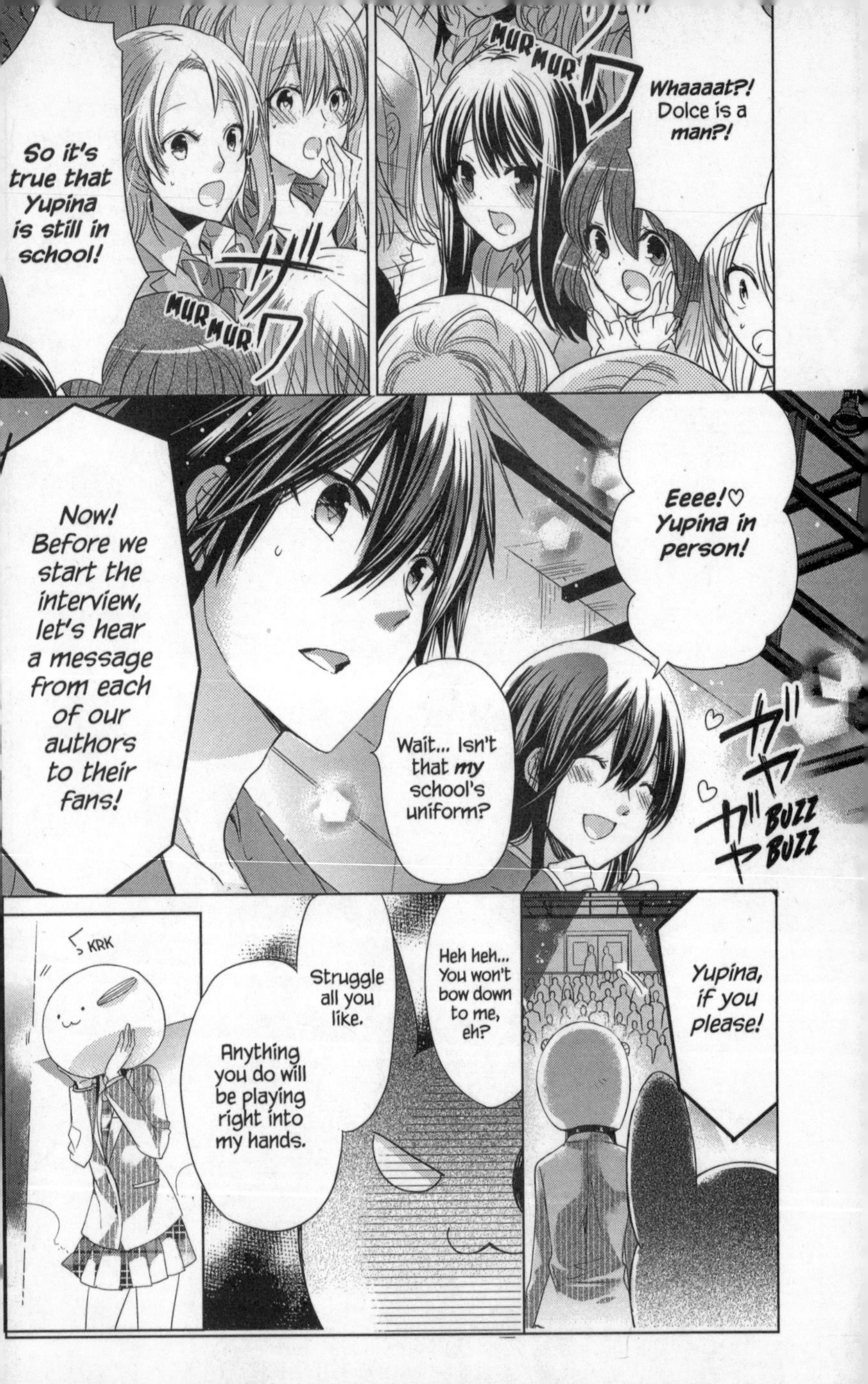
MUR MUR
Whaaaat?! Dolce is a man?!
So it's true that Yupina is still in school!
MUR MUR
Eeee!♡ Yupina in person!
BUZZ BUZZ
Now! Before we start the interview, let's hear a message from each of our authors to their fans!
Wait... Isn't that my school's uniform?
Yupina, if you please!
Heh heh... You won't bow down to me, eh?
Struggle all you like.
Anything you do will be playing right into my hands.
KRK

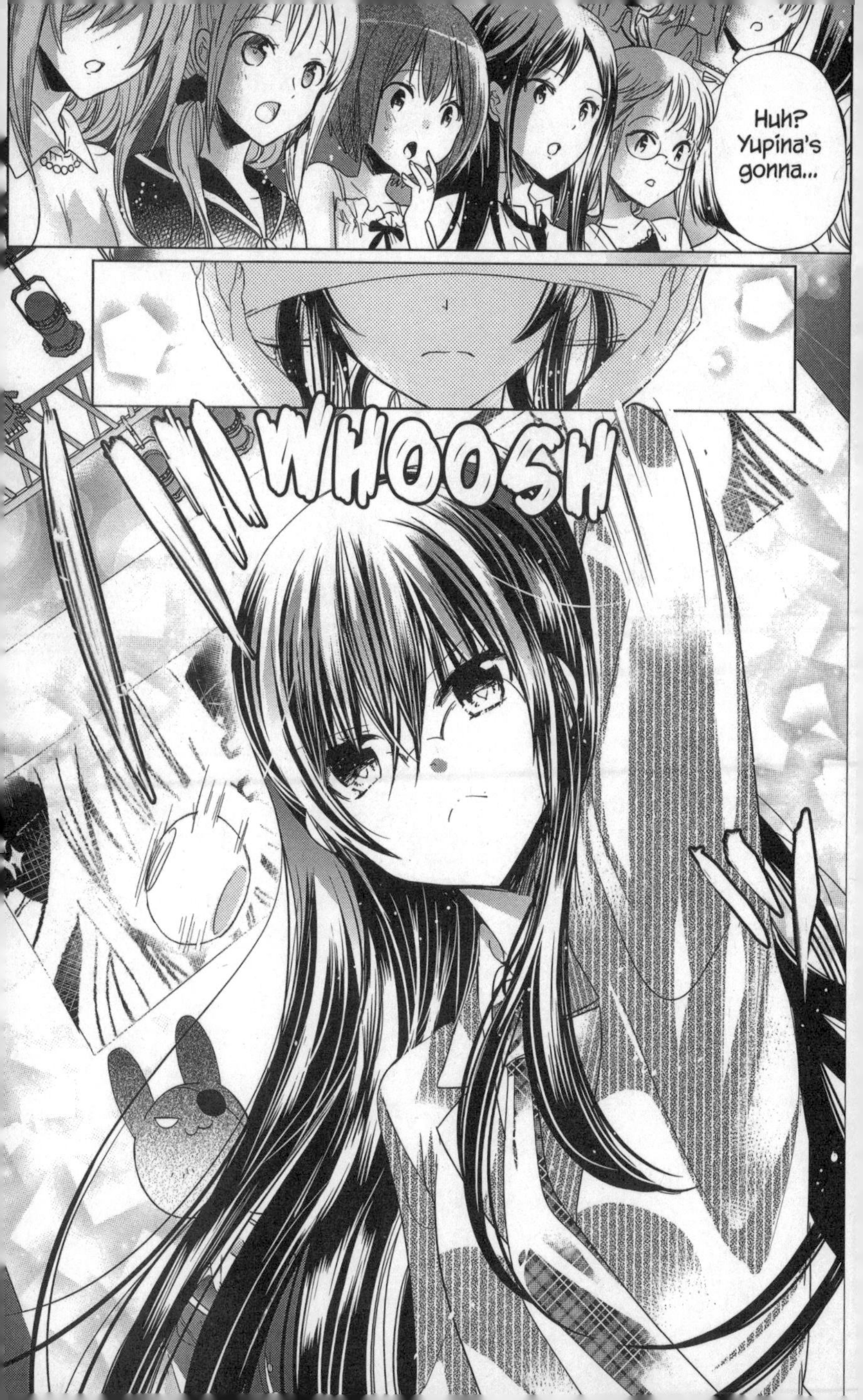
Huh? Yupina's gonna...
WHOOSH

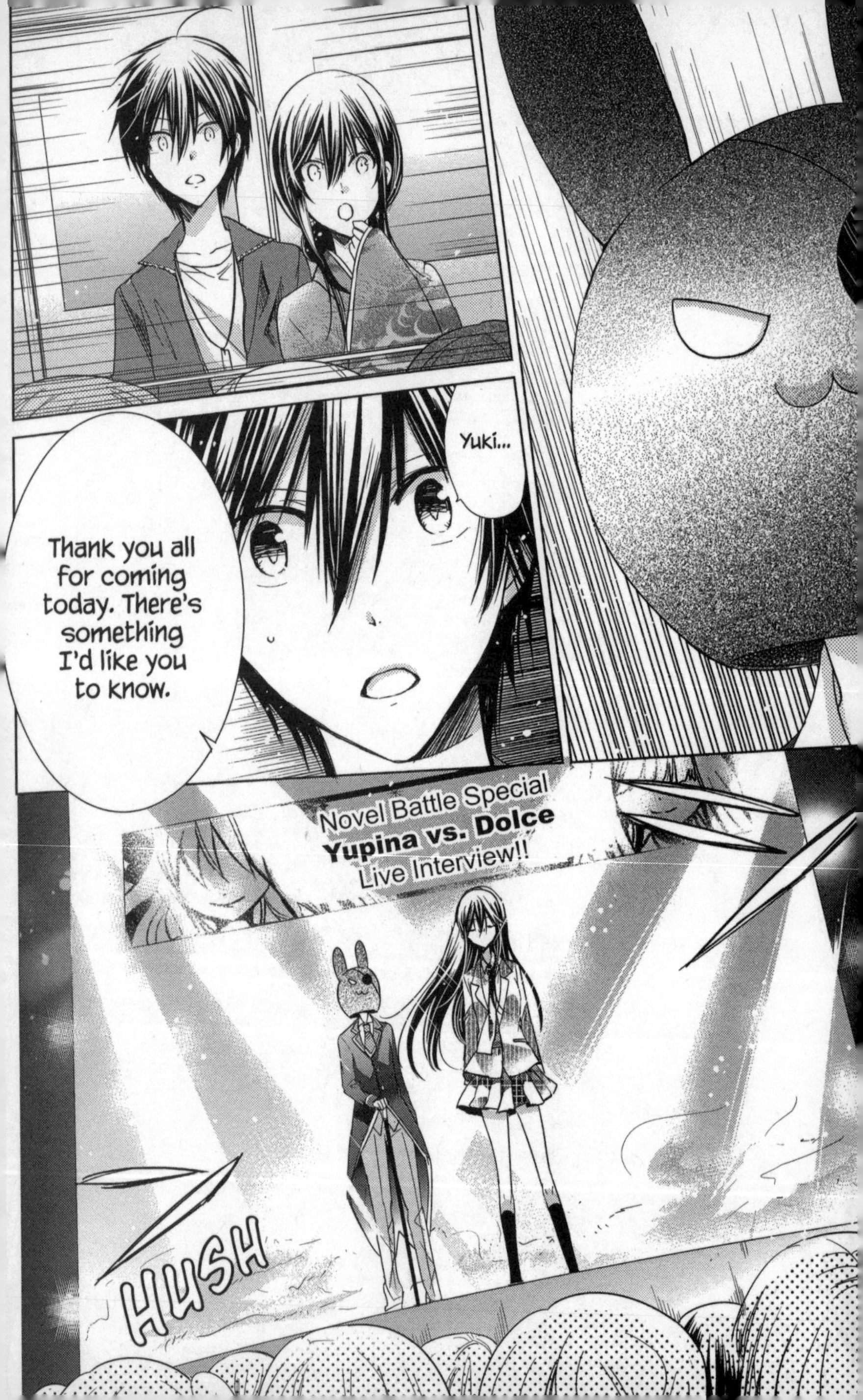
Yuki...
Thank you all for coming today. There's something I'd like you to know.
Novel Battle Special
Yupina vs. Dolce
Live Interview!!
HUSH

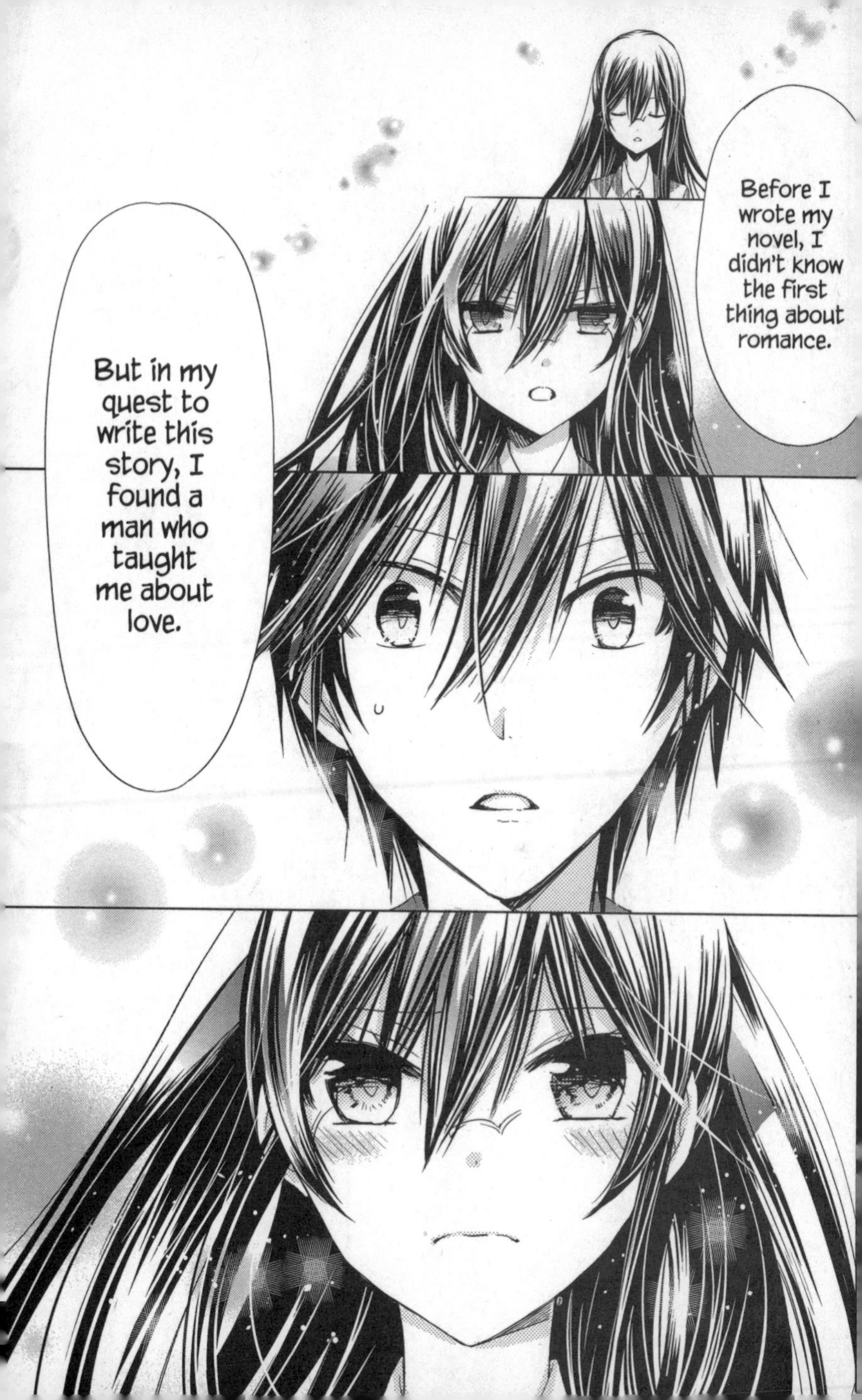
Before I wrote my novel, I didn't know the first thing about romance.
But in my quest to write this story, I found a man who taught me about love.

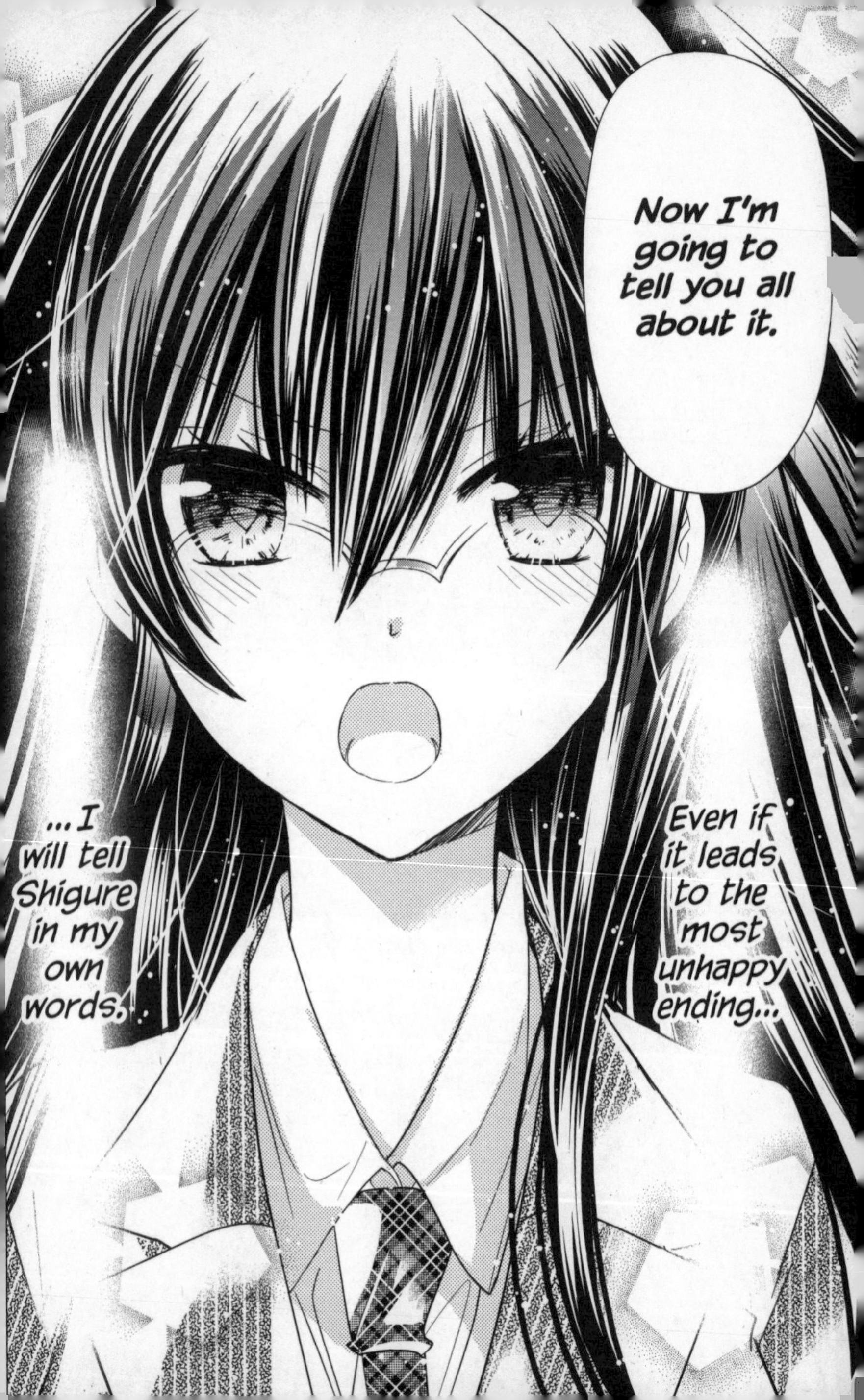
Now I'm going to tell you all about it.
Even if it leads to the most unhappy ending...
...I will tell Shigure in my own words.

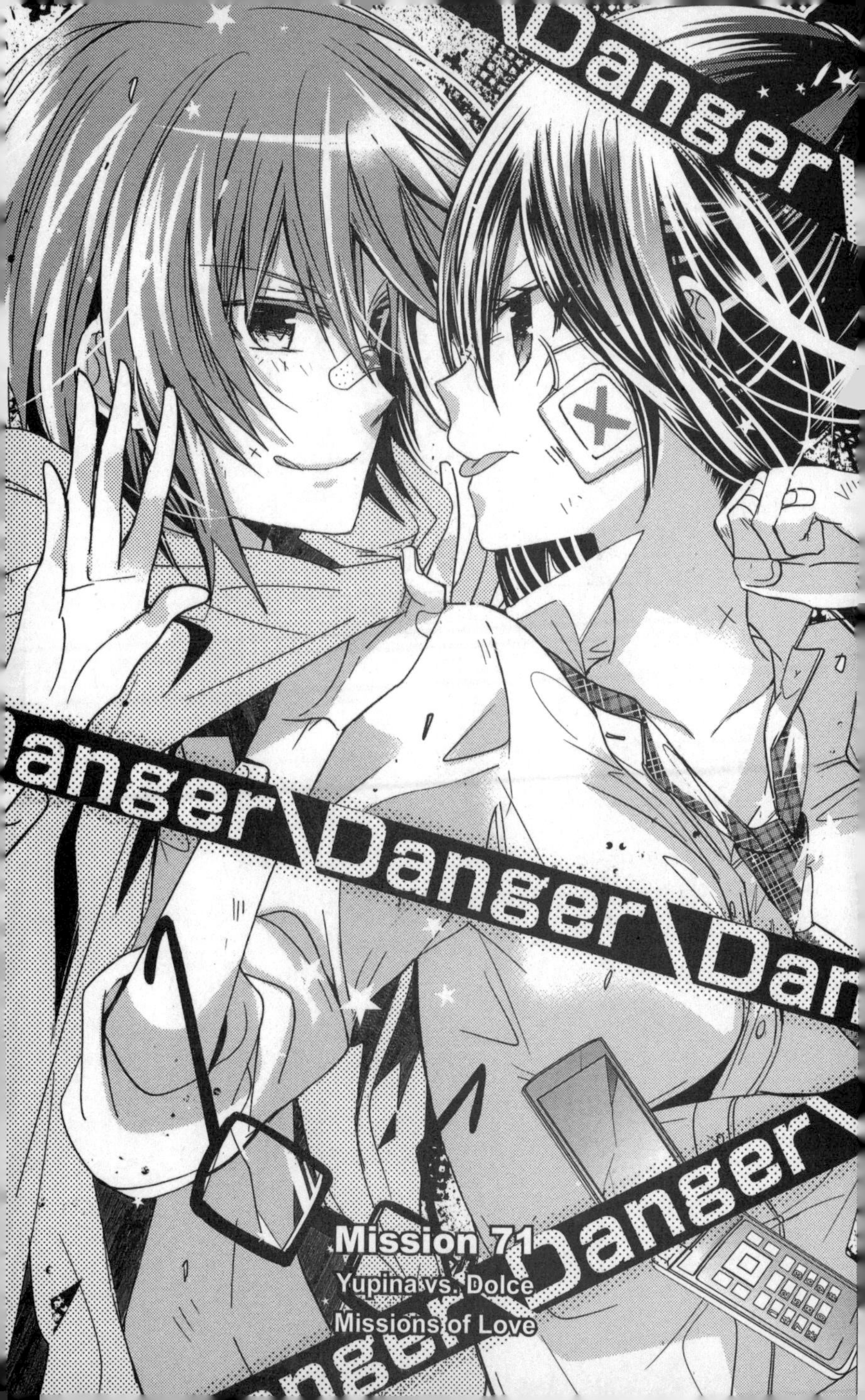
Danger Danger Danger
Mission 71
Yupina vs. Dolce
Missions of Love

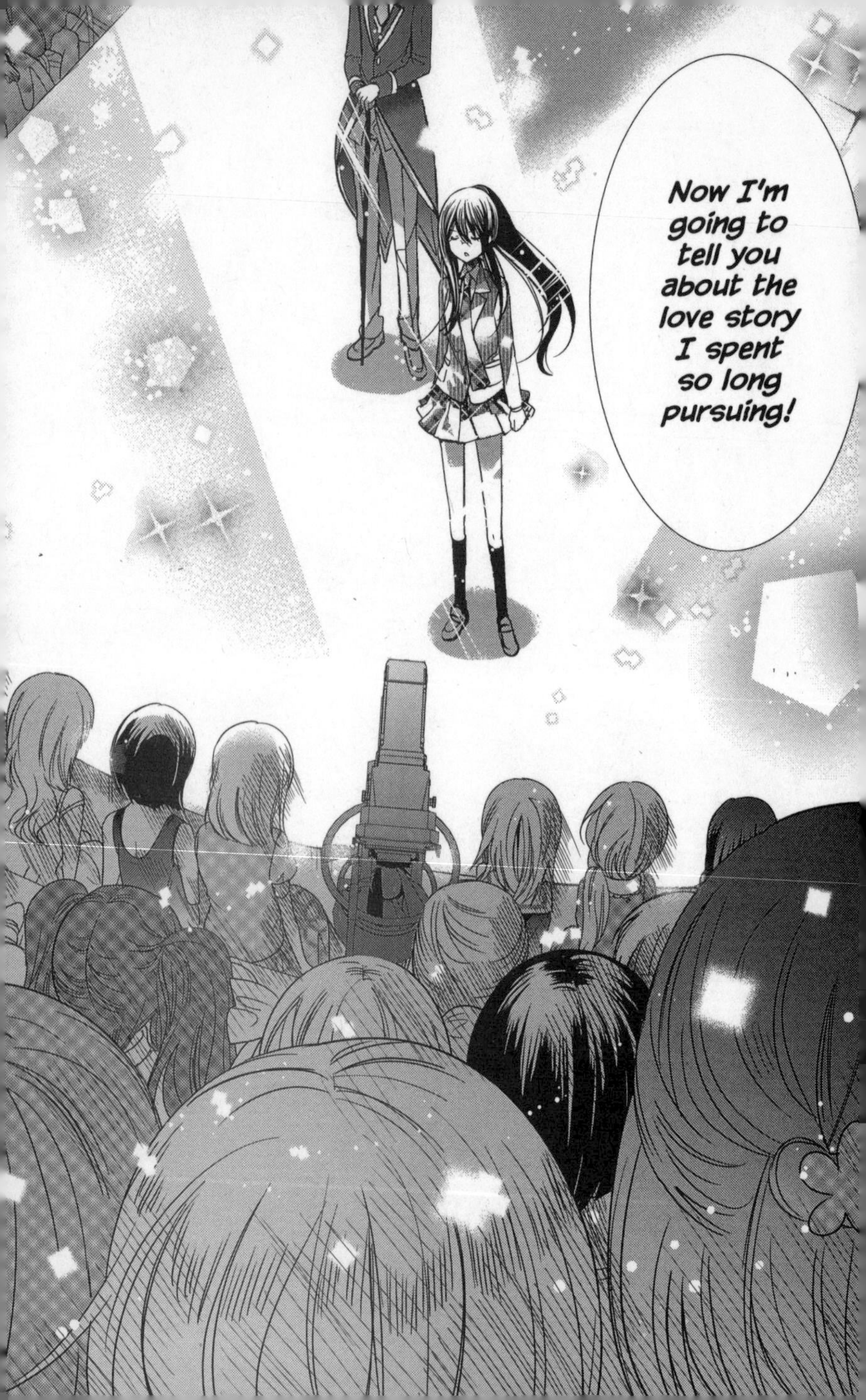
Now I'm going to tell you about the love story I spent so long pursuing!

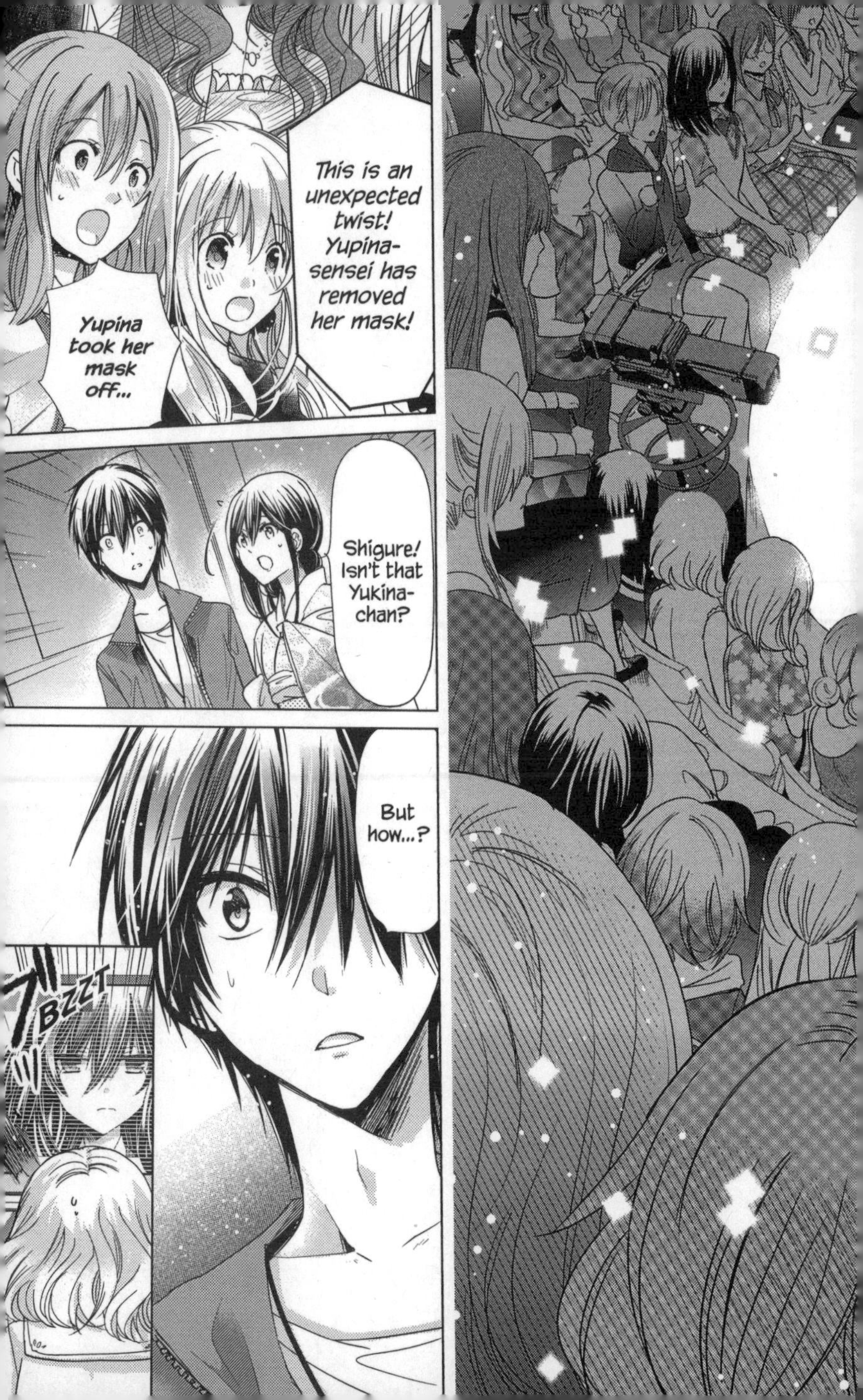
This is an unexpected twist! Yupina-sensei has removed her mask!
Yupina took her mask off...
Shigure! Isn't that Yukina-chan?
But how...?
BZZT

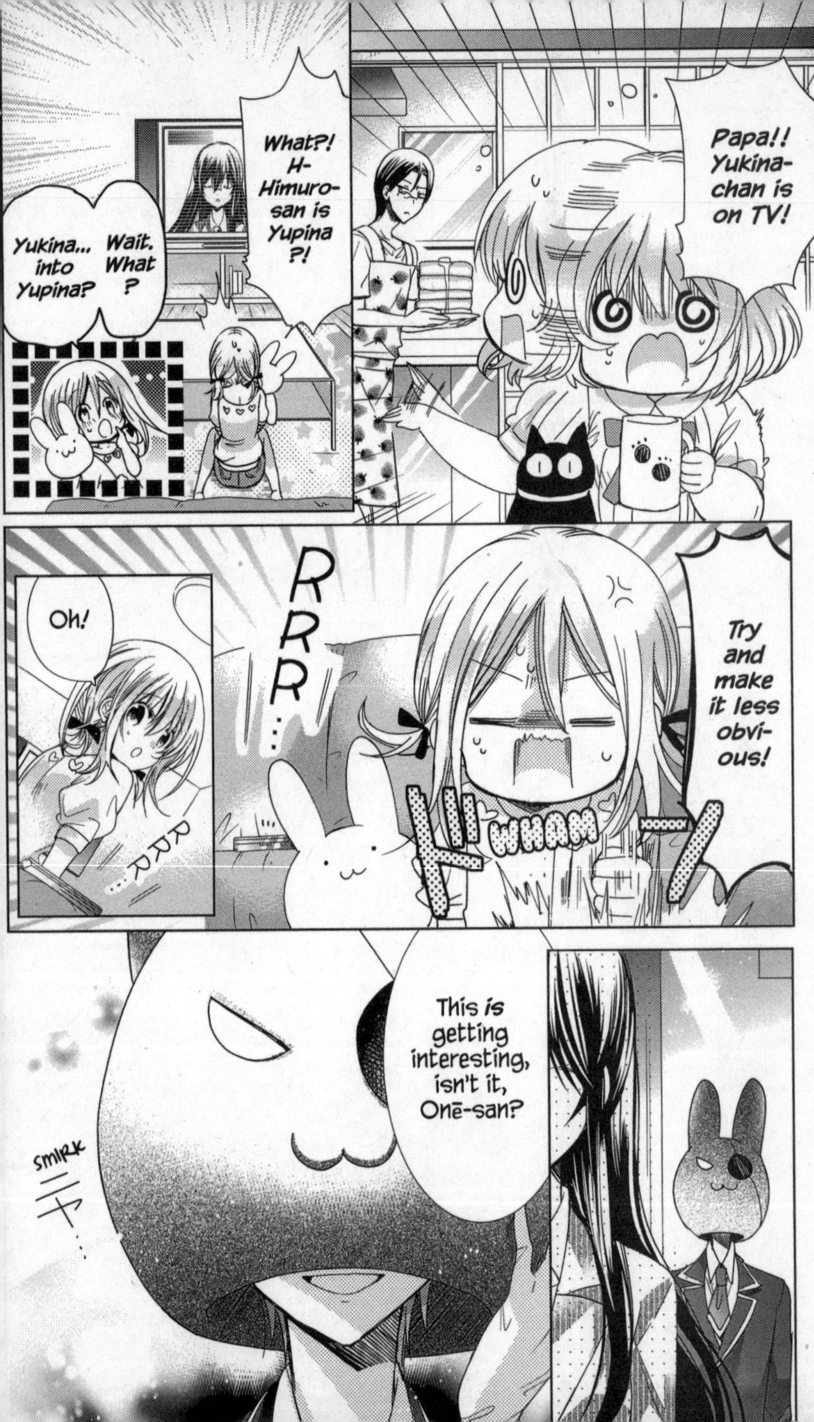
Papa!! Yukina-chan is on TV!
What?! H-Himuro-san is Yupina?!
Wait. What?
Yukina... into Yupina?
Try and make it less obvious!
RRR...
WHAM
Oh!
RRR...
This is getting interesting, isn't it, Onē-san?
SMIRK

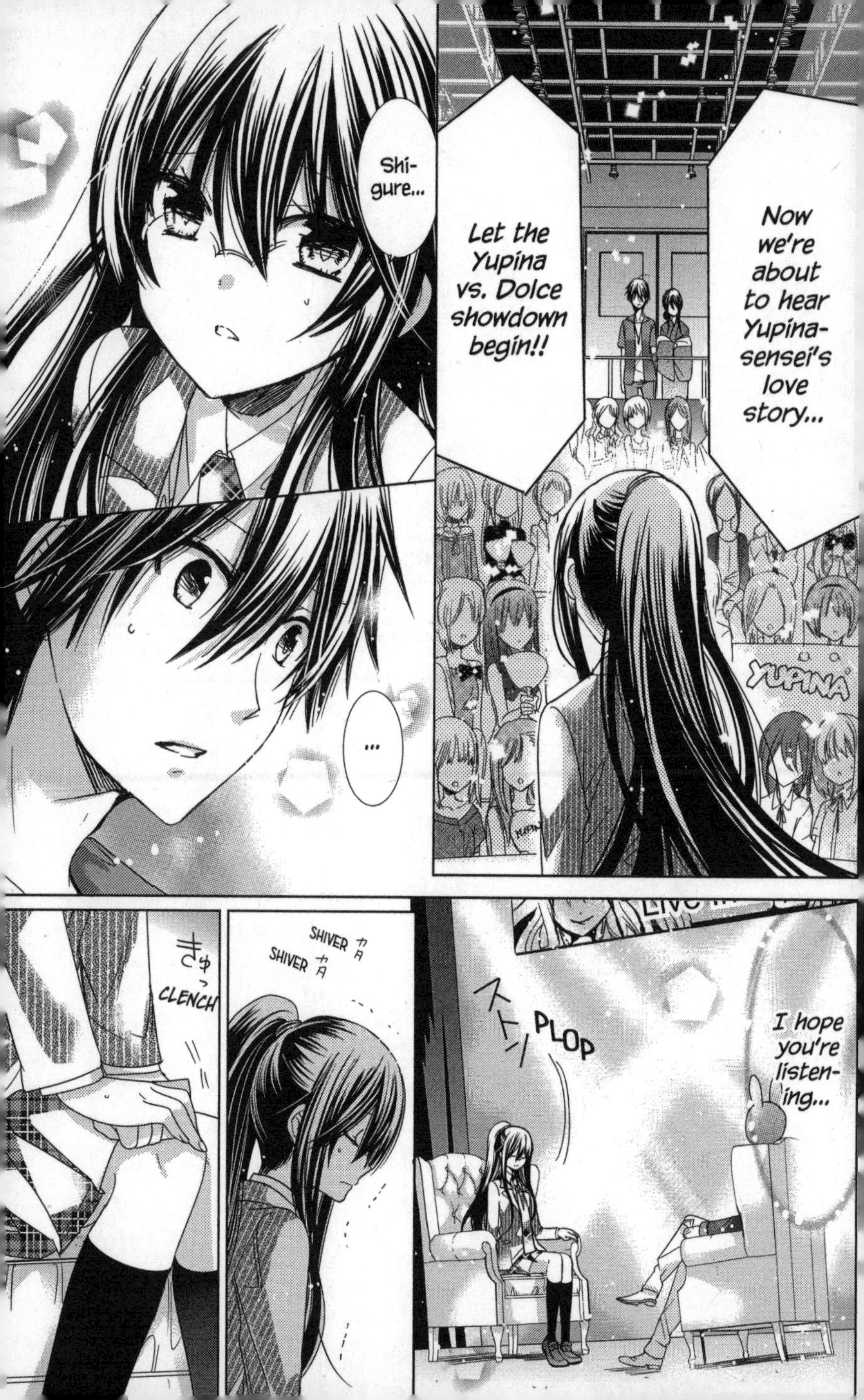
Now we're about to hear Yupina-sensei's love story...
Let the Yupina vs. Dolce showdown begin!!
YUPINA
YUPIN
Shi-gure...
...
I hope you're listening...
ストン
PLOP
SHIVER カタ
SHIVER カタ
きゅっ
CLENCH

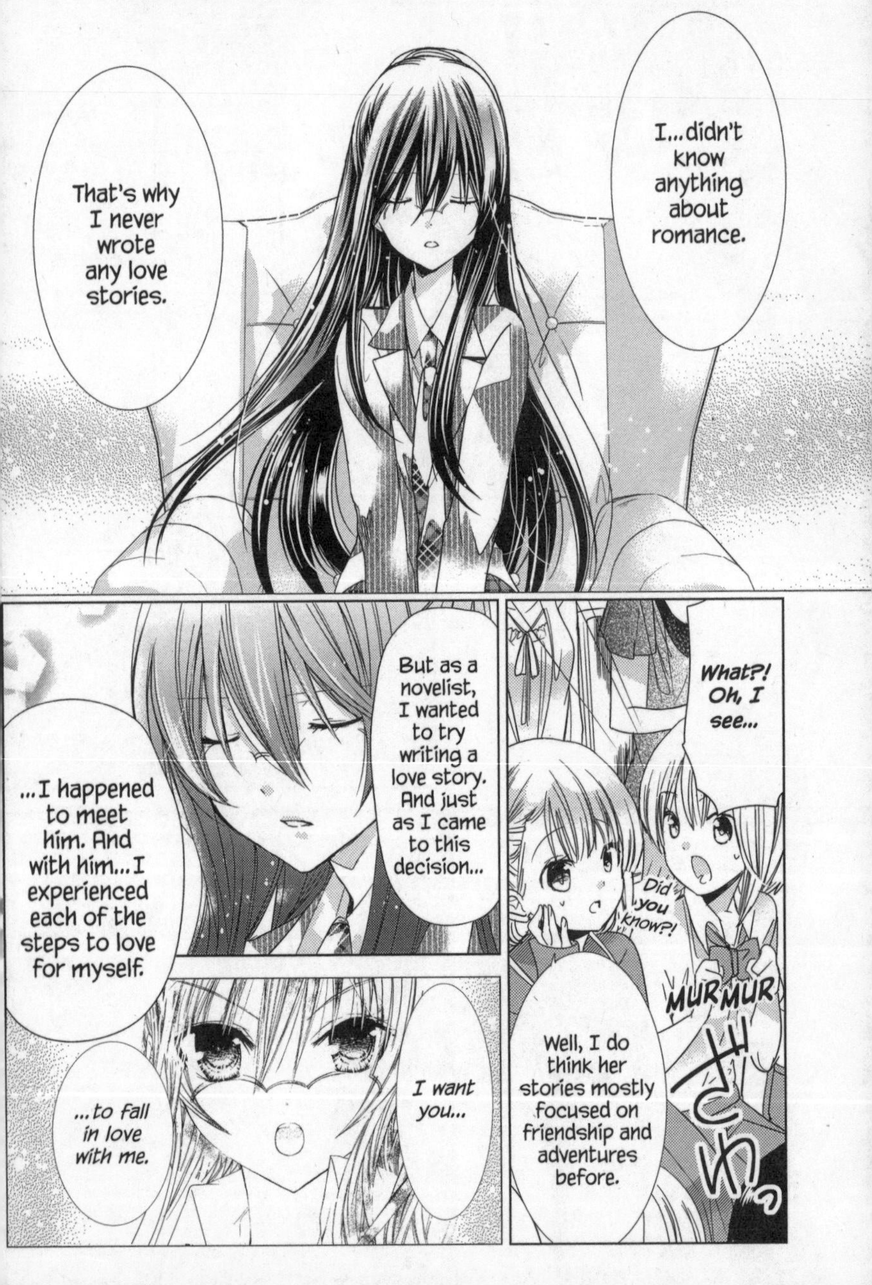
I...didn't know anything about romance.
That's why I never wrote any love stories.
What?! Oh, I see...
Did you know?!
MUR MUR
Well, I do think her stories mostly focused on friendship and adventures before.
But as a novelist, I wanted to try writing a love story. And just as I came to this decision...
...I happened to meet him. And with him...I experienced each of the steps to love for myself.
I want you...
...to fall in love with me.

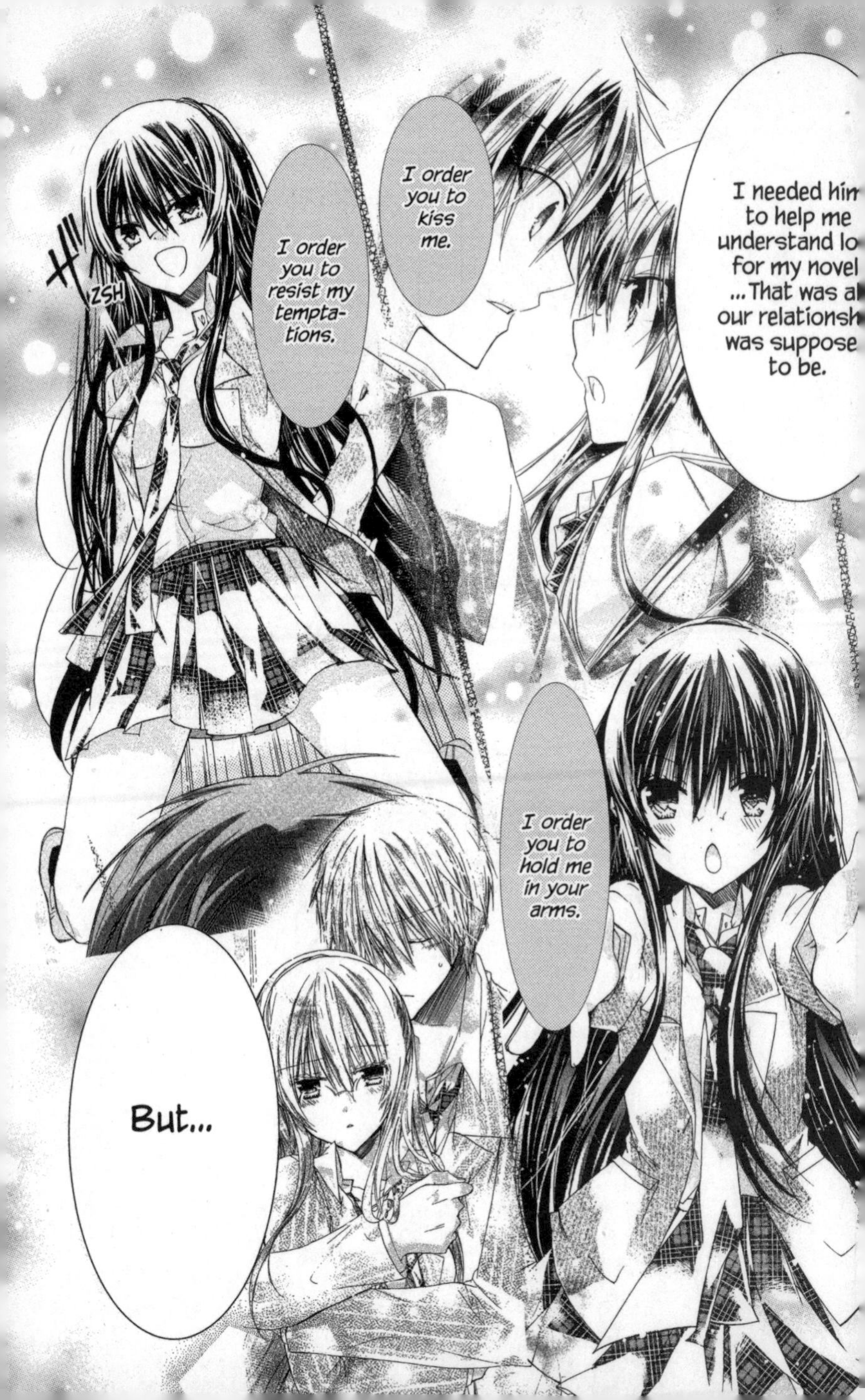
I needed hin to help me understand lo for my novel ...That was al our relationsh was suppose to be.
I order you to kiss me.
I order you to resist my tempta-tions.
ZSH
I order you to hold me in your arms.
But...

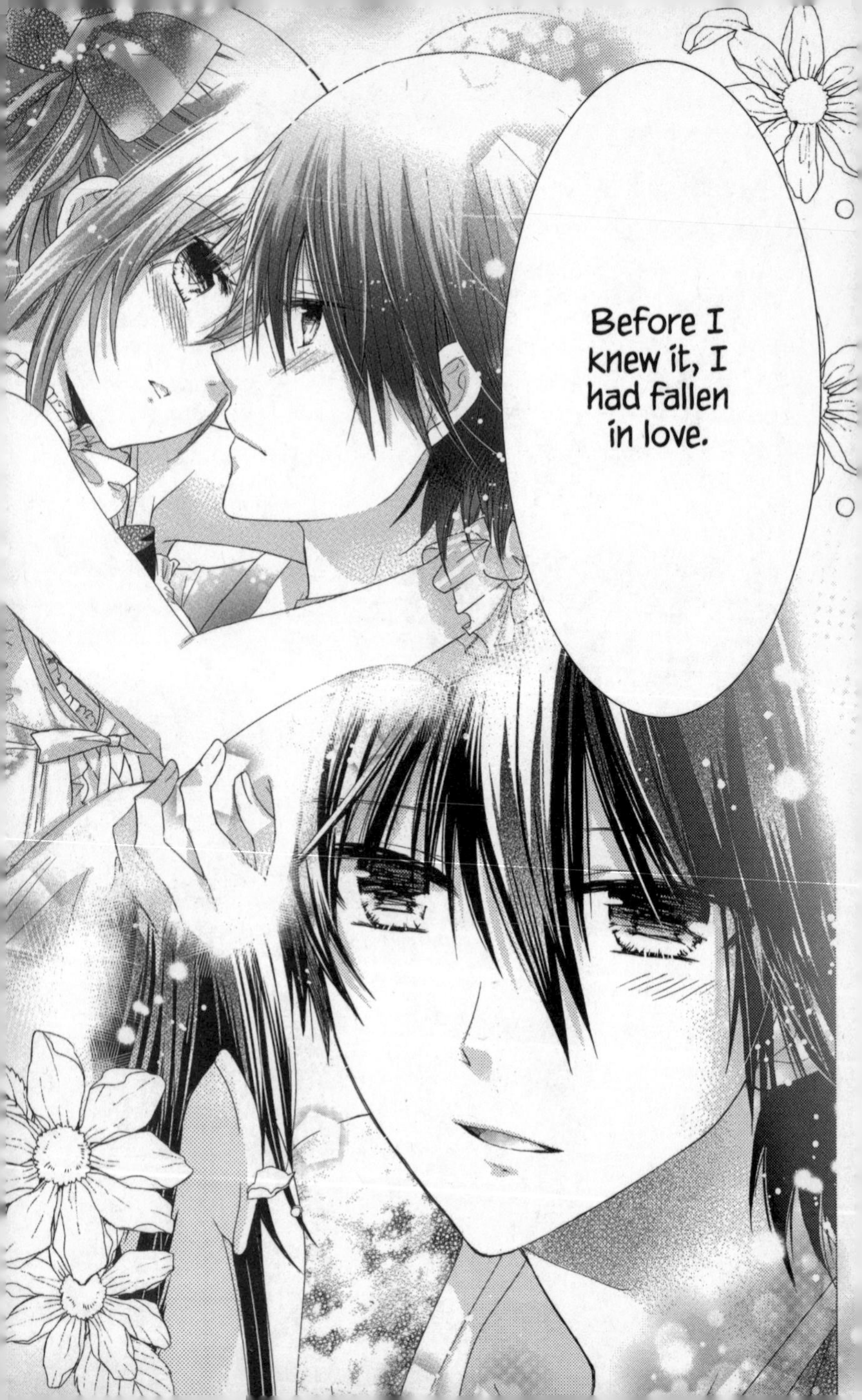
Before I knew it, I had fallen in love.

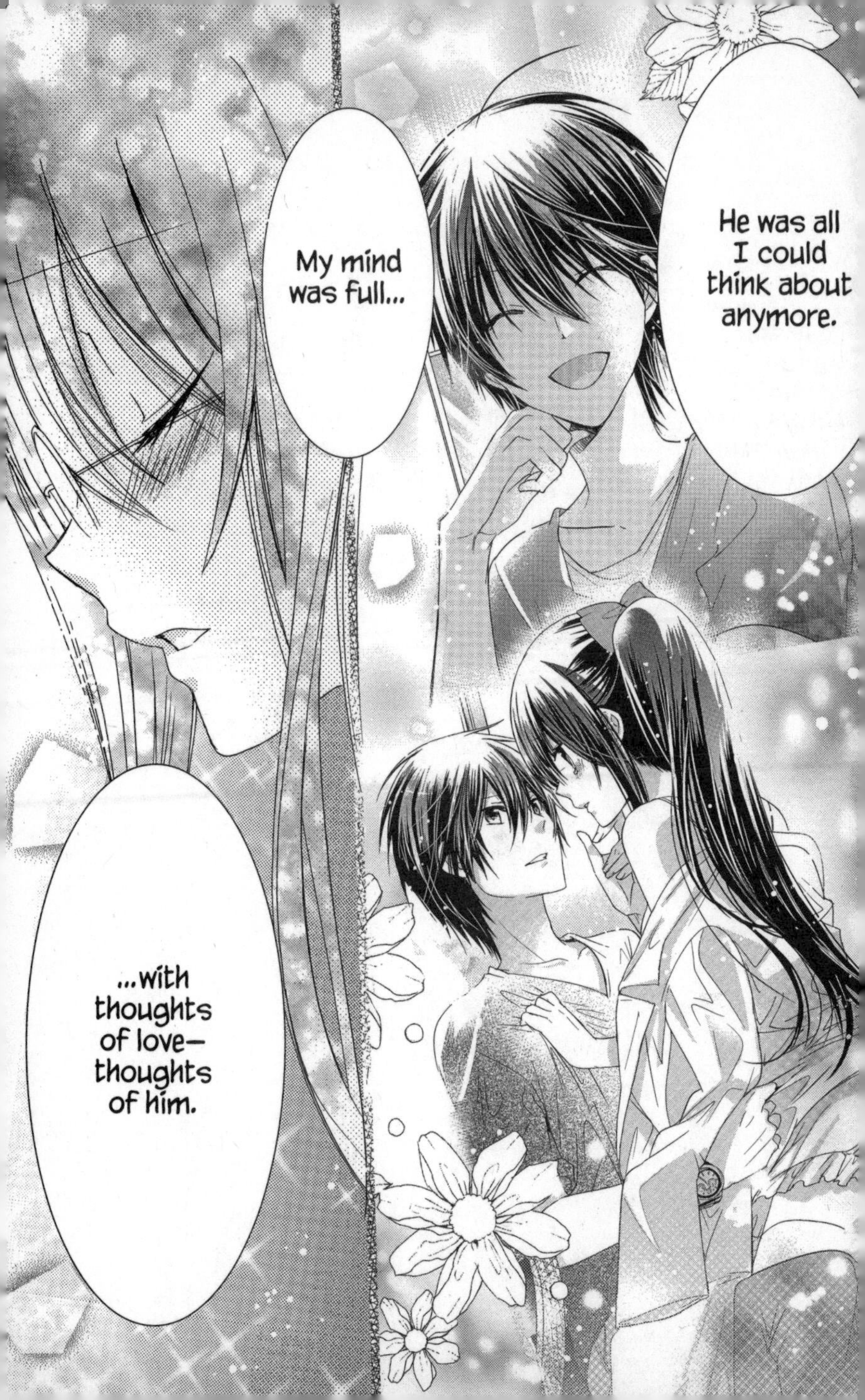
He was all I could think about anymore.
My mind was full...
...with thoughts of love—thoughts of him.

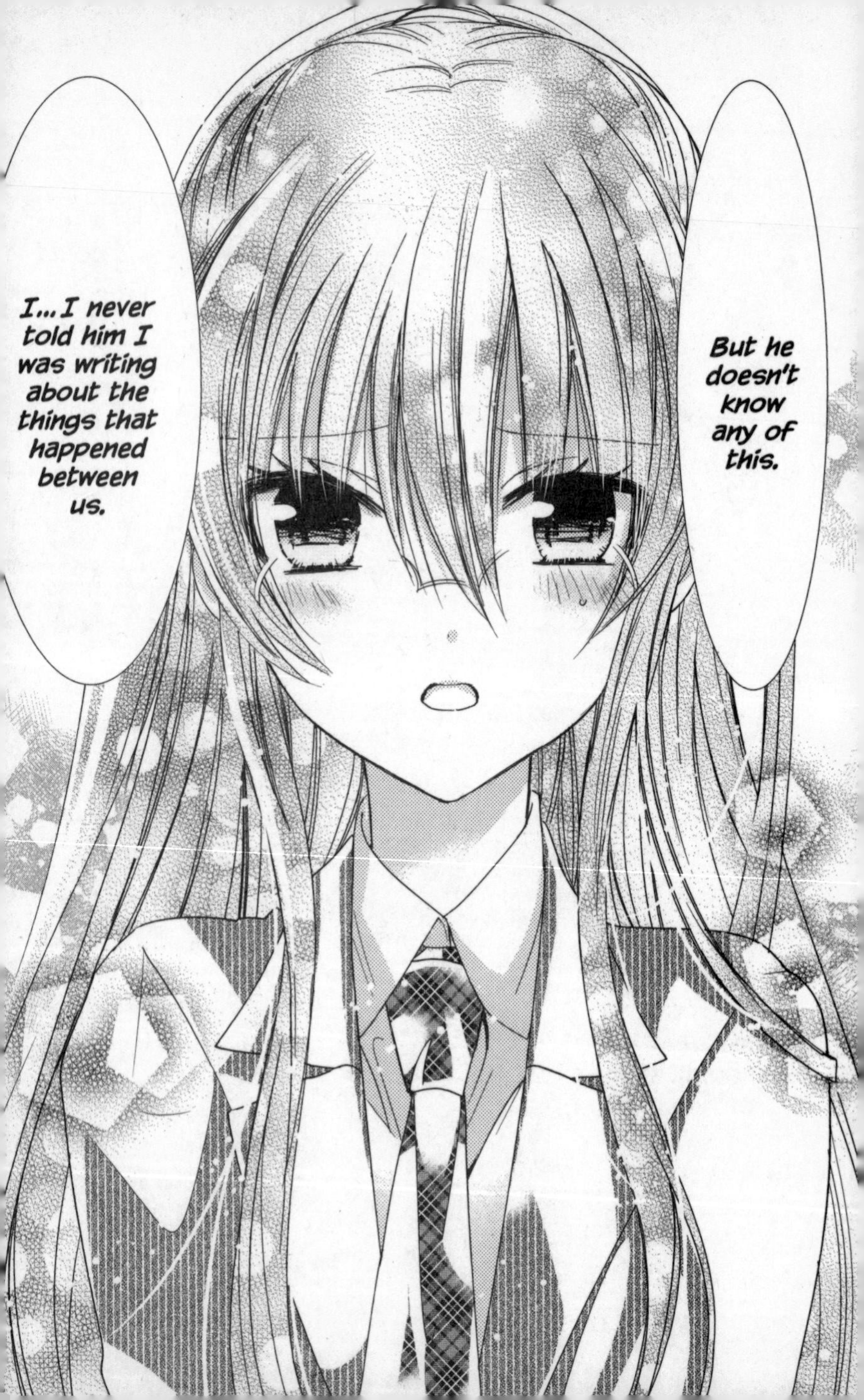
But he doesn't know any of this.
I...I never told him I was writing about the things that happened between us.

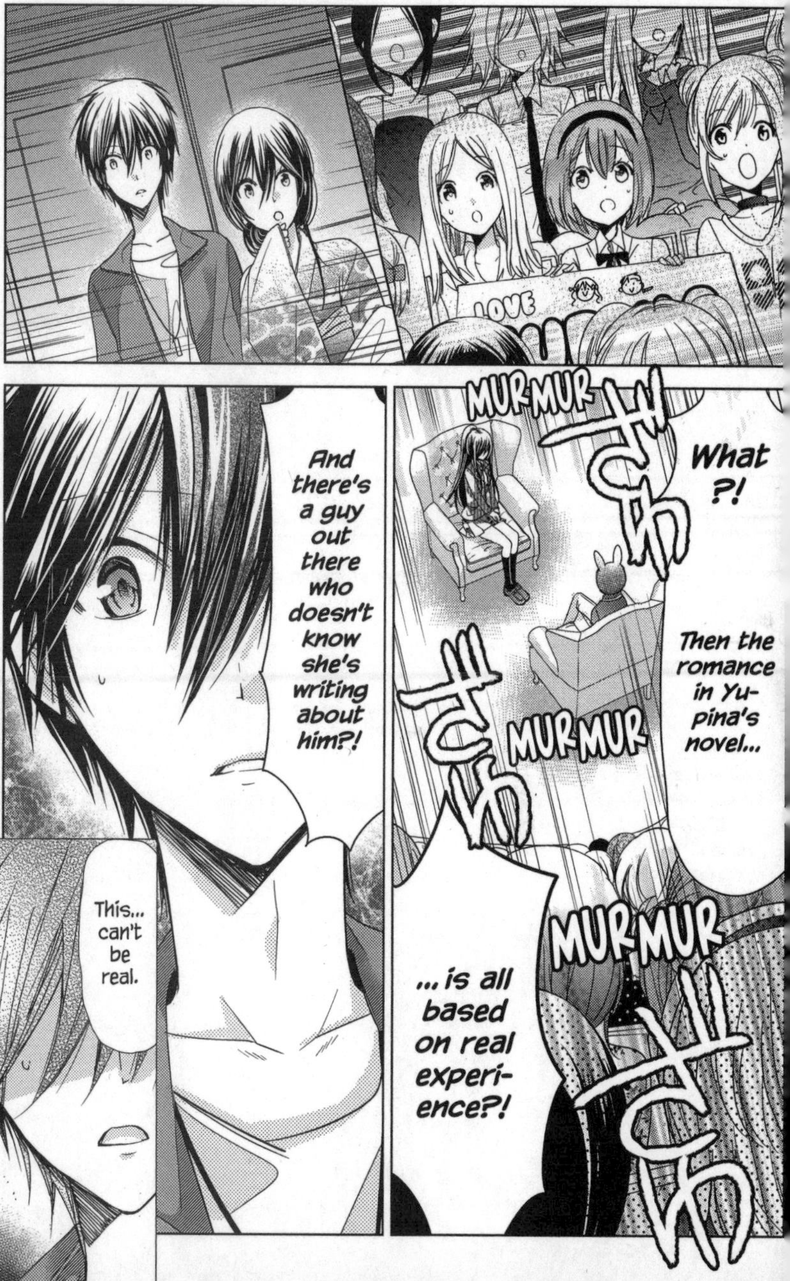
LOVE
MURMUR
ざわ
What?!
Then the romance in Yupina's novel...
ざわ
MURMUR
...is all based on real experience?!
MURMUR
ざわ
And there's a guy out there who doesn't know she's writing about him?!
This... can't be real.

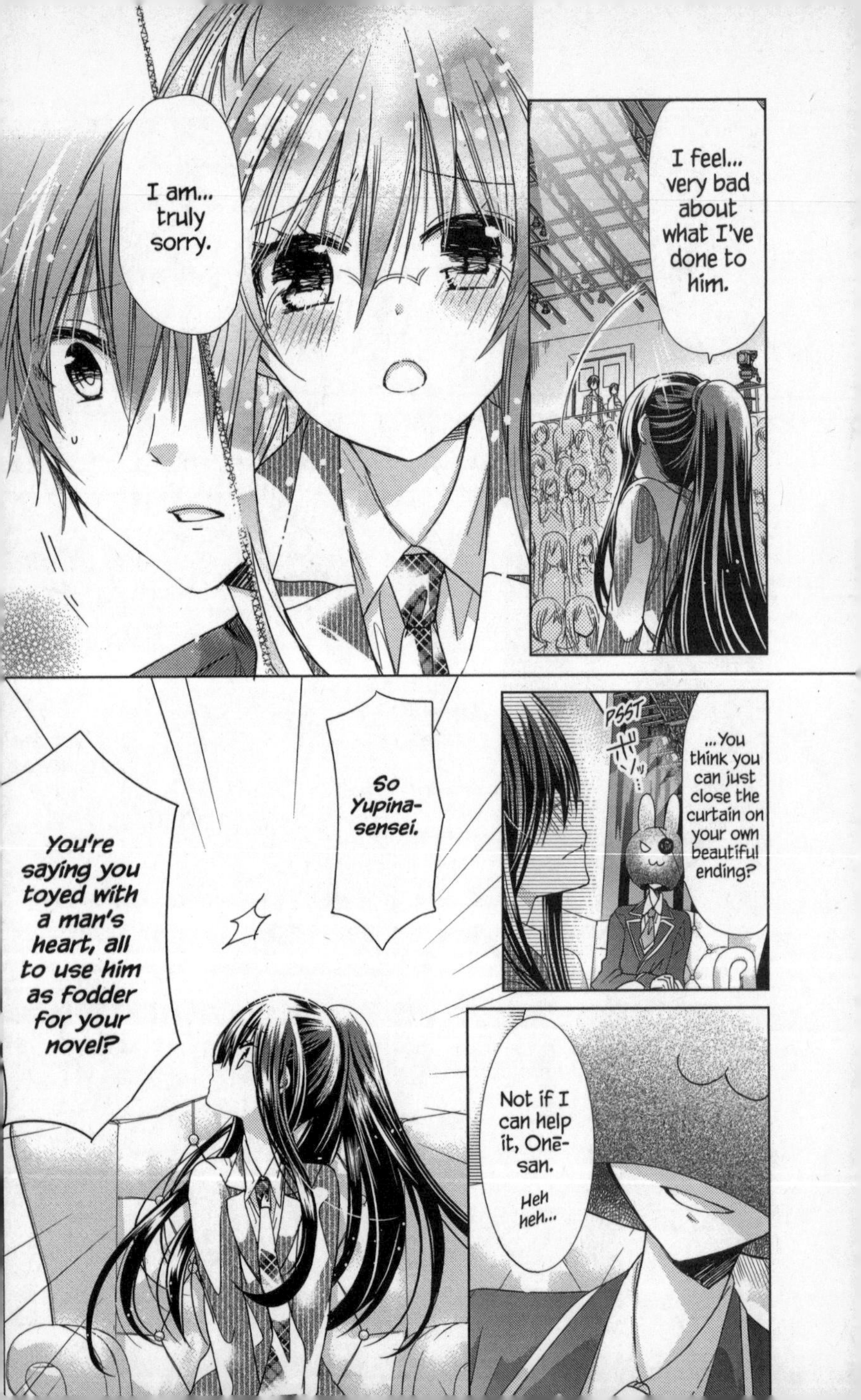
I feel... very bad about what I've done to him.
I am... truly sorry.
PSST
...You think you can just close the curtain on your own beautiful ending?
Not if I can help it, Onē-san.
Heh heh...
So Yupina-sensei.
You're saying you toyed with a man's heart, all to use him as fodder for your novel?

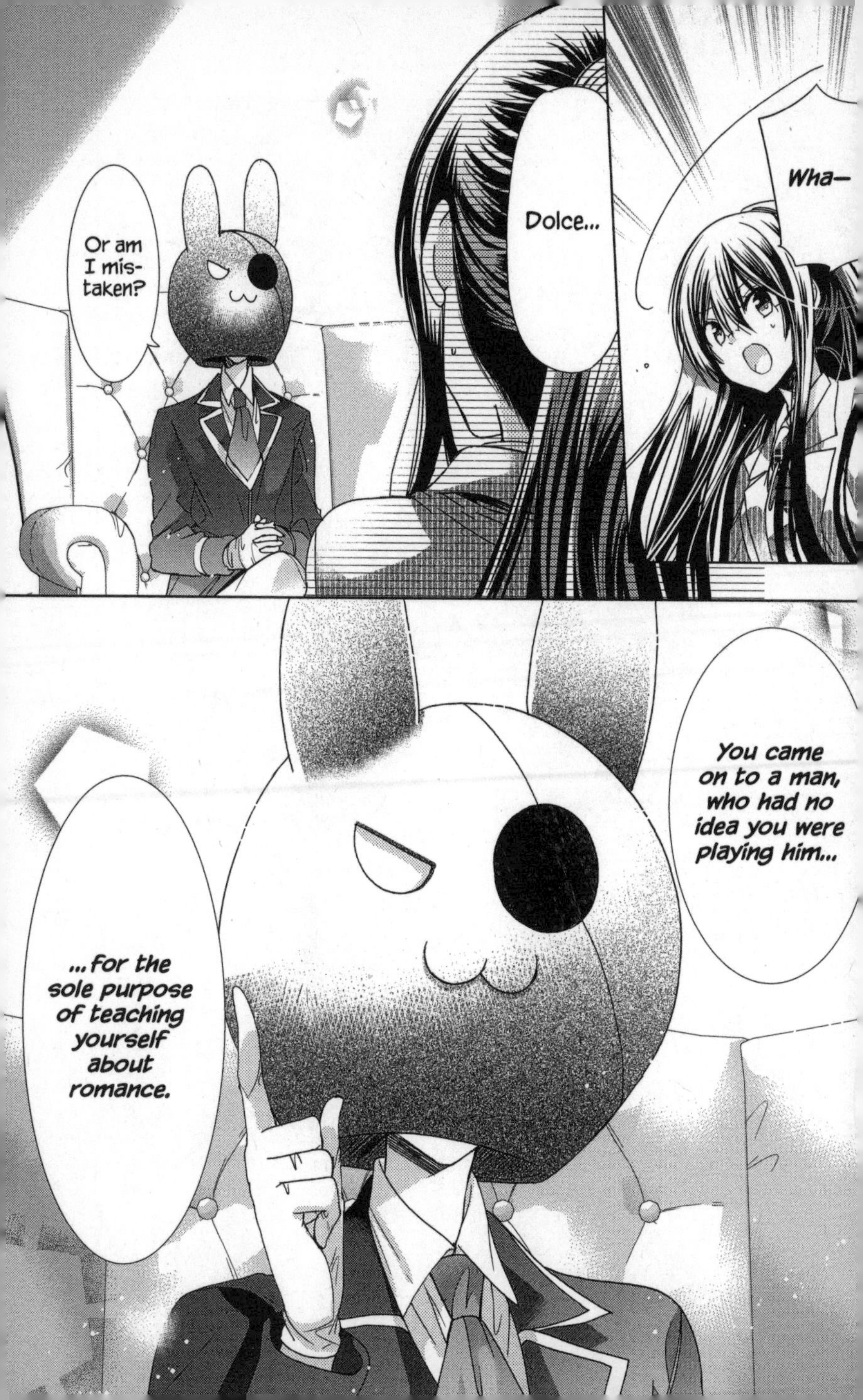
Wha—
Dolce...
Or am I mis-taken?
You came on to a man, who had no idea you were playing him...
...for the sole purpose of teaching yourself about romance.

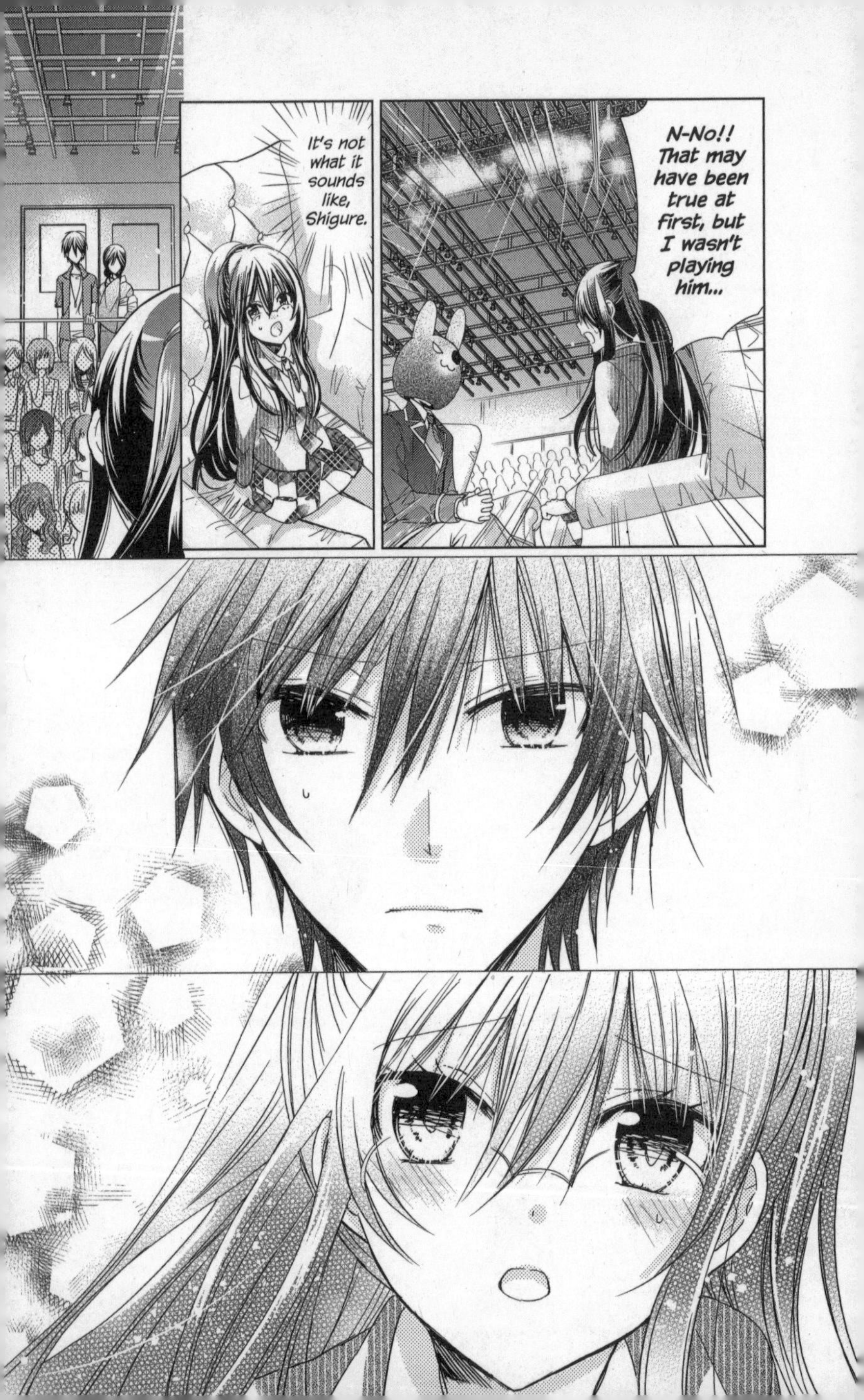
N-No!! That may have been true at first, but I wasn't playing him...
It's not what it sounds like, Shigure.

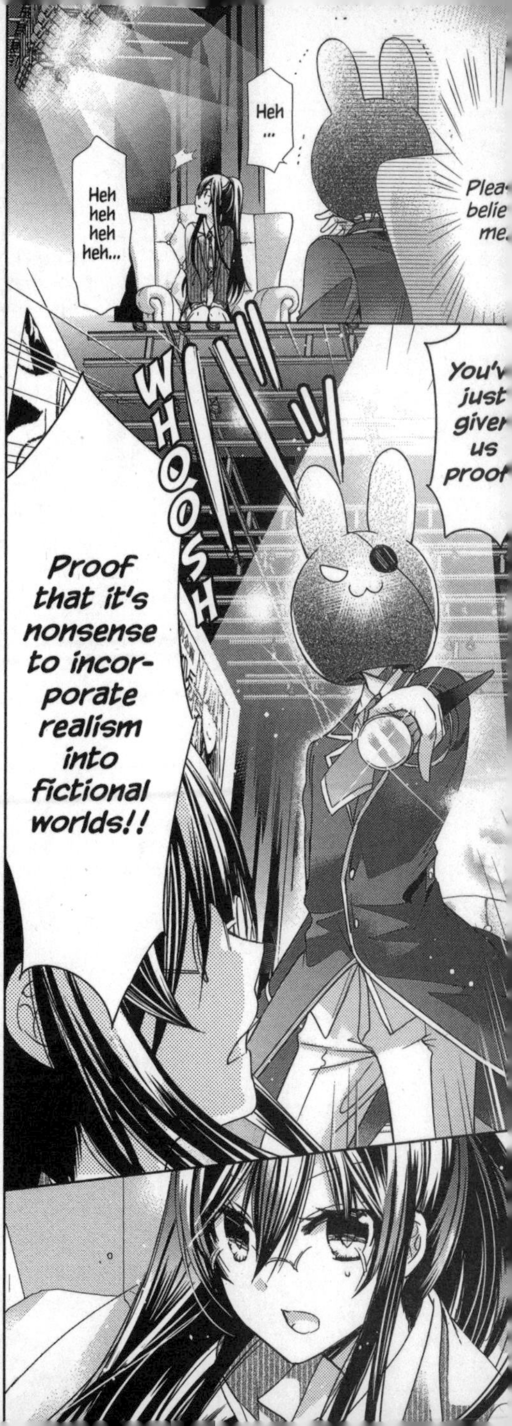
Plea-
belie
me.
Heh ...
Heh heh heh heh...
You'v just giver us proof
WHOOOSH
Proof that it's nonsense to incorporate realism into fictional worlds!!

How to Make Snow Babies

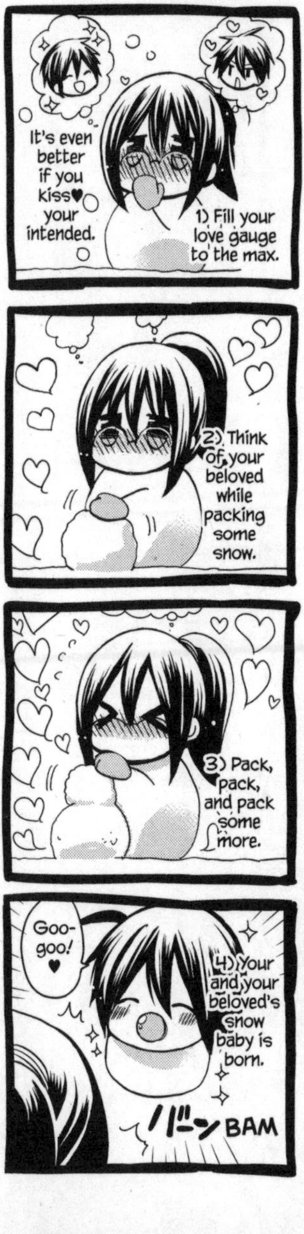
1) Fill your love gauge to the max.
It's even better if you kiss♥ your intended.
2) Think of your beloved while packing some snow.
3) Pack, pack, and pack some more.
4) Your and your beloved's snow baby is born.
Goo-goo!♥
バーン BAM

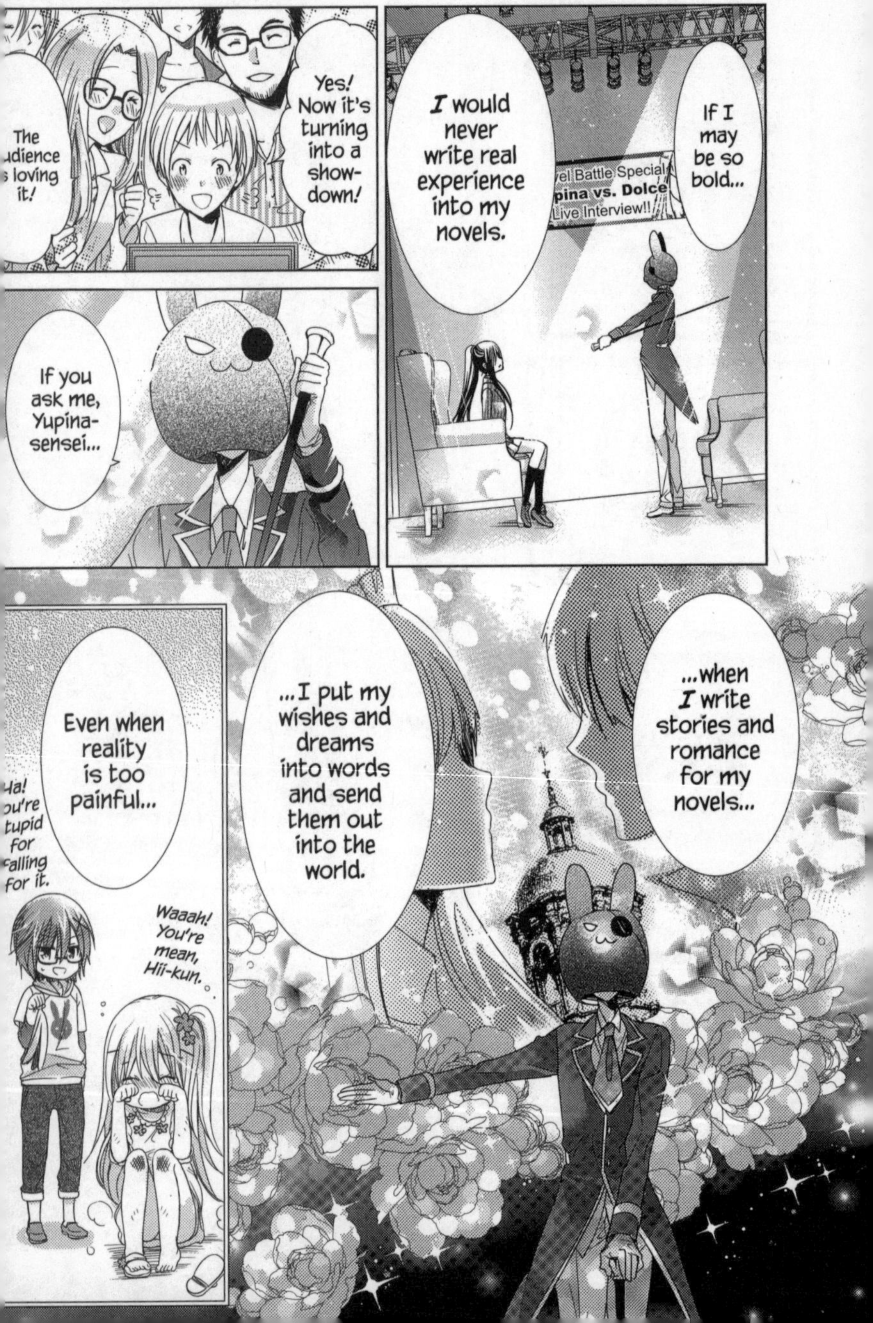
If I may be so bold...
I would never write real experience into my novels.
vs. Dolce
Live Interview!!
Yes! Now it's turning into a show-down!
The udience s loving it!
If you ask me, Yupina-sensei...
...when I write stories and romance for my novels...
...I put my wishes and dreams into words and send them out into the world.
Even when reality is too painful...
Ha! ou're tupid for alling for it.
Waaah! You're mean, Hii-kun.

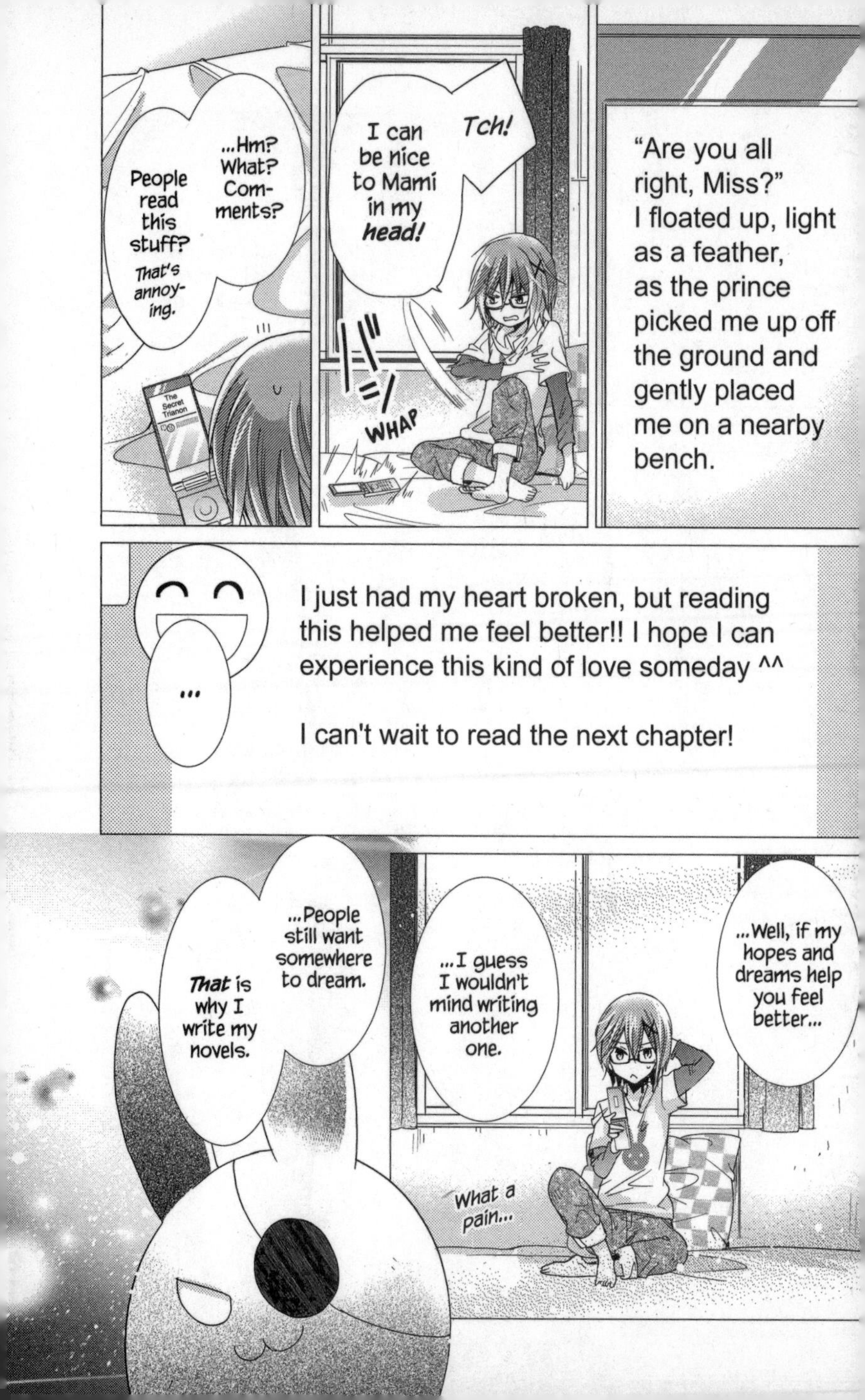
"Are you all right, Miss?" I floated up, light as a feather, as the prince picked me up off the ground and gently placed me on a nearby bench.
Tch!
I can be nice to Mami in my head!
WHAP
...Hm? What? Comments?
People read this stuff?
That's annoying.
The Secret Trianon
I just had my heart broken, but reading this helped me feel better!! I hope I can experience this kind of love someday ^^
I can't wait to read the next chapter!
...
...Well, if my hopes and dreams help you feel better...
...I guess I wouldn't mind writing another one.
What a pain...
...People still want somewhere to dream.
That is why I write my novels.

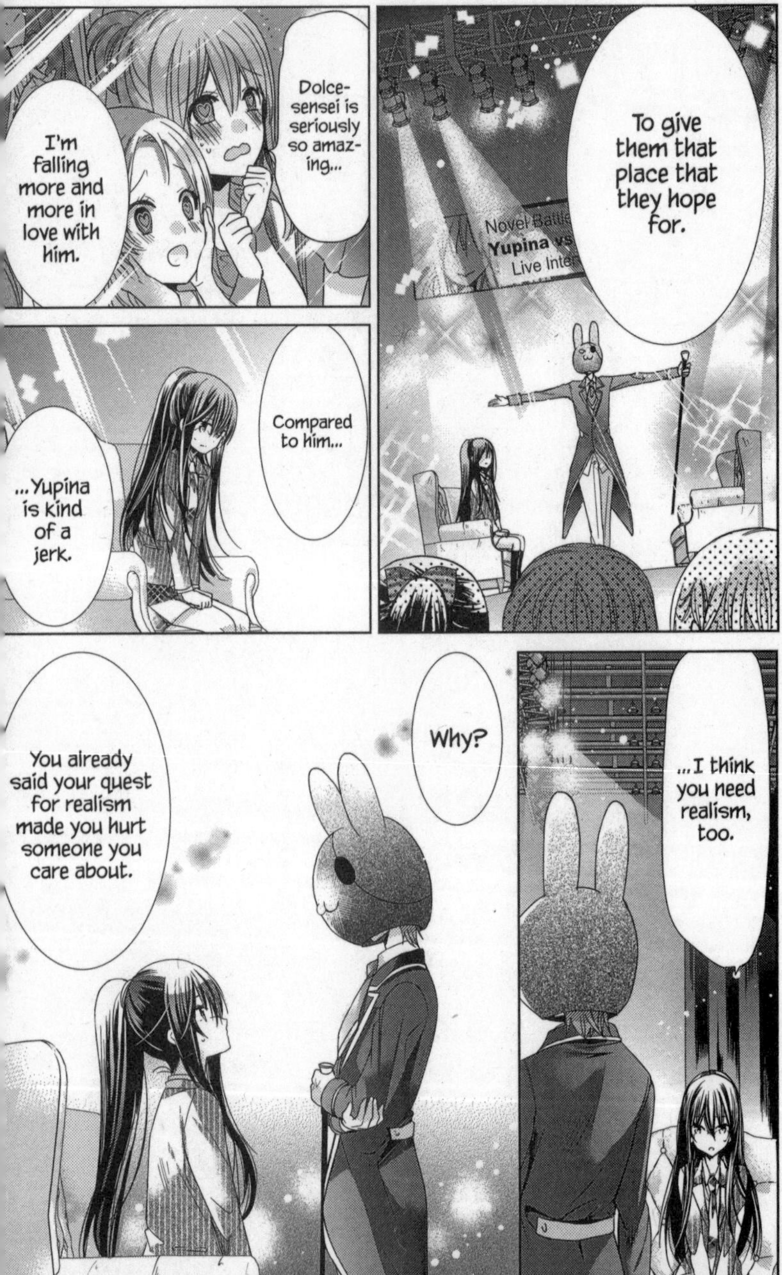
To give them that place that they hope for.
Dolce-sensei is seriously so amaz-ing...
I'm falling more and more in love with him.
Compared to him...
...Yupina is kind of a jerk.
...I think you need realism, too.
Why?
You already said your quest for realism made you hurt someone you care about.

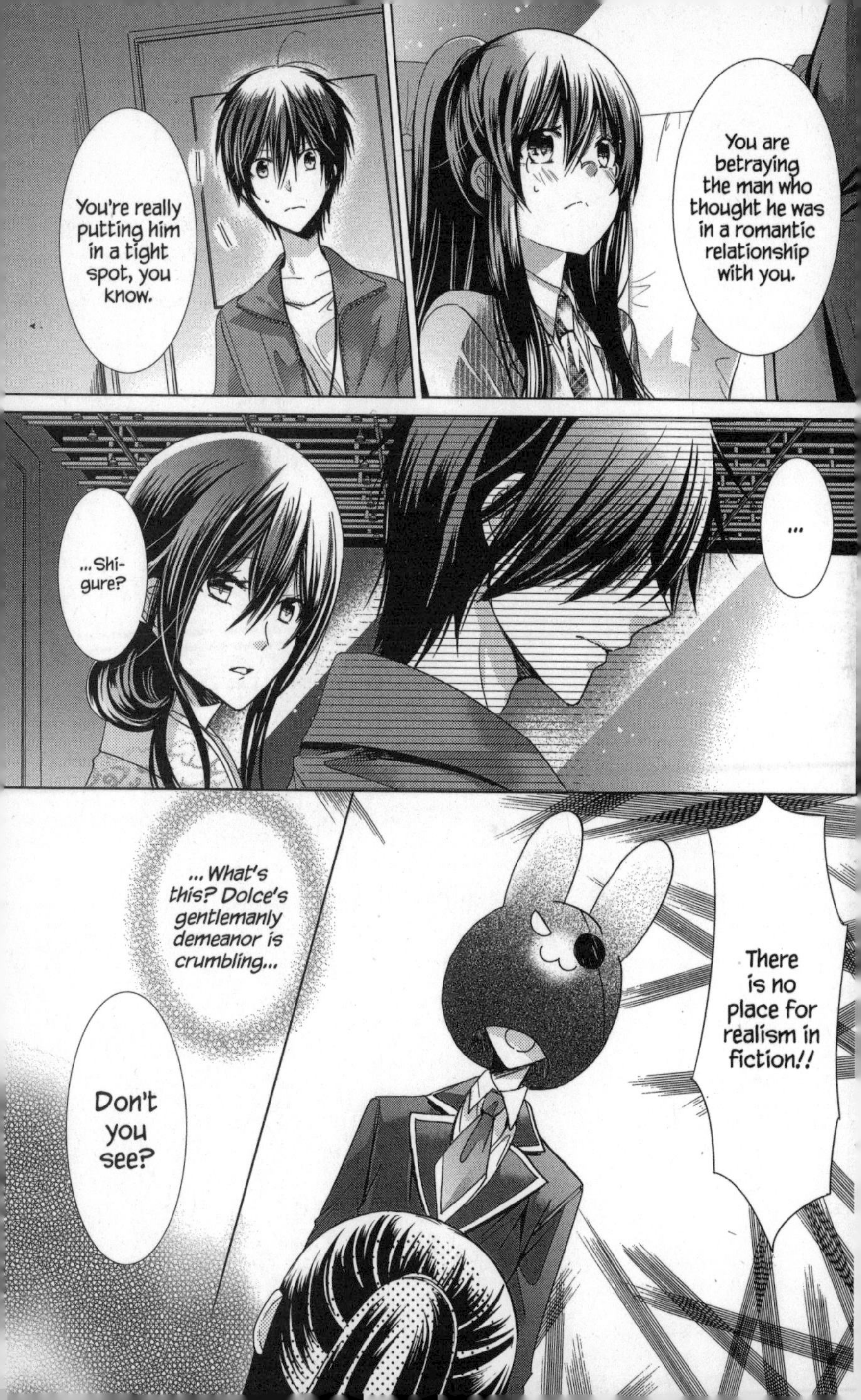
You are betraying the man who thought he was in a romantic relationship with you.
You're really putting him in a tight spot, you know.
...
...Shi-gure?
There is no place for realism in fiction!!
...What's this? Dolce's gentlemanly demeanor is crumbling...
Don't you see?

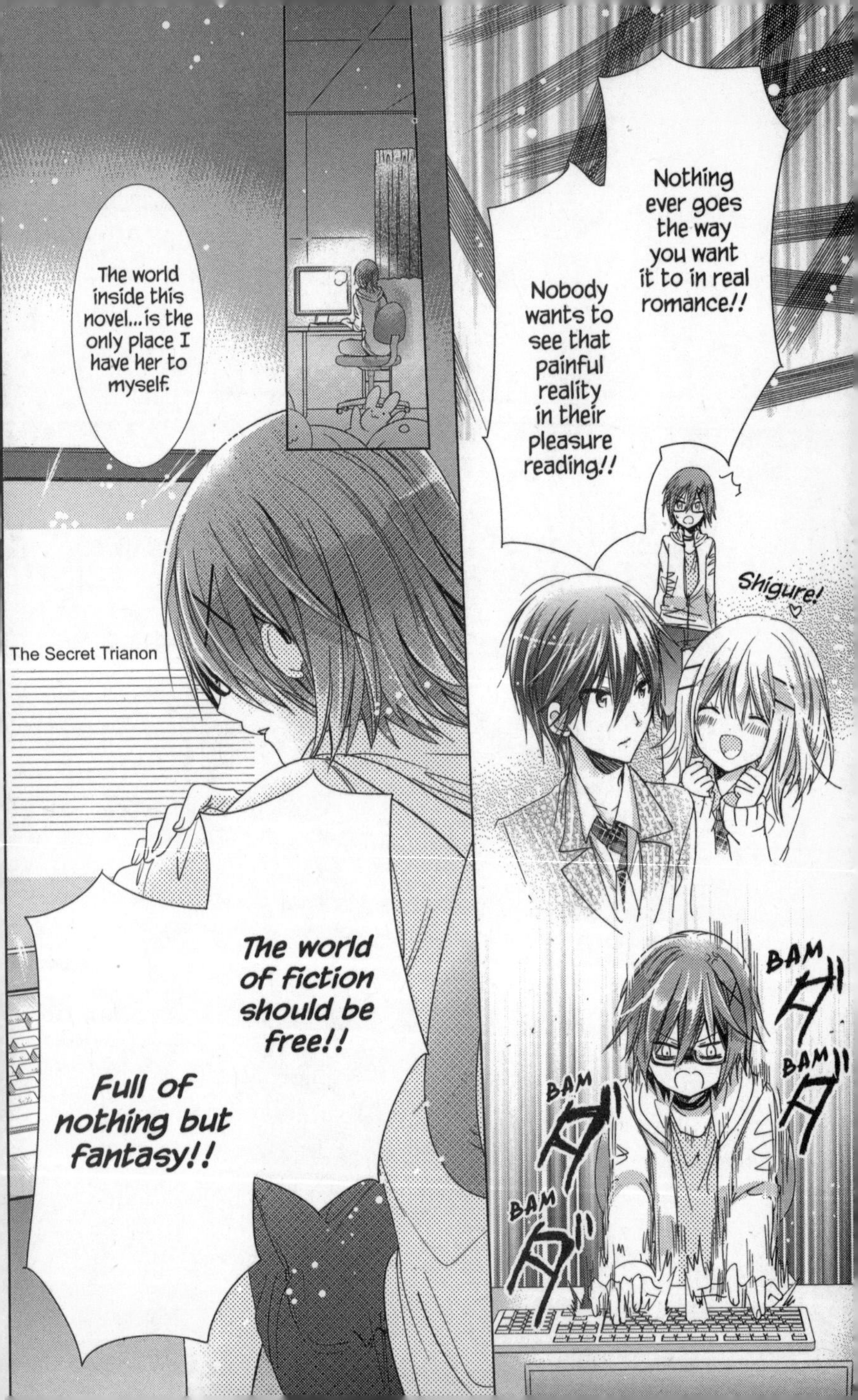
Nothing ever goes the way you want it to in real romance!!
Nobody wants to see that painful reality in their pleasure reading!!
Shigure!
BAM
BAM
BAM
BAM
The world inside this novel...is the only place I have her to myself.
The Secret Trianon
The world of fiction should be free!!
Full of nothing but fantasy!!

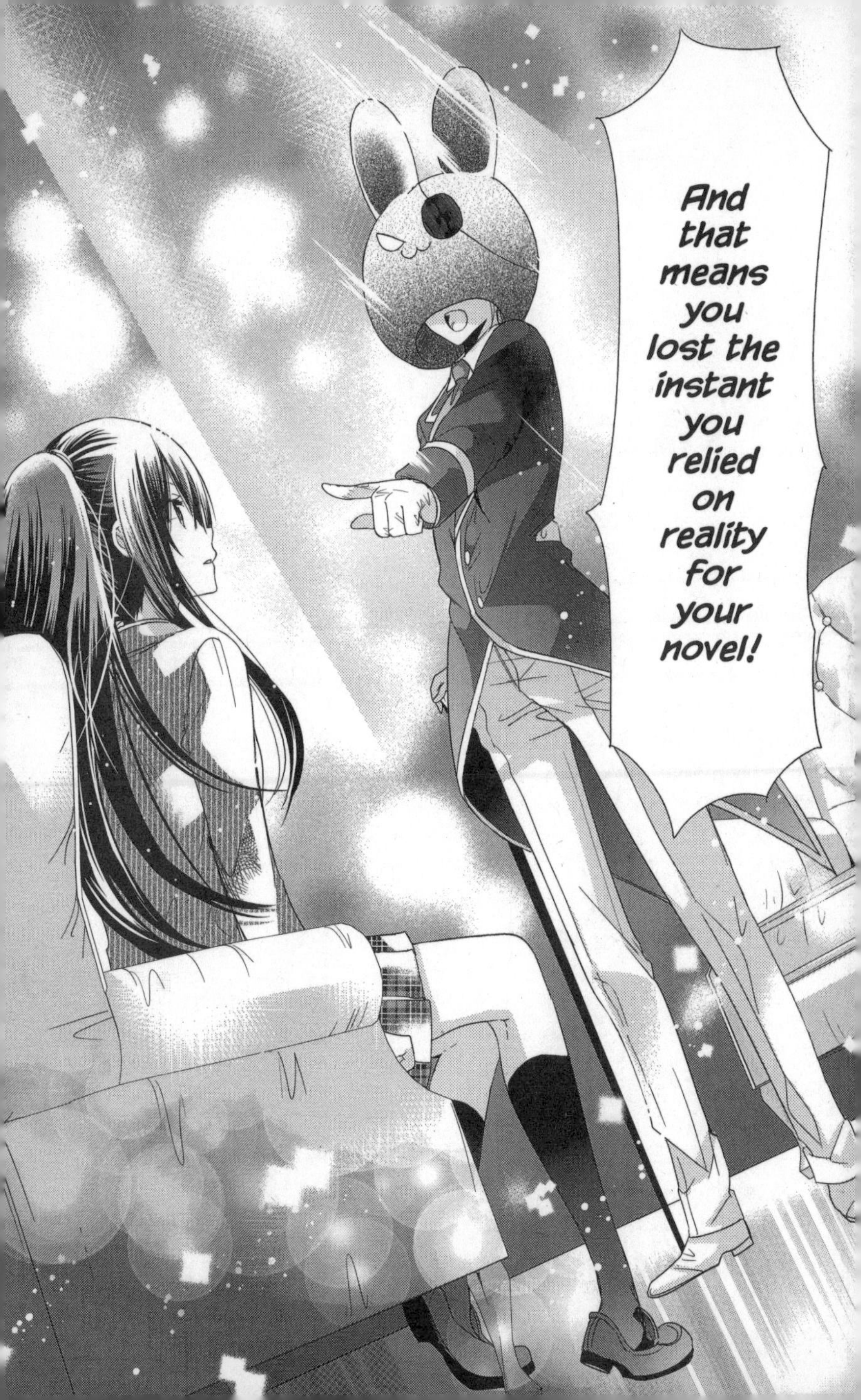
And that means you lost the instant you relied on reality for your novel!

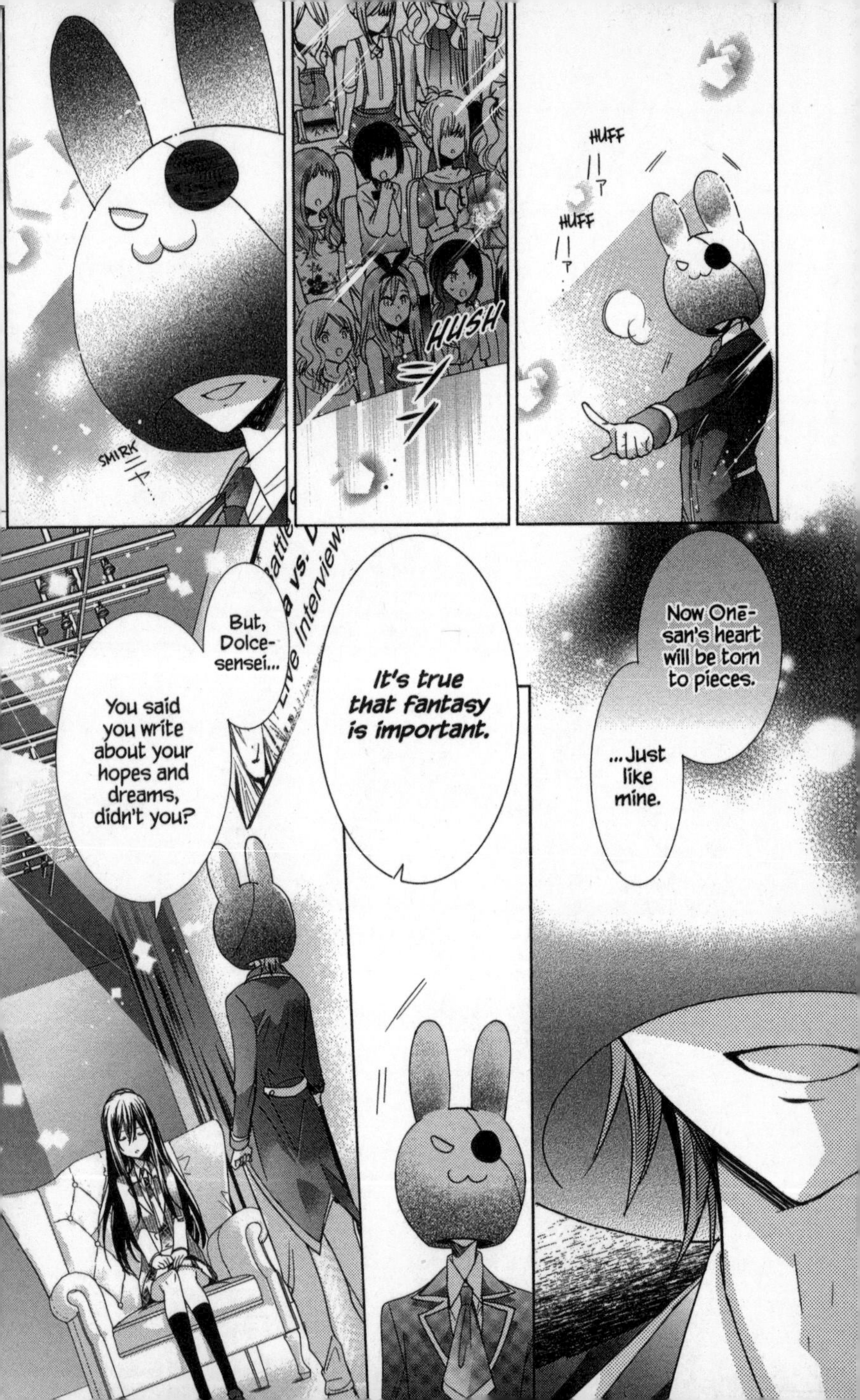
HUFF
HUFF
HUSH
SMIRK
Now Onē-san's heart will be torn to pieces.
...Just like mine.
It's true that fantasy is important.
But, Dolce-sensei...
You said you write about your hopes and dreams, didn't you?

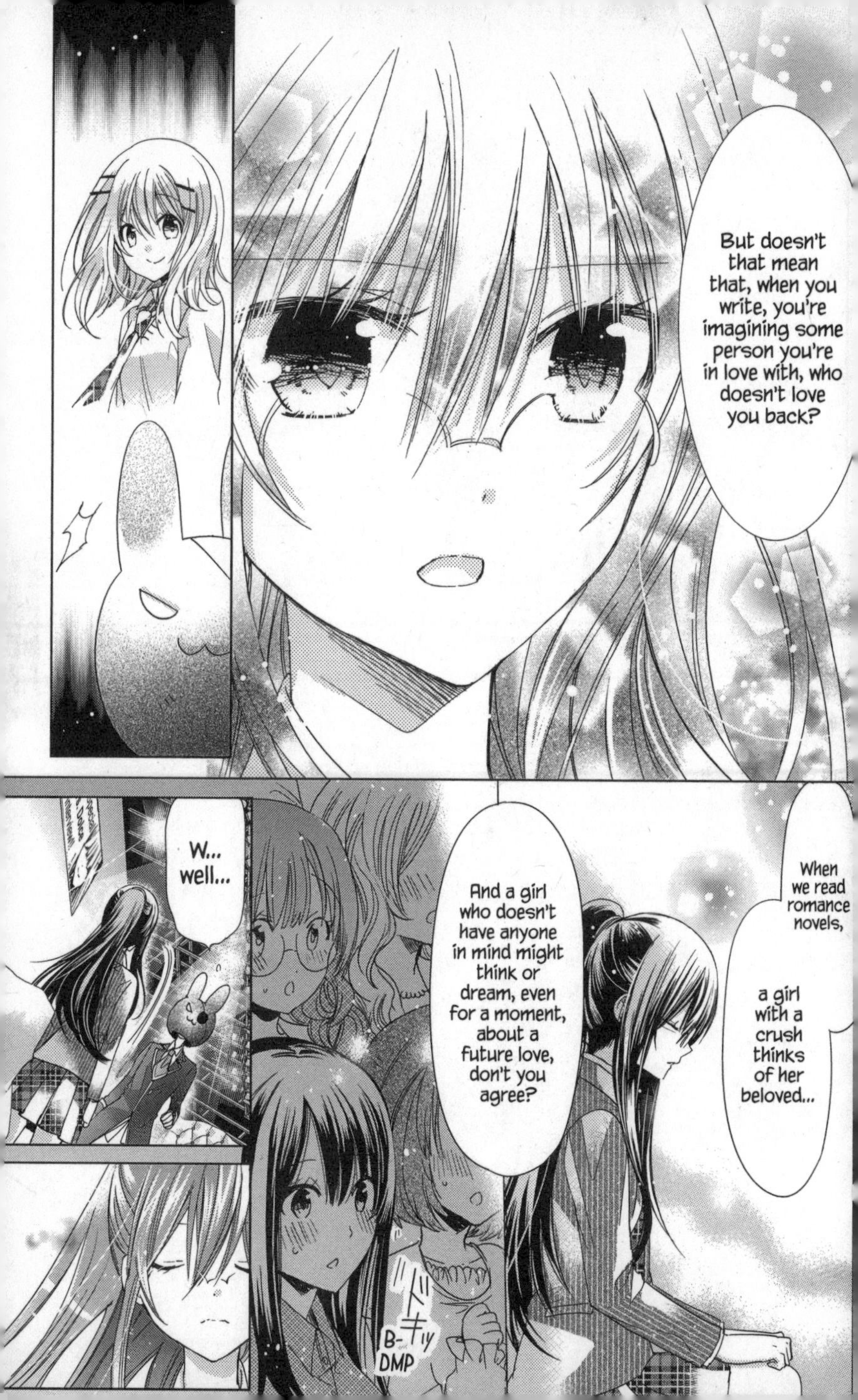
But doesn't that mean that, when you write, you're imagining some person you're in love with, who doesn't love you back?
When we read romance novels,
a girl with a crush thinks of her beloved...
And a girl who doesn't have anyone in mind might think or dream, even for a moment, about a future love, don't you agree?
W... well...
B-DMP

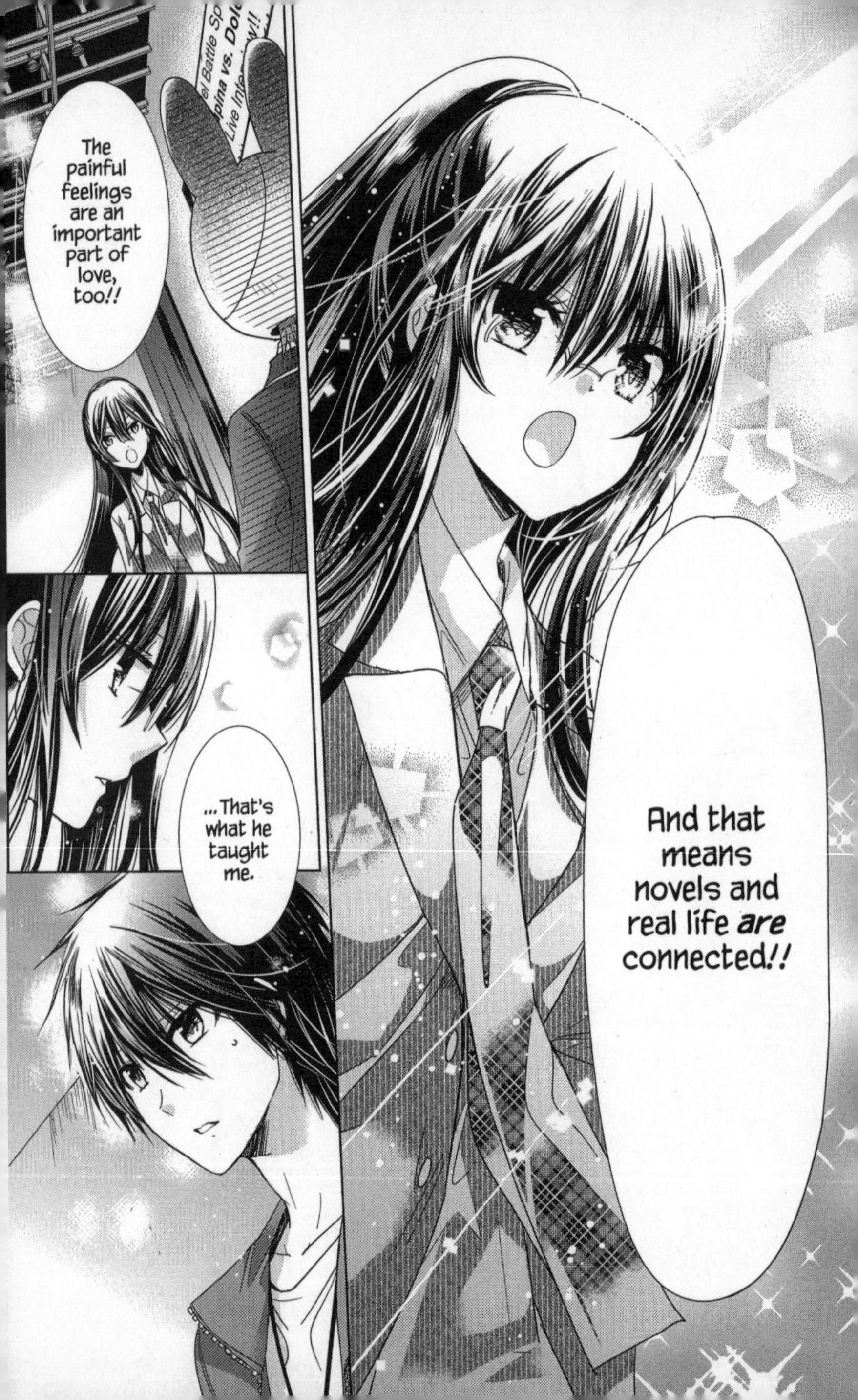
And that means novels and real life *are* connected!!
The painful feelings are an important part of love, too!!
...That's what he taught me.

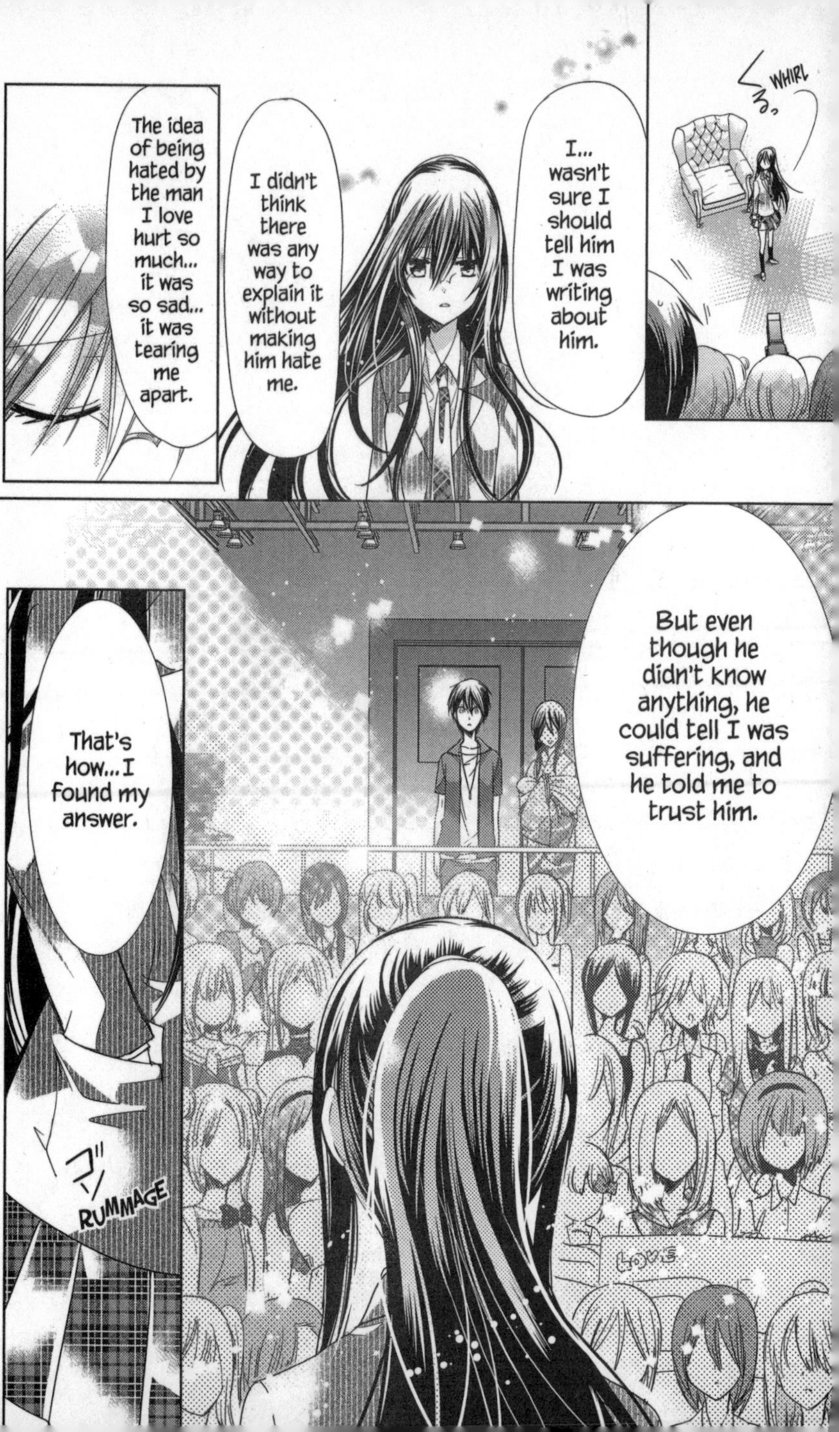
WHIRL
I... wasn't sure I should tell him I was writing about him.
I didn't think there was any way to explain it without making him hate me.
The idea of being hated by the man I love hurt so much... it was so sad... it was tearing me apart.
But even though he didn't know anything, he could tell I was suffering, and he told me to trust him.
That's how... I found my answer.
RUMMAGE

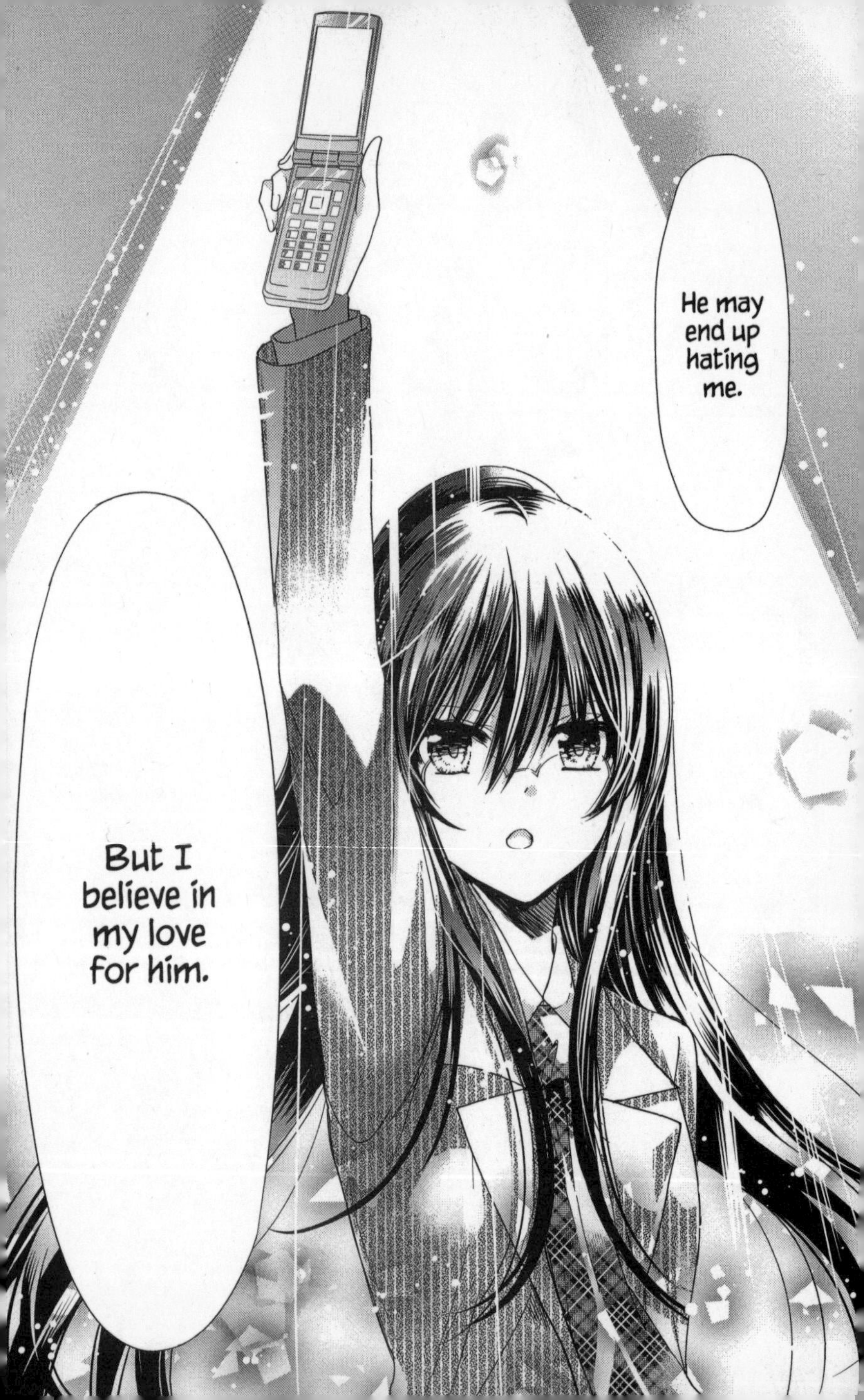
He may end up hating me.
But I believe in my love for him.

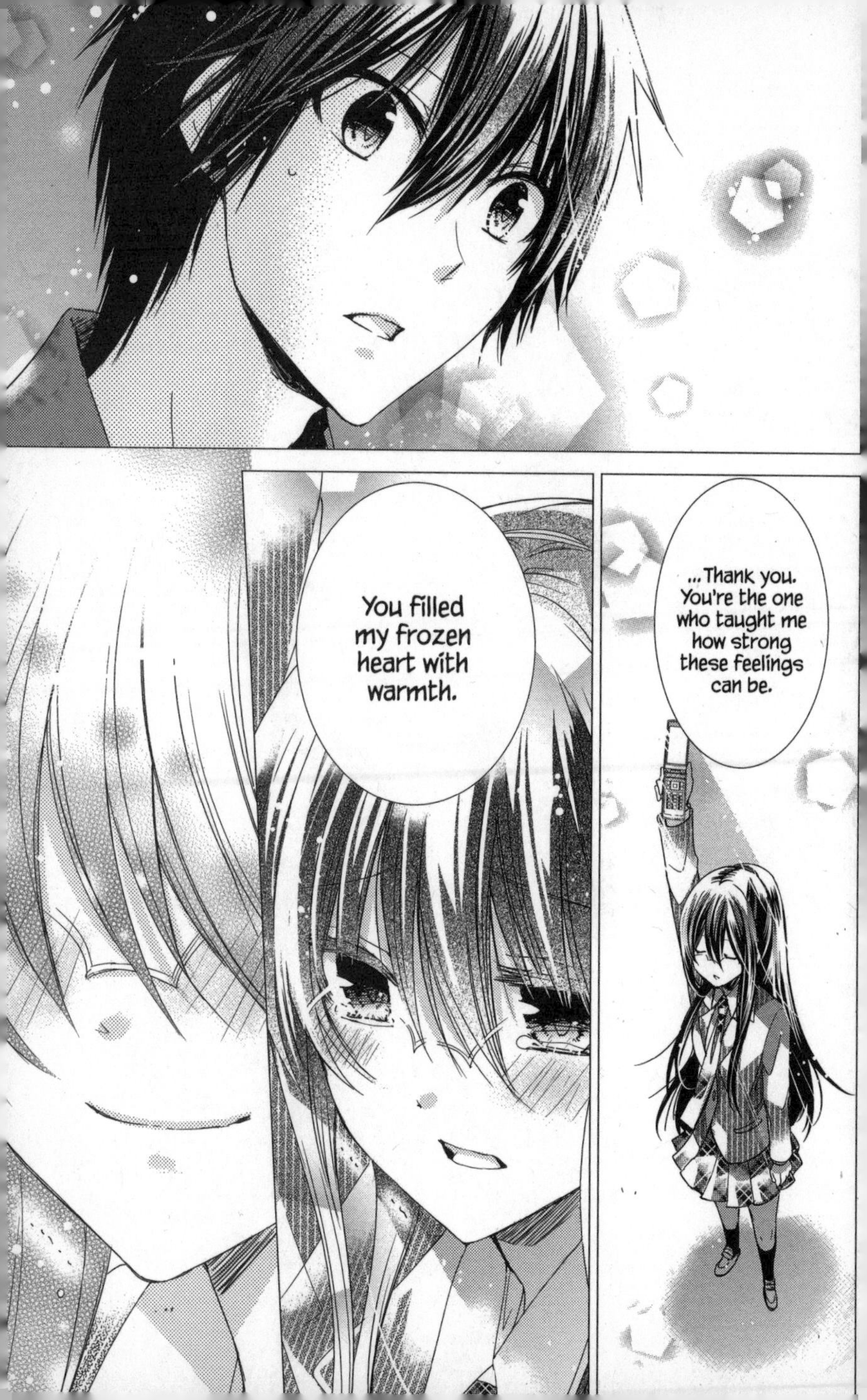
...Thank you. You're the one who taught me how strong these feelings can be.
You filled my frozen heart with warmth.

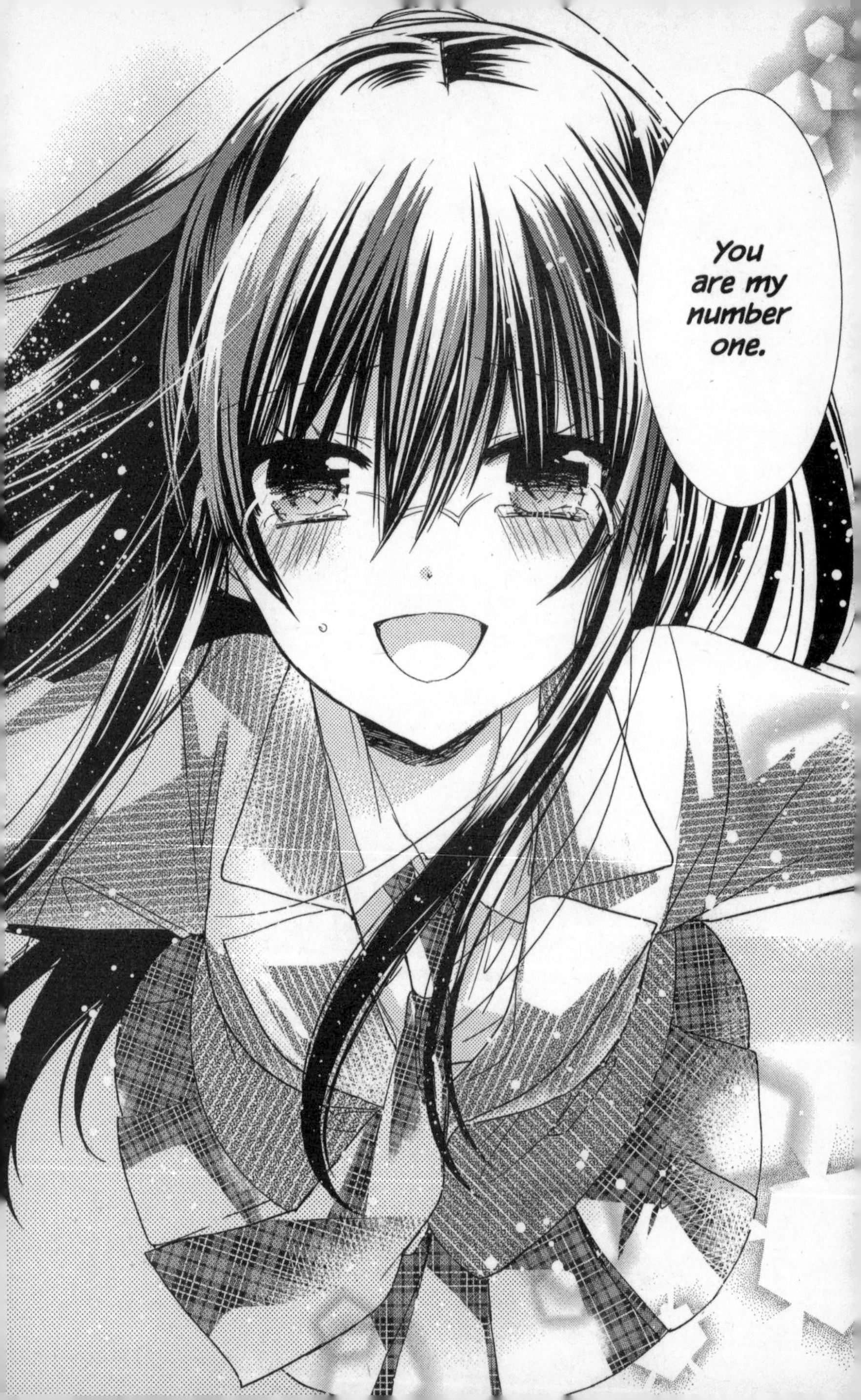
You are my number one.

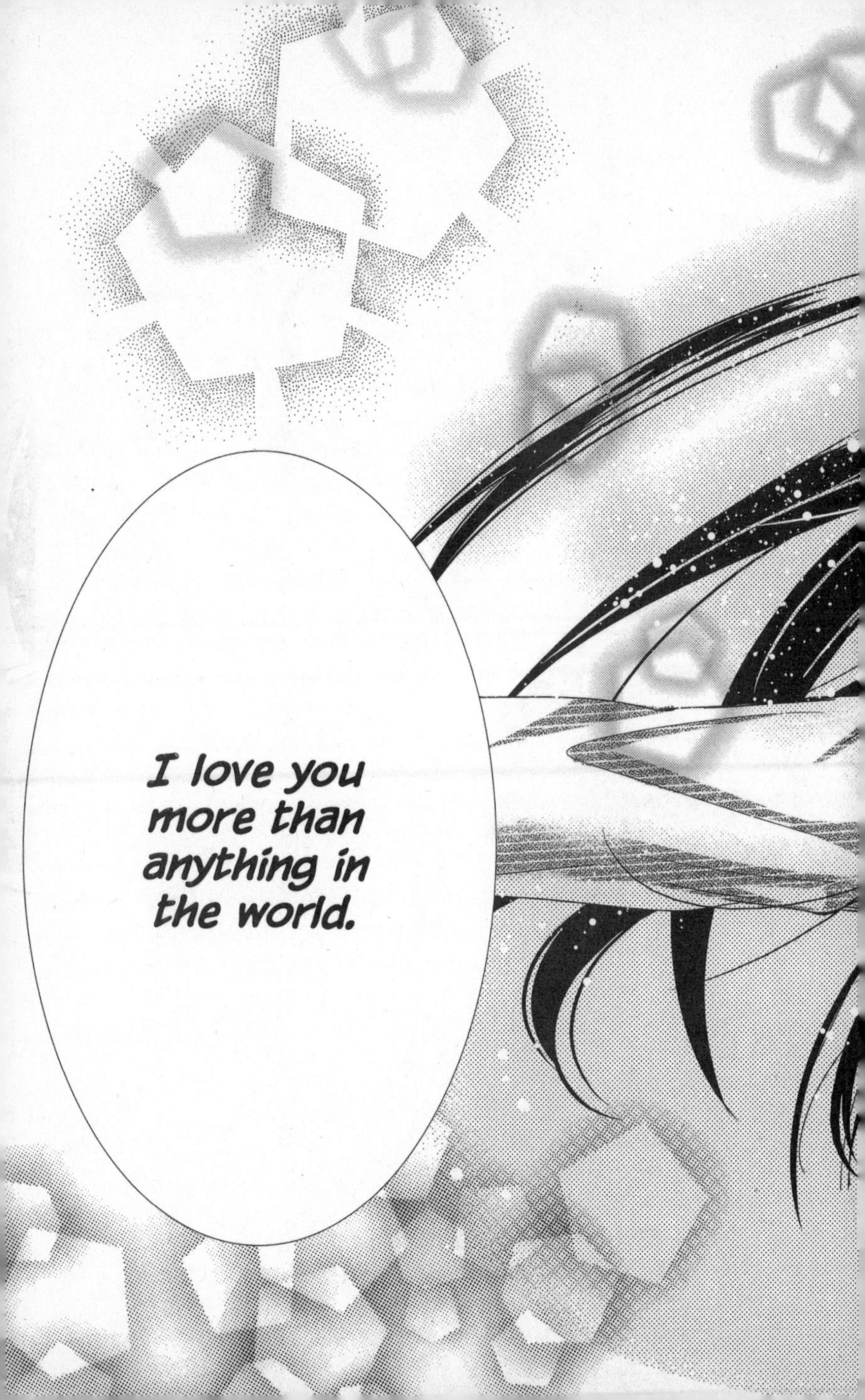
I love you more than anything in the world.

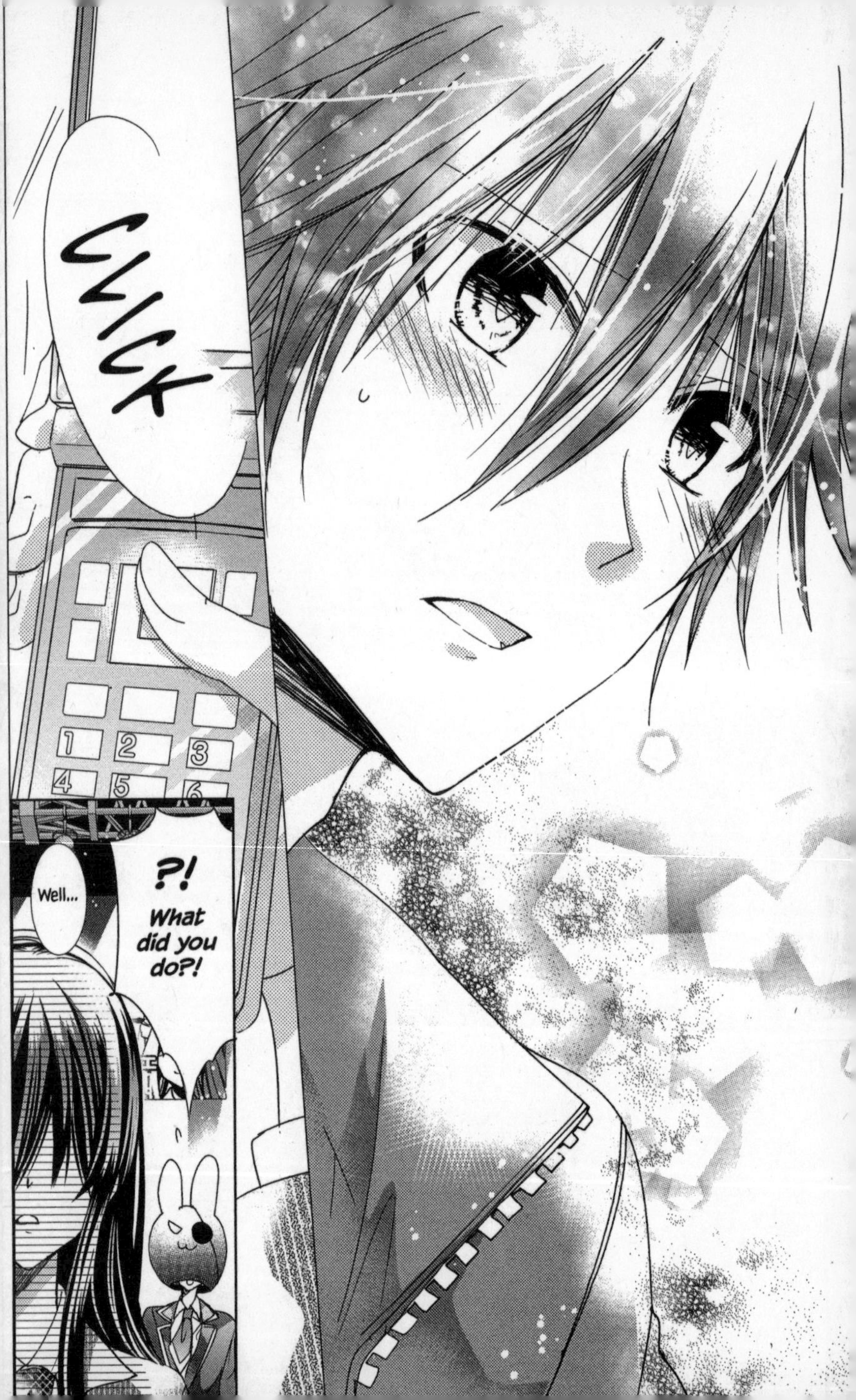
CLICK
?! What did you do?!
Well...

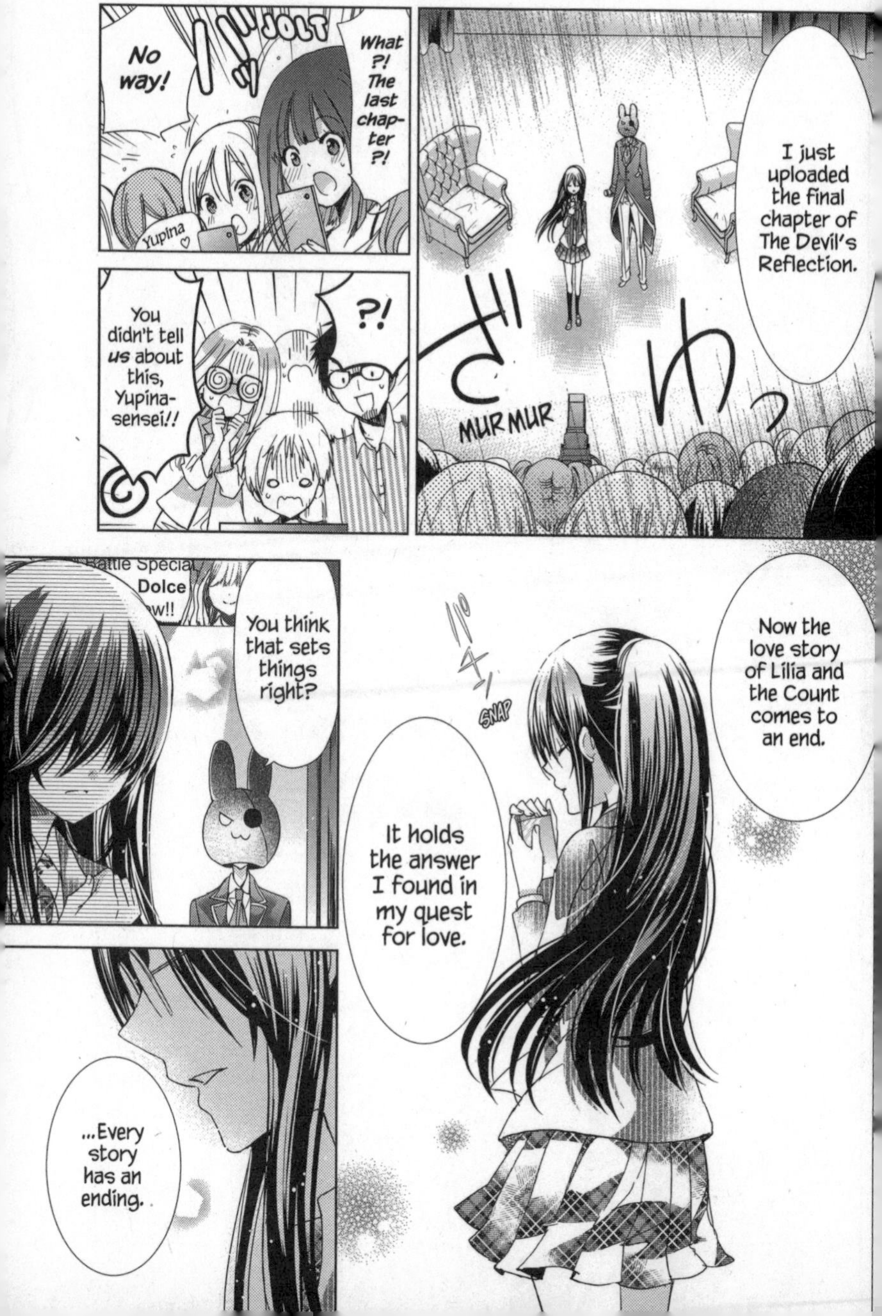
I just uploaded the final chapter of The Devil's Reflection.
MURMUR
What?! The last chapter?!
JOLT
No way!
Yupina ♡
?!
You didn't tell us about this, Yupina-sensei!!
Now the love story of Lilia and the Count comes to an end.
SNAP
It holds the answer I found in my quest for love.
Dolce
You think that sets things right?
...Every story has an ending.

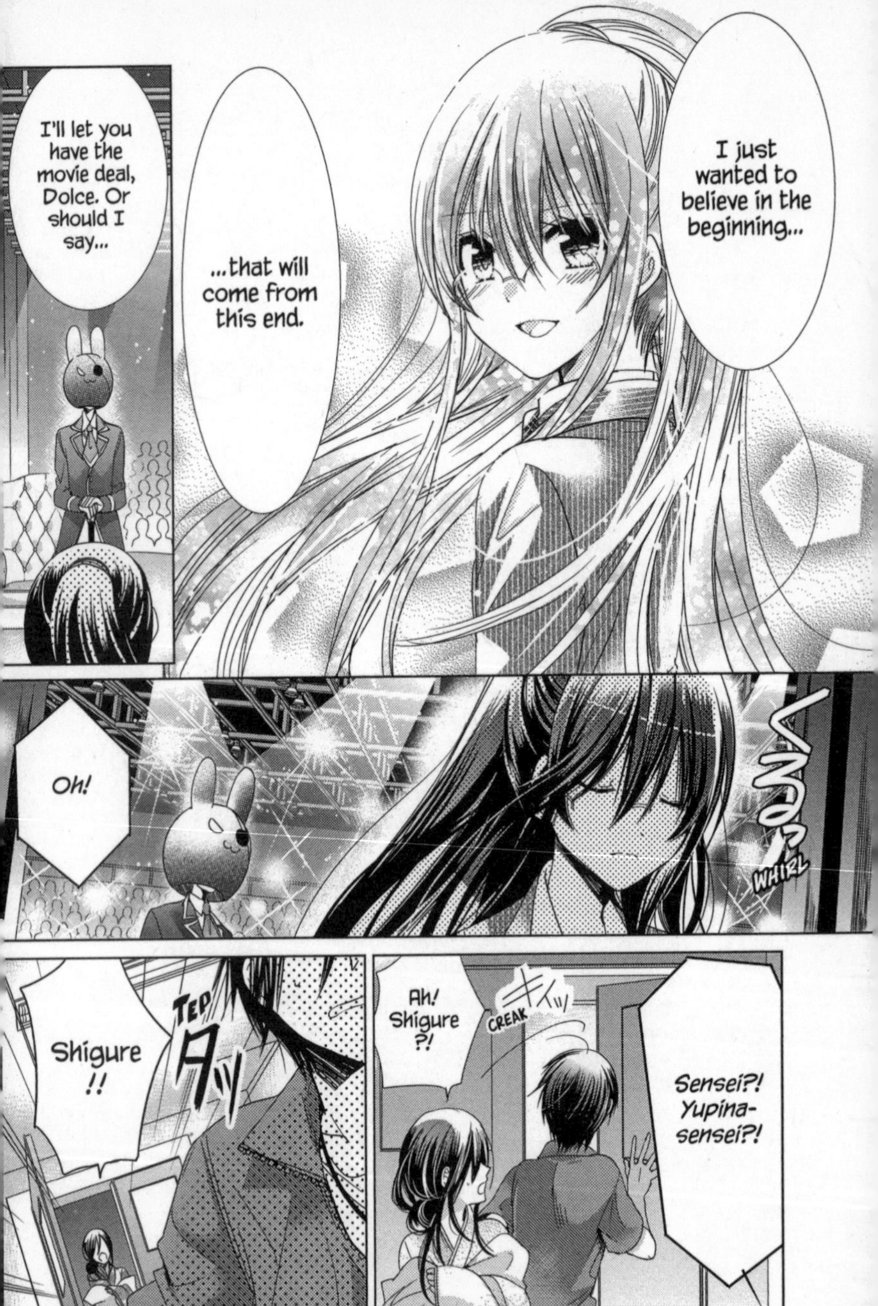
I just wanted to believe in the beginning...
...that will come from this end.
I'll let you have the movie deal, Dolce. Or should I say...
WHIRL
Oh!
Sensei?! Yupina-sensei?!
CREAK
Ah! Shigure?!
TEP
Shigure!!

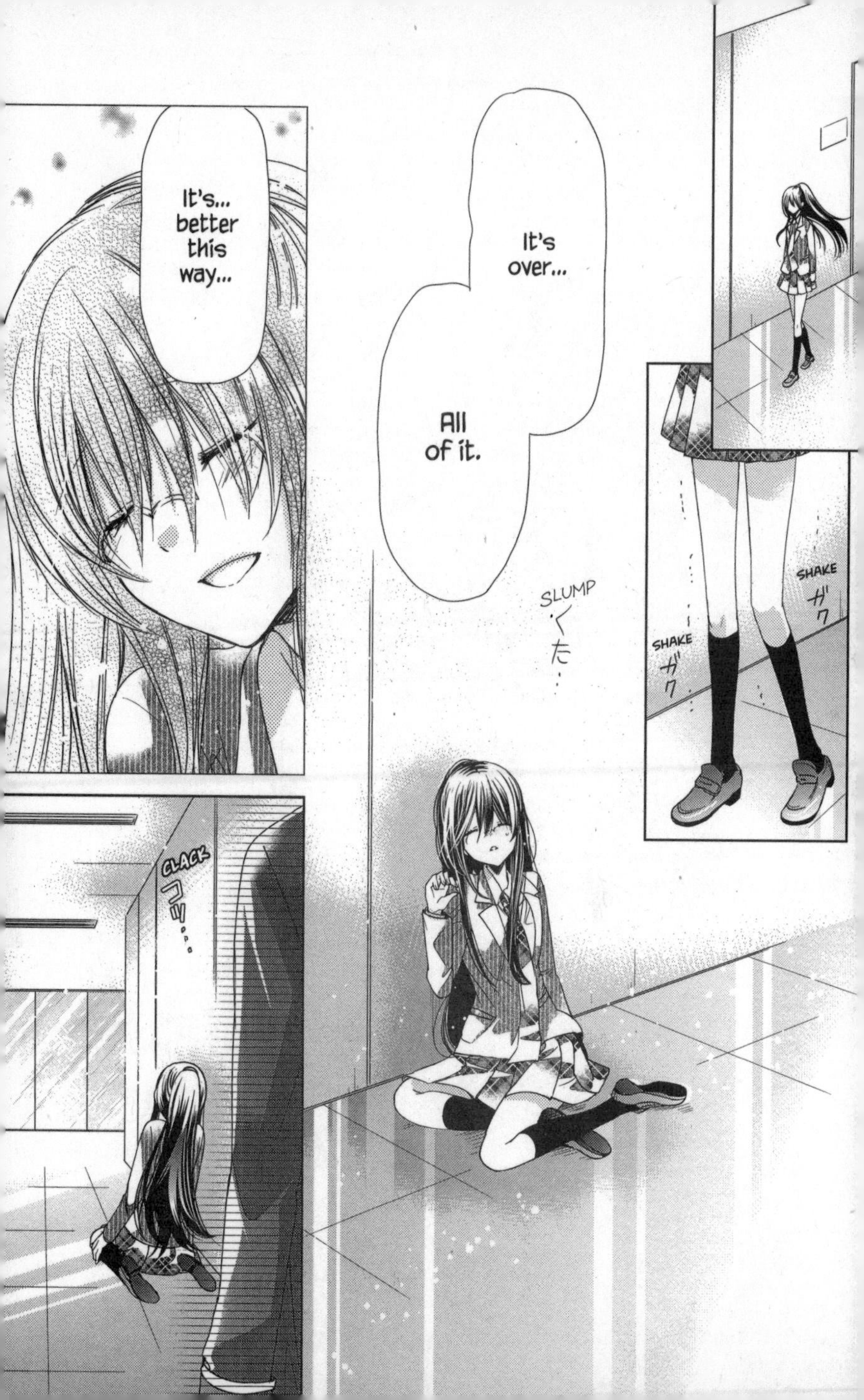
SHAKE ガク
SHAKE ガク
It's over...
All of it.
SLUMP くた…
It's... better this way...
CLACK コツ…

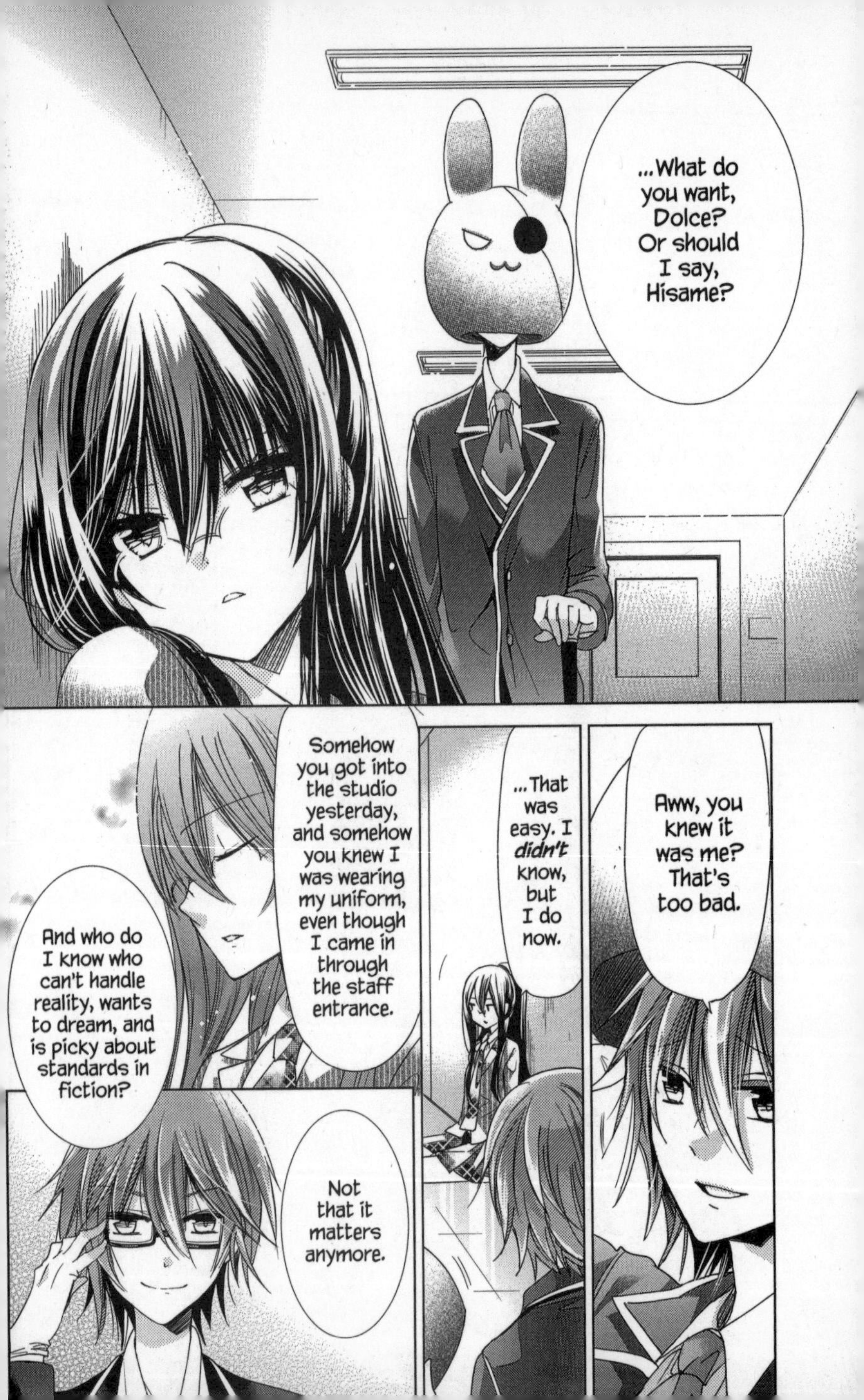
...What do you want, Dolce? Or should I say, Hisame?
Aww, you knew it was me? That's too bad.
...That was easy. I *didn't* know, but I do now.
Somehow you got into the studio yesterday, and somehow you knew I was wearing my uniform, even though I came in through the staff entrance.
And who do I know who can't handle reality, wants to dream, and is picky about standards in fiction?
Not that it matters anymore.

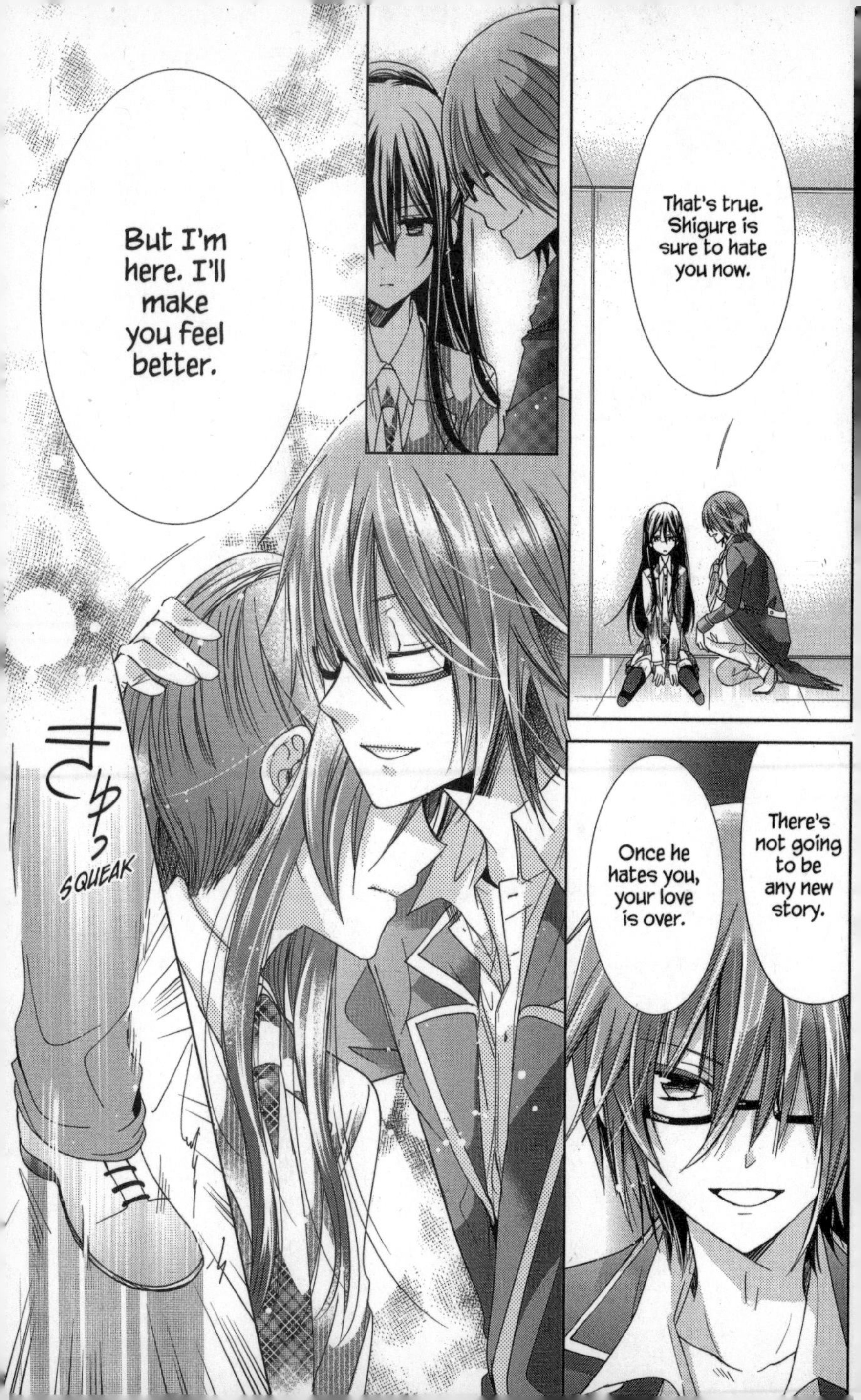
That's true. Shigure is sure to hate you now.
There's not going to be any new story.
Once he hates you, your love is over.
But I'm here. I'll make you feel better.
SQUEAK

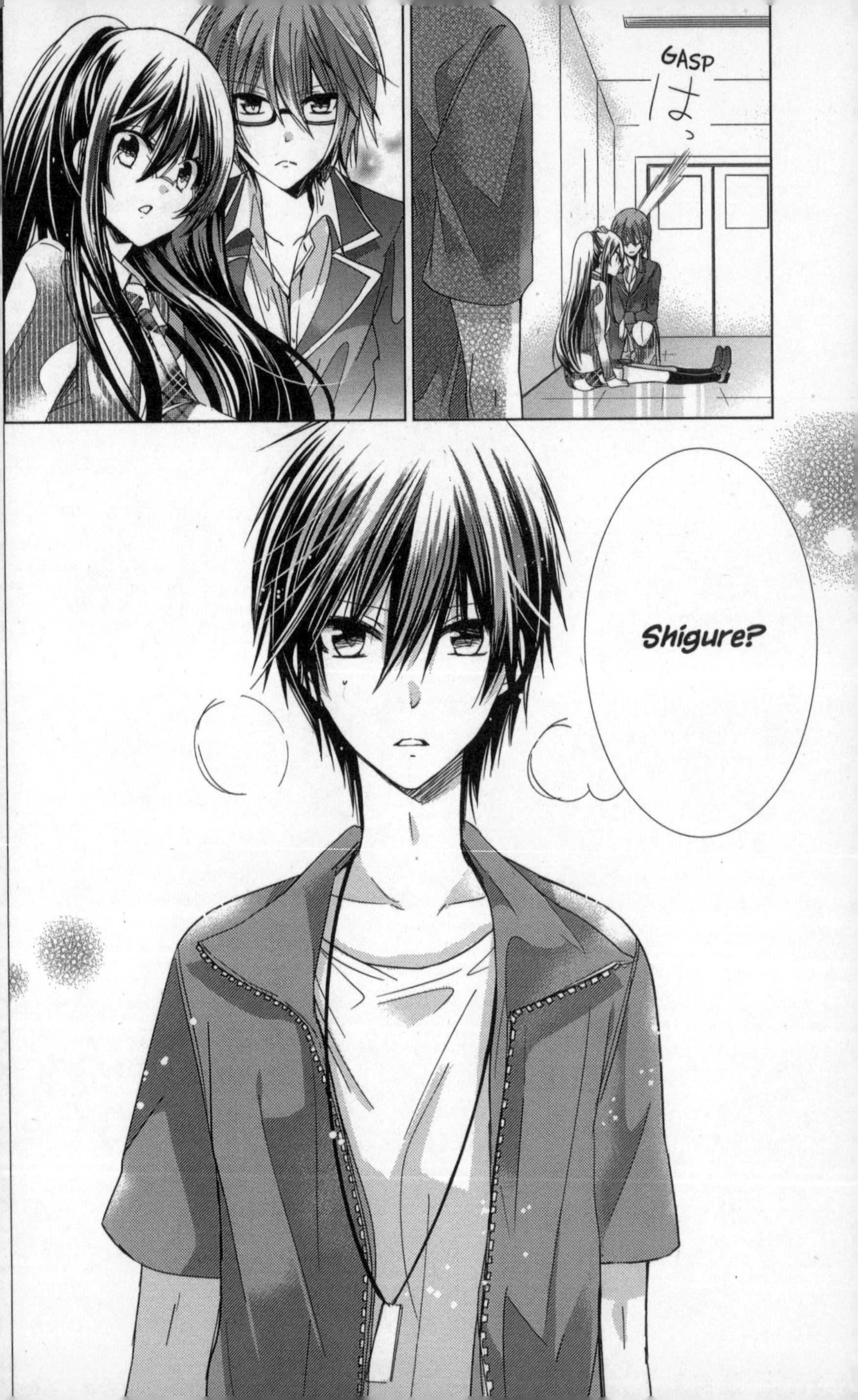
GASP
はっ
Shigure?

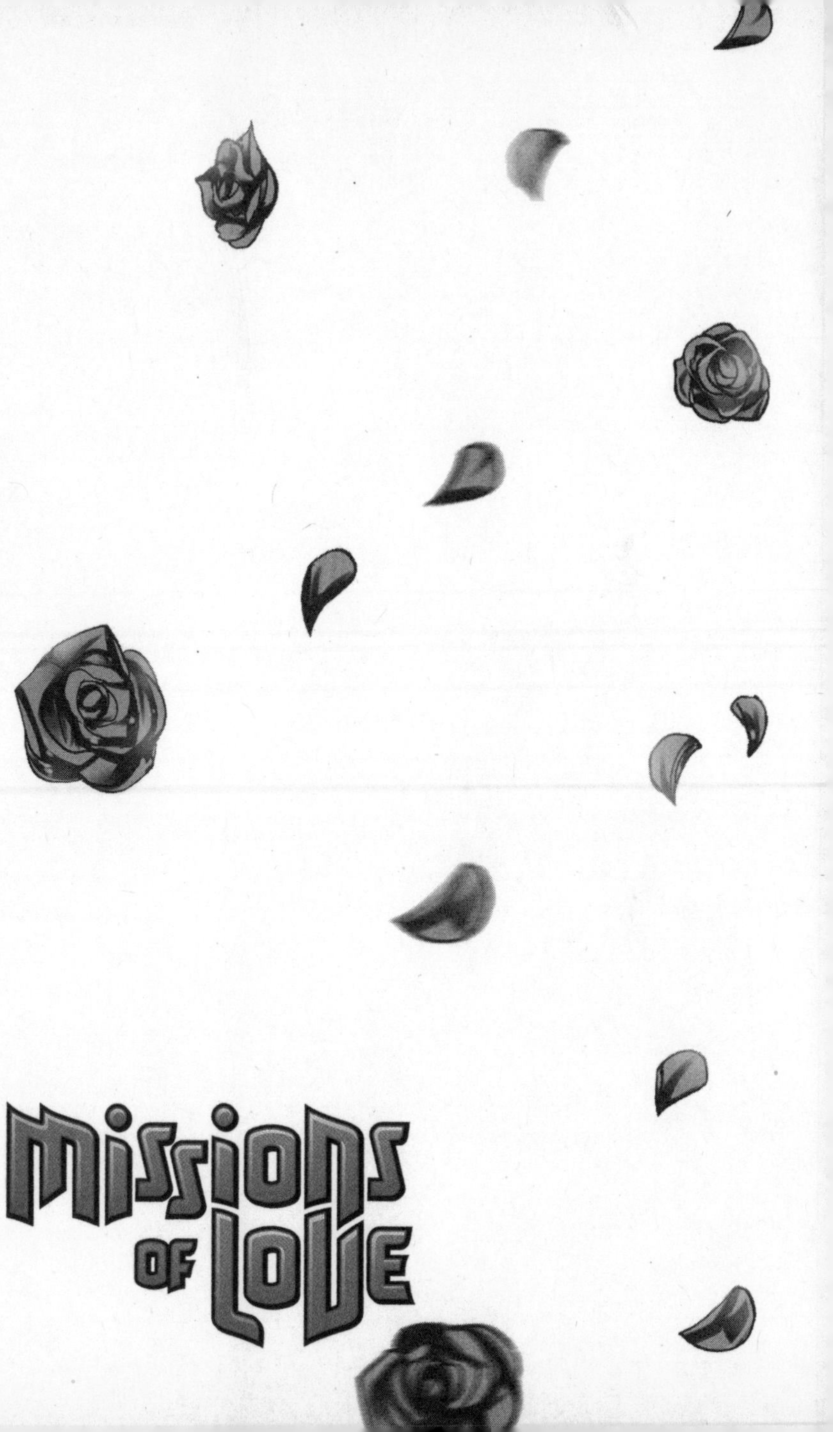
MISSIONS OF LOVE

Missions of Love

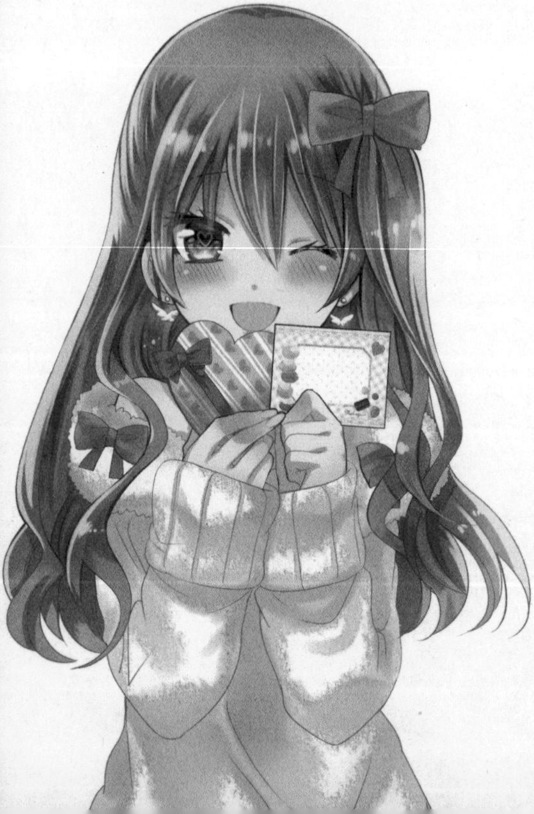

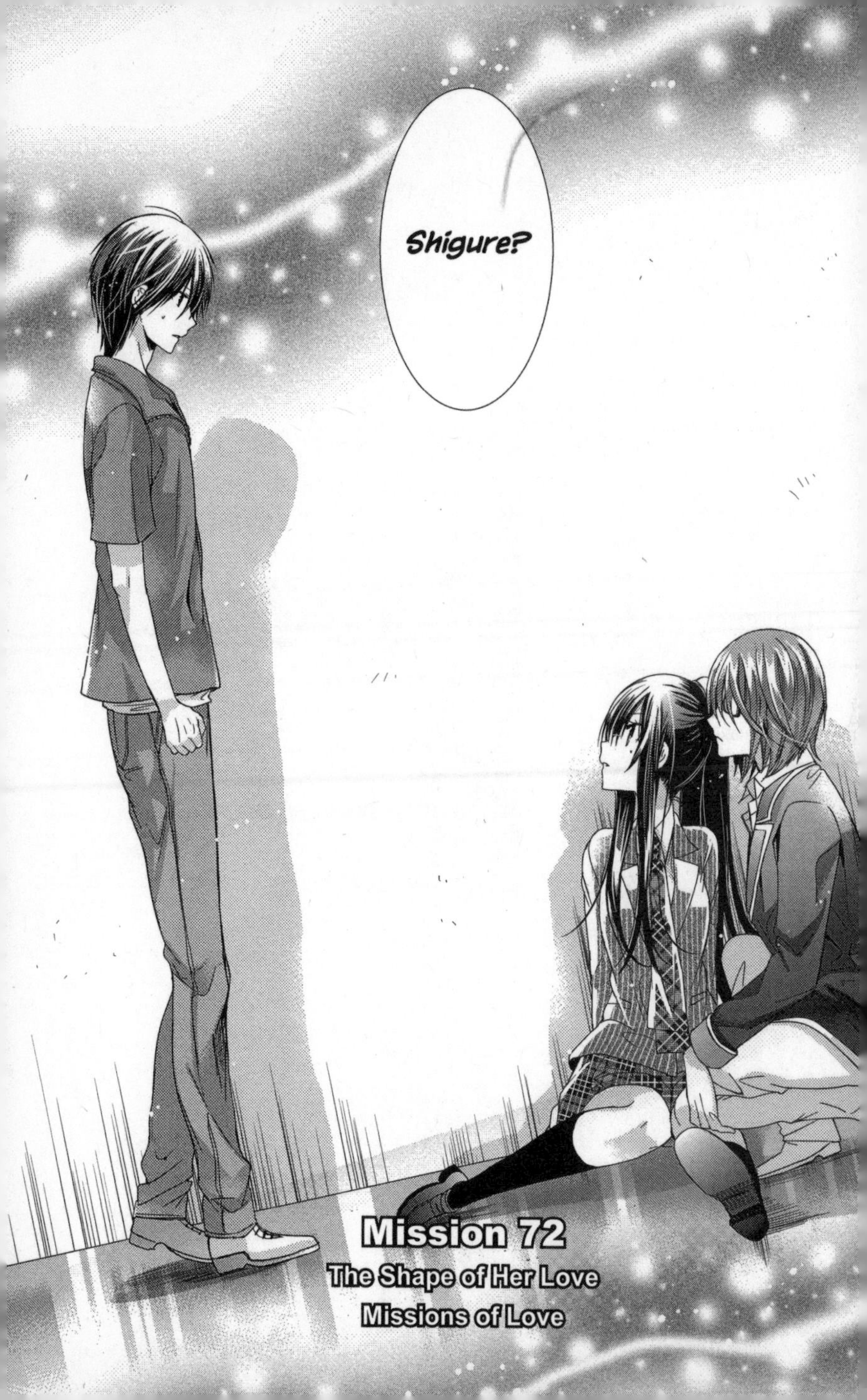
Shigure?
Mission 72
The Shape of Her Love
Missions of Love

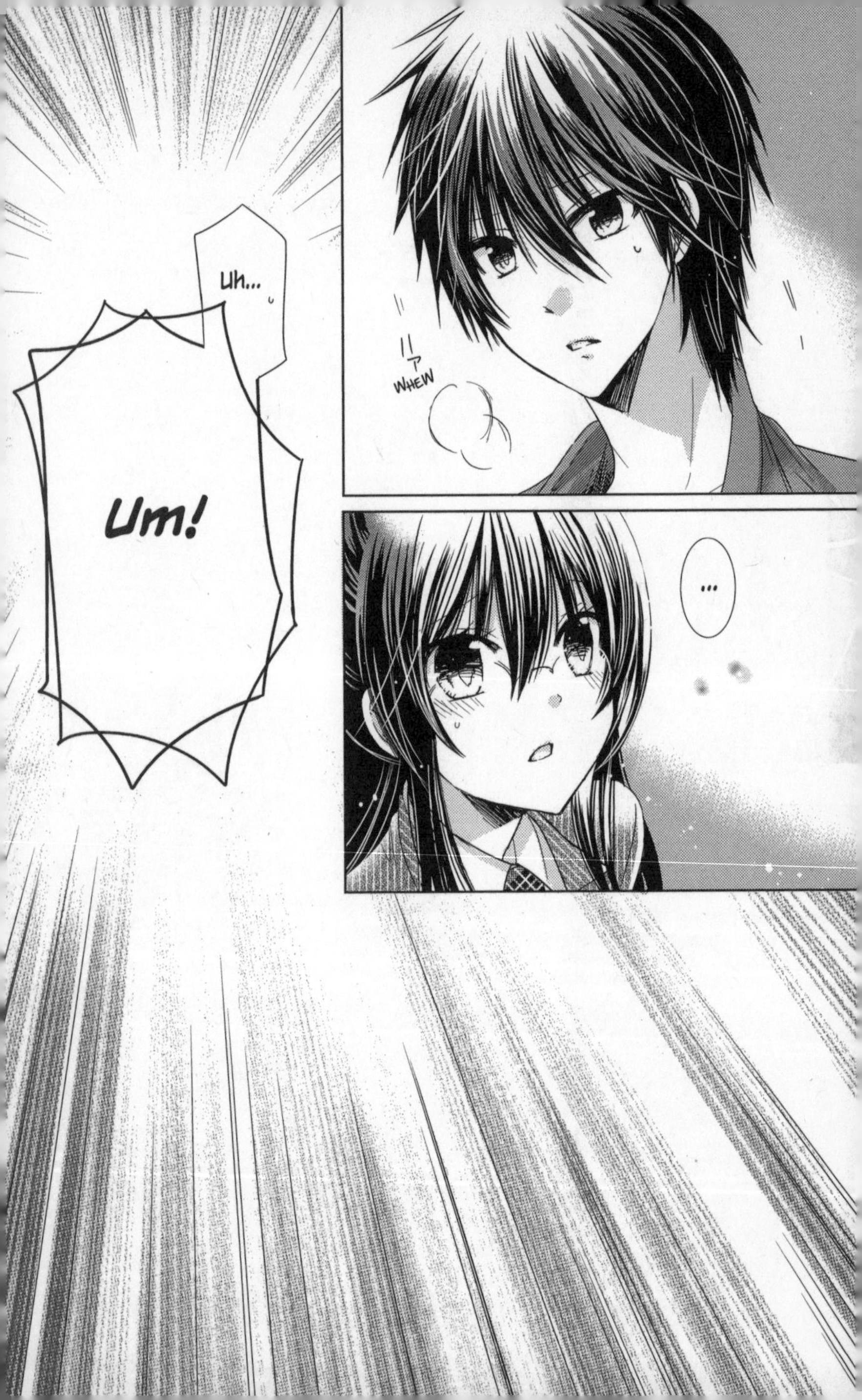
Uh...
WHEW
...
Um!

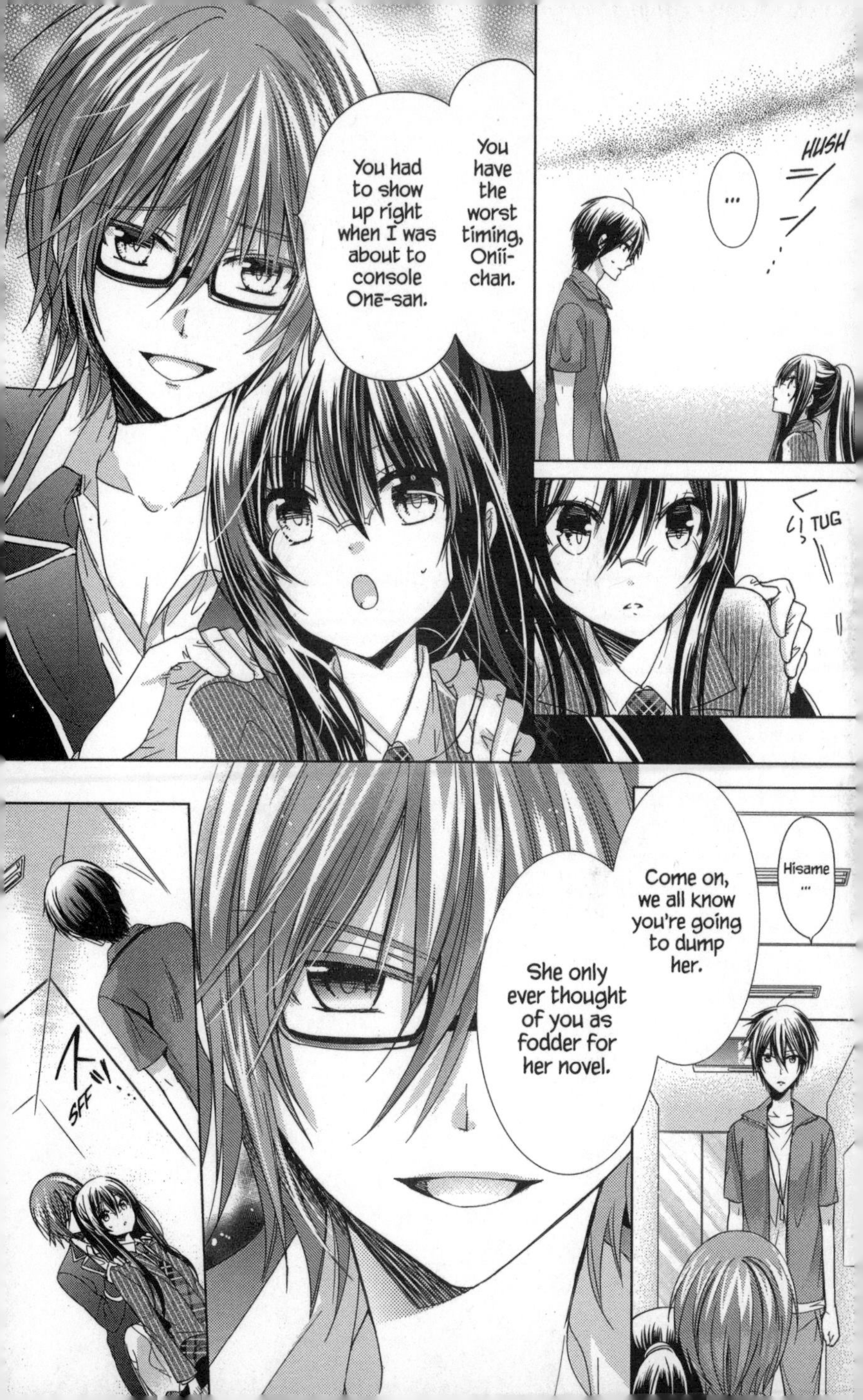
HUSH
...
TUG
You have the worst timing, Onii-chan.
You had to show up right when I was about to console Onē-san.
Hisame...
Come on, we all know you're going to dump her.
She only ever thought of you as fodder for her novel.
SFF

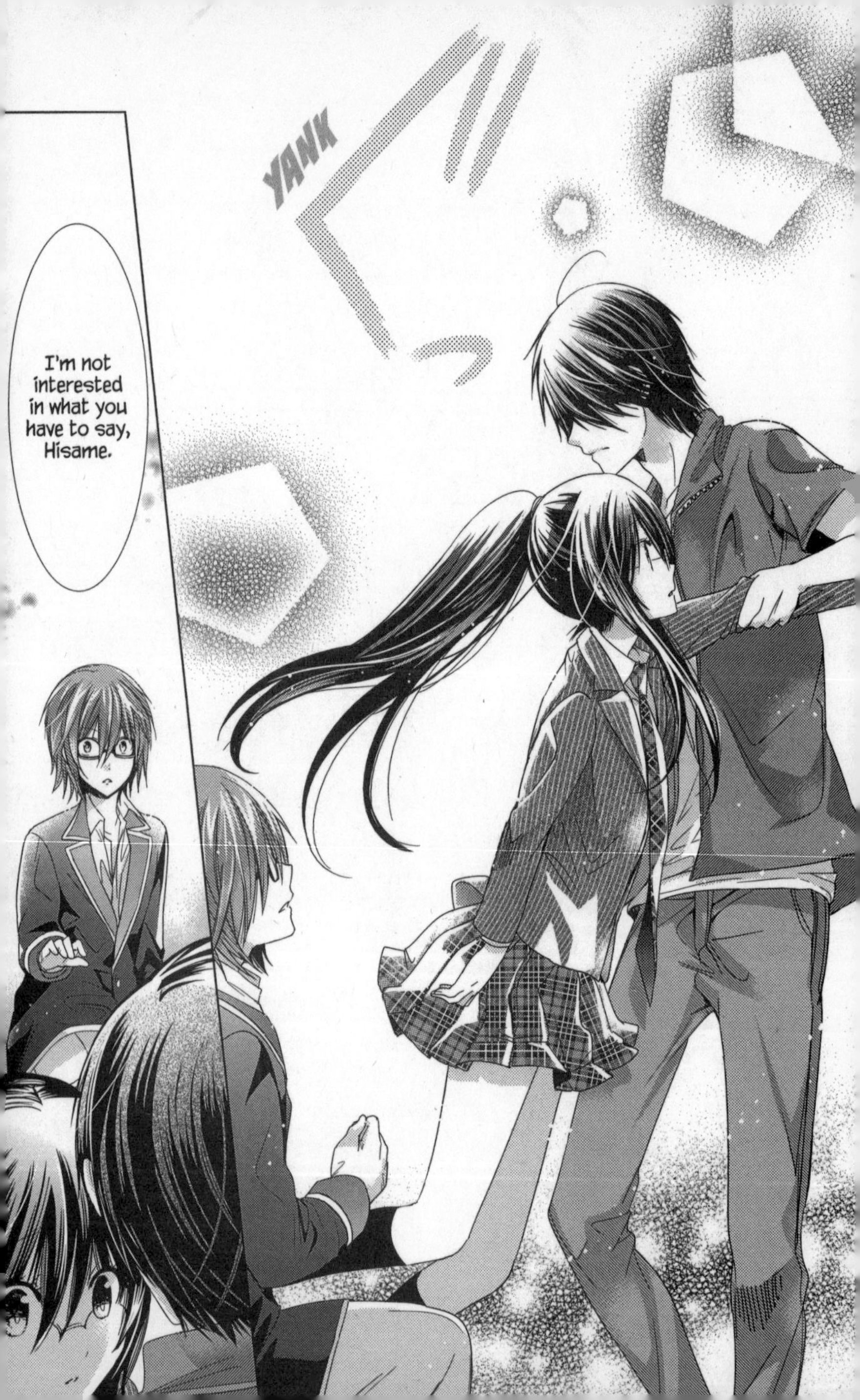
YANK
I'm not interested in what you have to say, Hisame.

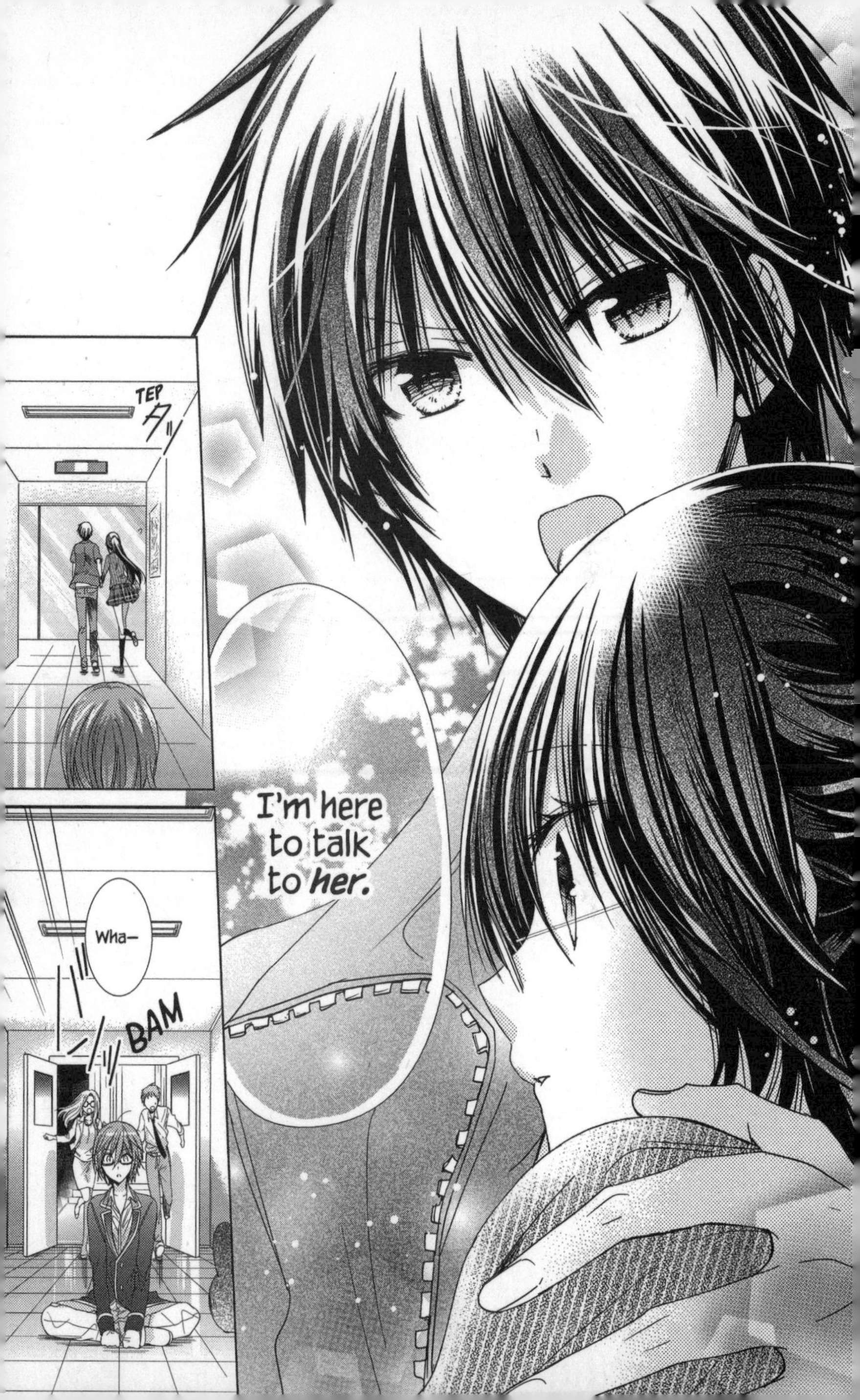
I'm here to talk to her.
TEP
Wha-
BAM

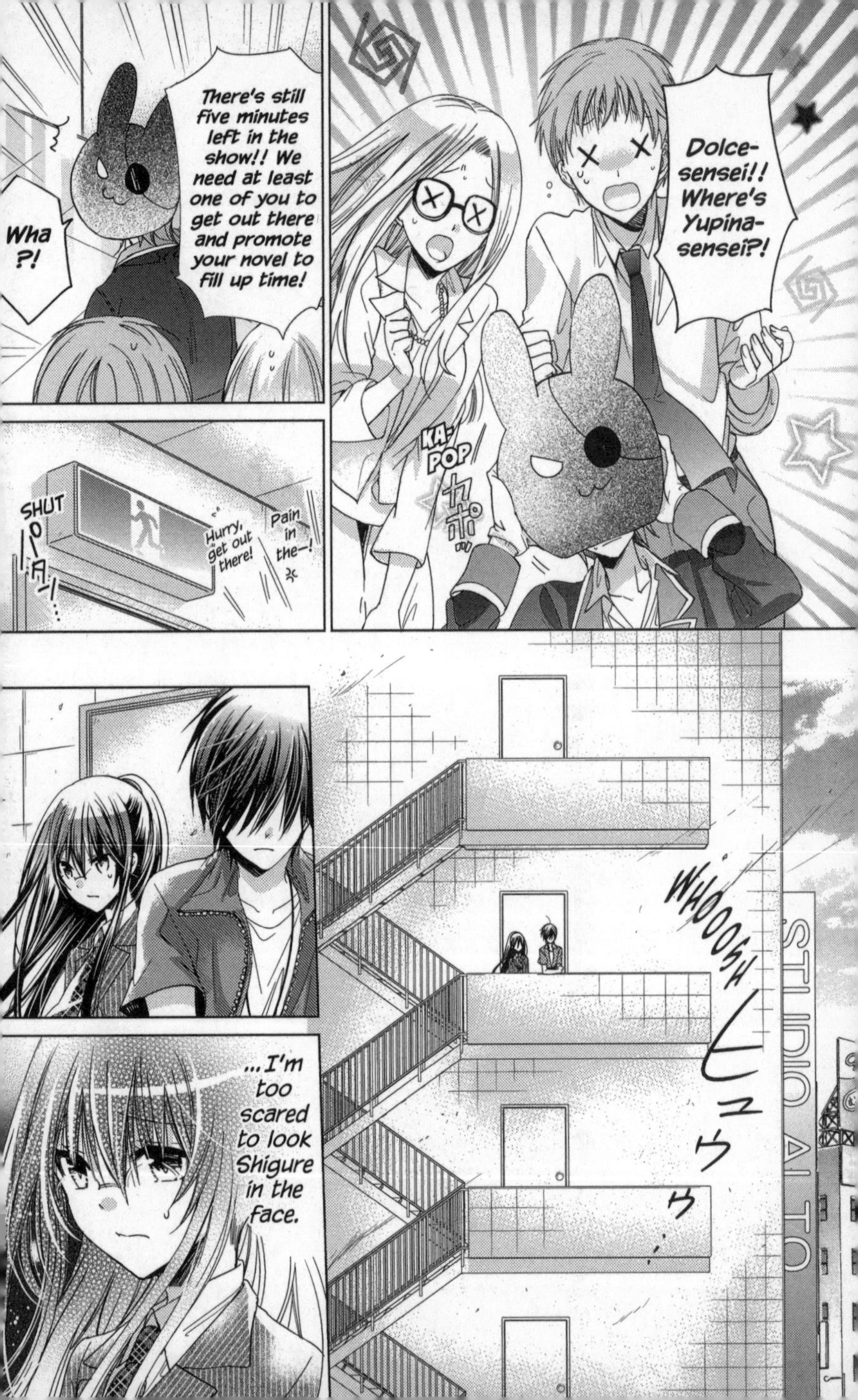
Dolce-sensei!! Where's Yupina-sensei?!
KA-POP
There's still five minutes left in the show!! We need at least one of you to get out there and promote your novel to fill up time!
Wha?!
Pain in the—!
Hurry, get out there!
SHUT
WHOOOSH
...I'm too scared to look Shigure in the face.

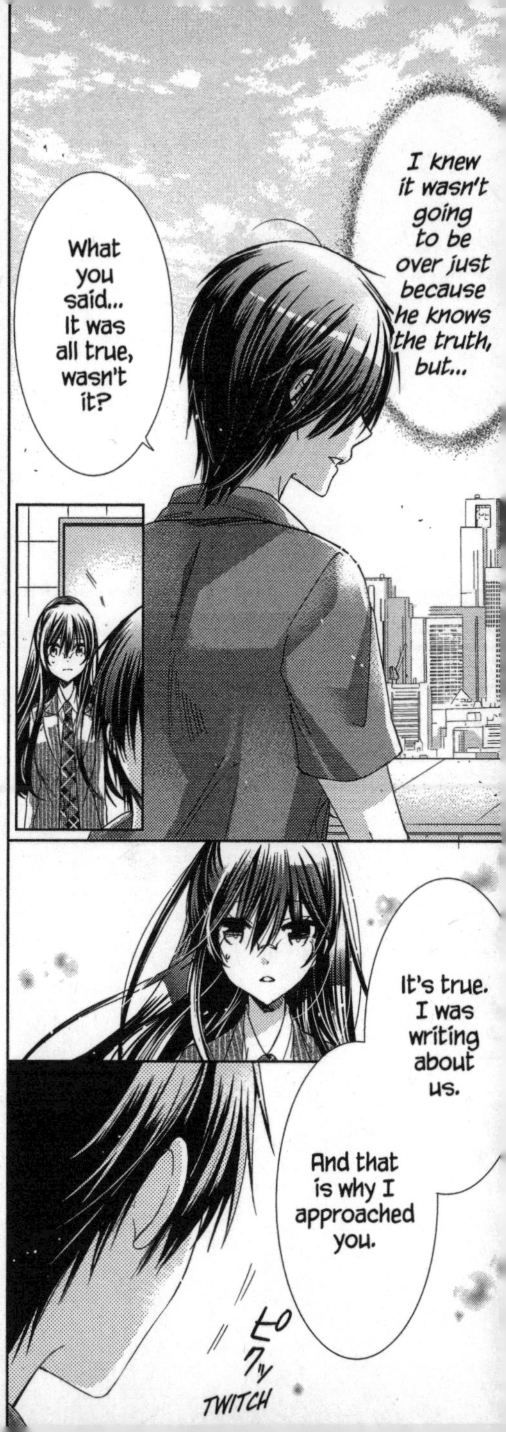
I knew it wasn't going to be over just because he knows the truth, but...
What you said... It was all true, wasn't it?
It's true. I was writing about us.
And that is why I approached you.
TWITCH

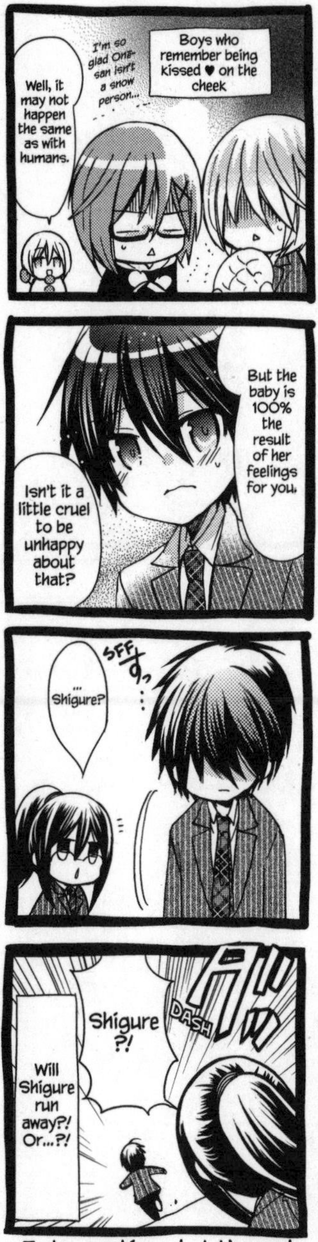
Boys who remember being kissed ♥ on the cheek
I'm so glad Ono-san isn't a snow person...
Well, it may not happen the same as with humans.
But the baby is 100% the result of her feelings for you.
Isn't it a little cruel to be unhappy about that?
SFF
...Shigure?
DASH
Shigure?!
Will Shigure run away?! Or...?!

To be continued at the end of this volume!

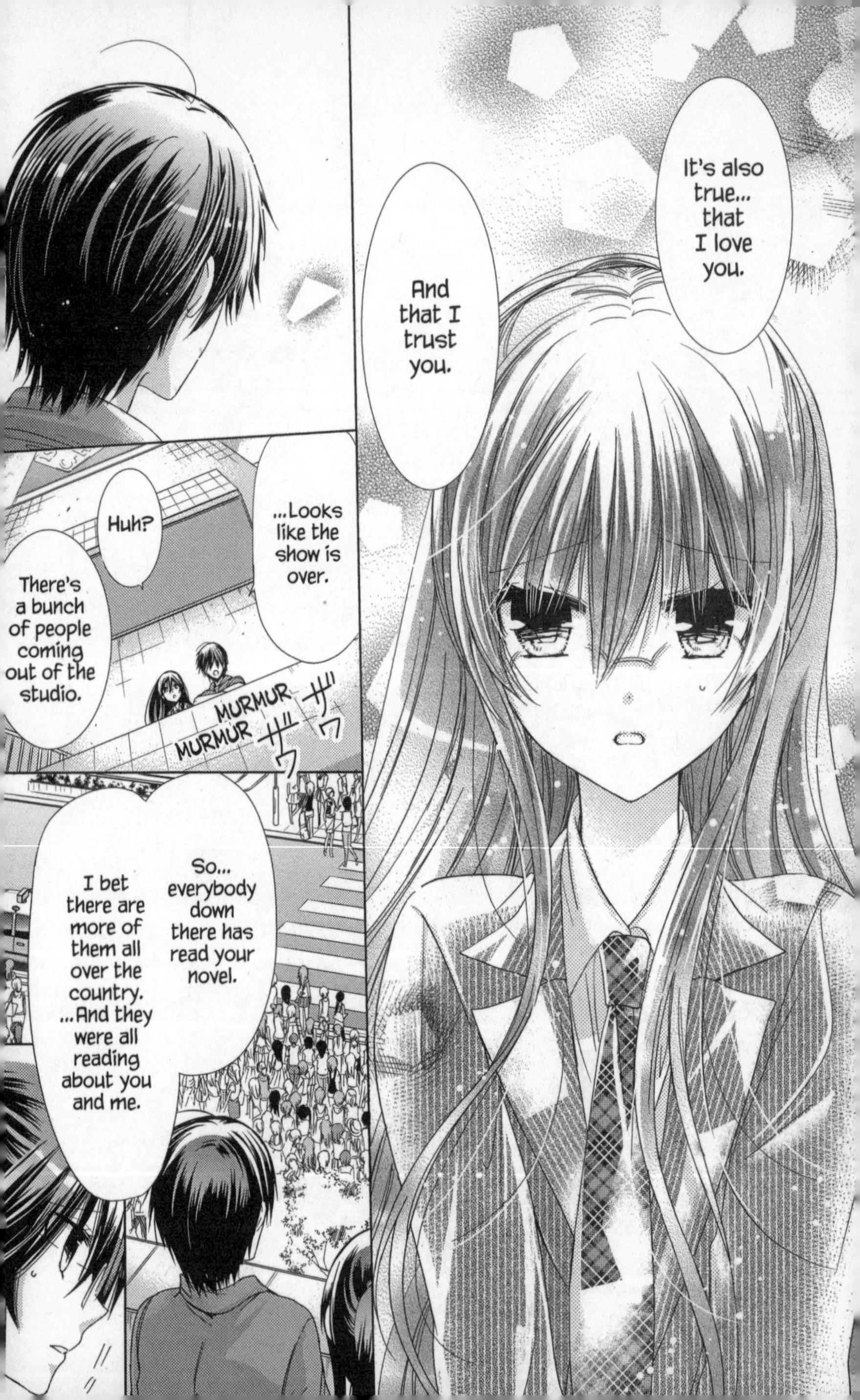
It's also true... that I love you.
And that I trust you.
...Looks like the show is over.
Huh?
There's a bunch of people coming out of the studio.
MURMUR
MURMUR
ザワ
ザワ
So... everybody down there has read your novel.
I bet there are more of them all over the country. ...And they were all reading about you and me.

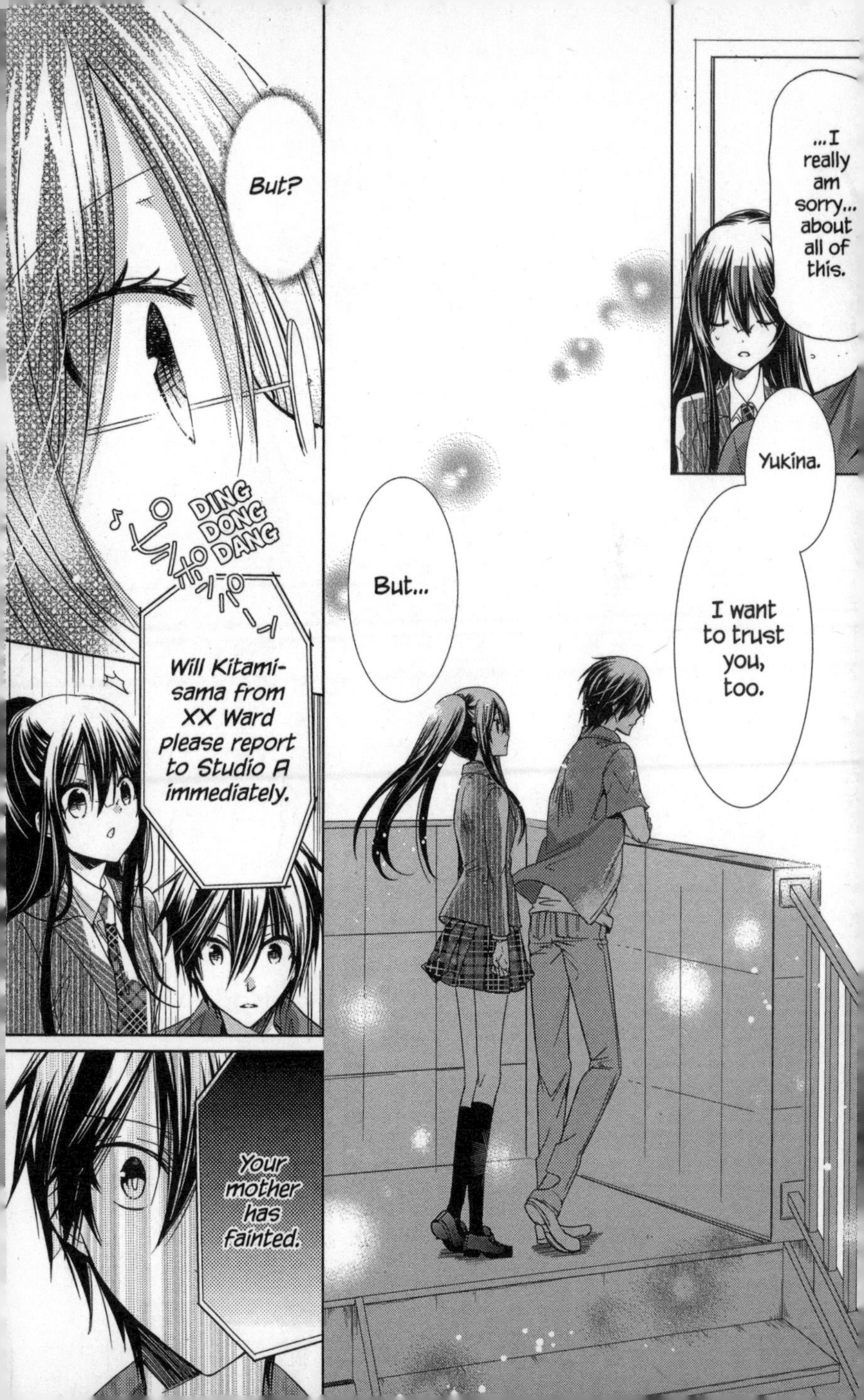
...I really am sorry... about all of this.
Yukina.
I want to trust you, too.
But...
But?
DING DONG DANG
Will Kitami-sama from XX Ward please report to Studio A immediately.
Your mother has fainted.

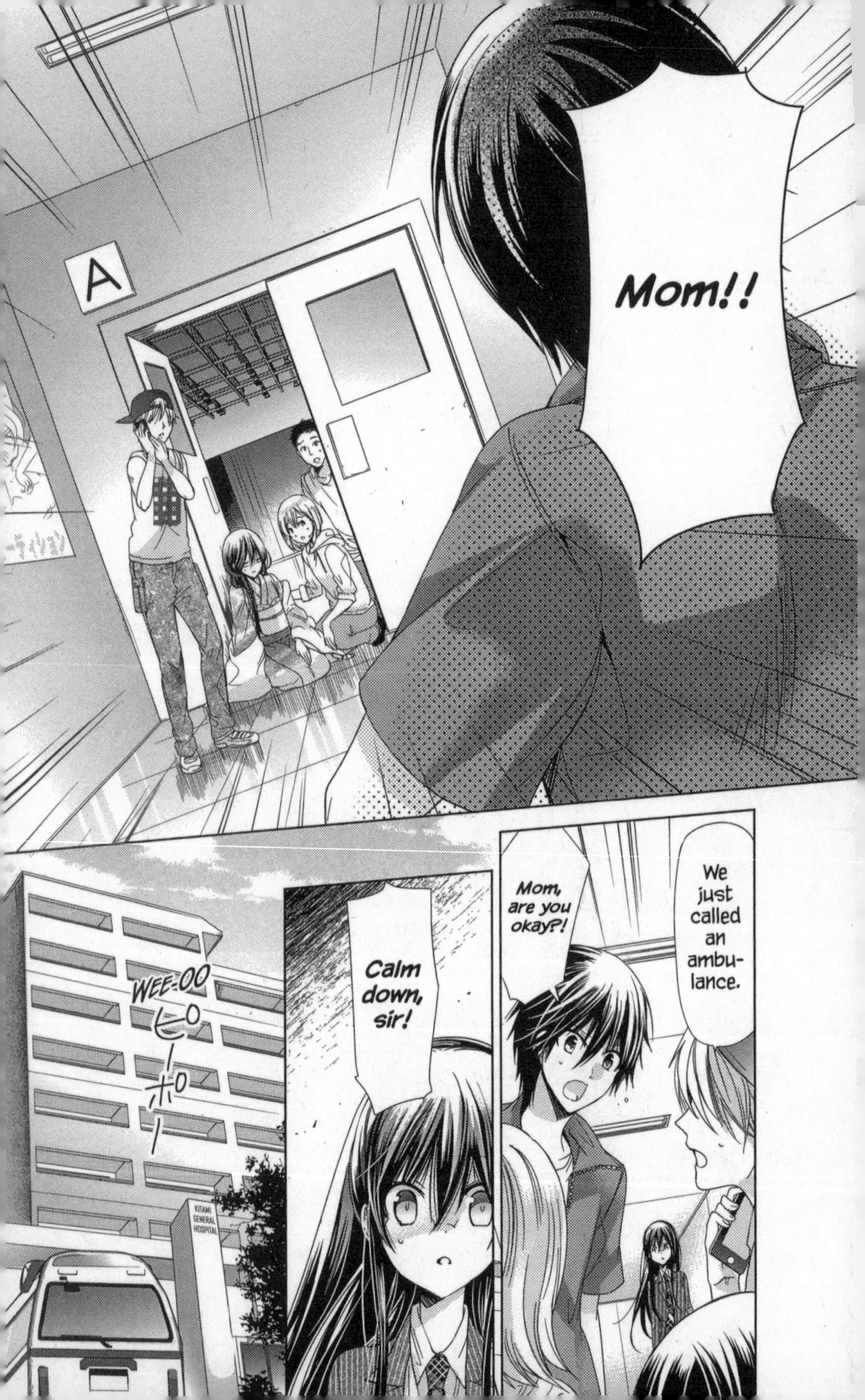
Mom!!
We just called an ambulance.
Mom, are you okay?!
Calm down, sir!
WEE-OO
ピーポー
KITAMI GENERAL HOSPITAL

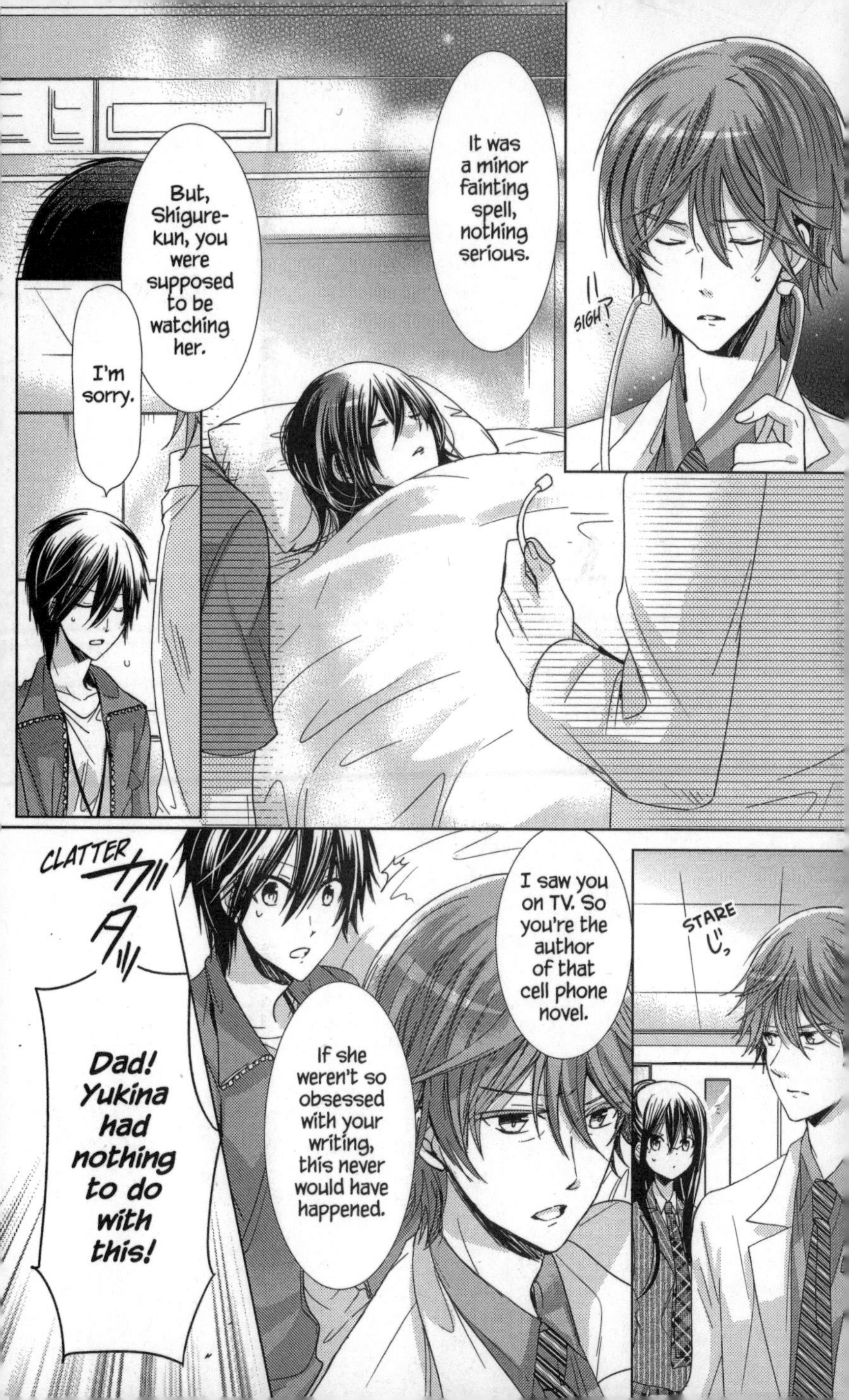

It was a minor fainting spell, nothing serious.
SIGH
But, Shigure-kun, you were supposed to be watching her.
I'm sorry.
STARE
I saw you on TV. So you're the author of that cell phone novel.
If she weren't so obsessed with your writing, this never would have happened.
CLATTER
Dad! Yukina had nothing to do with this!

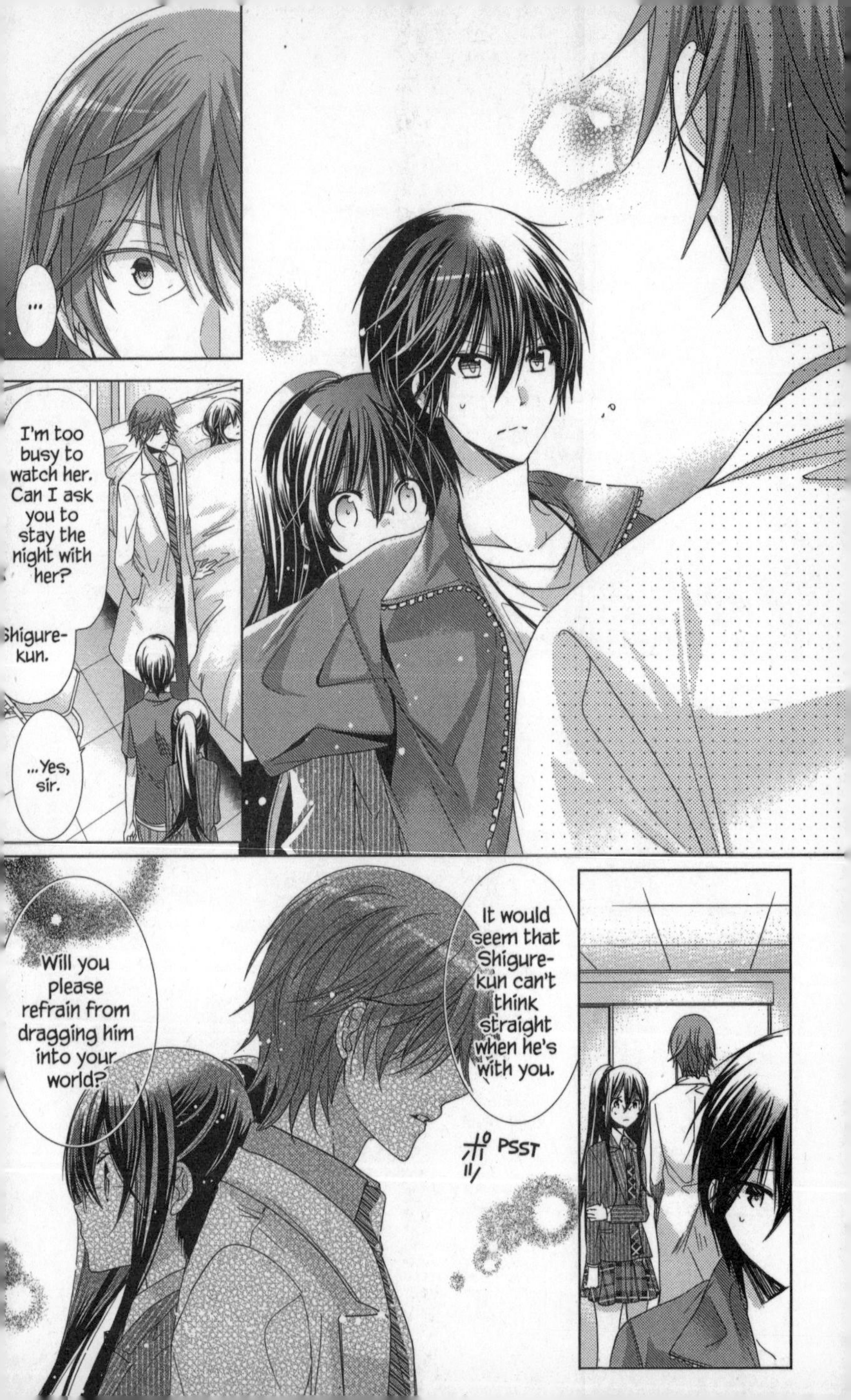
...
I'm too busy to watch her. Can I ask you to stay the night with her?
Shigure-kun.
...Yes, sir.
It would seem that Shigure-kun can't think straight when he's with you.
PSST
Will you please refrain from dragging him into your world?

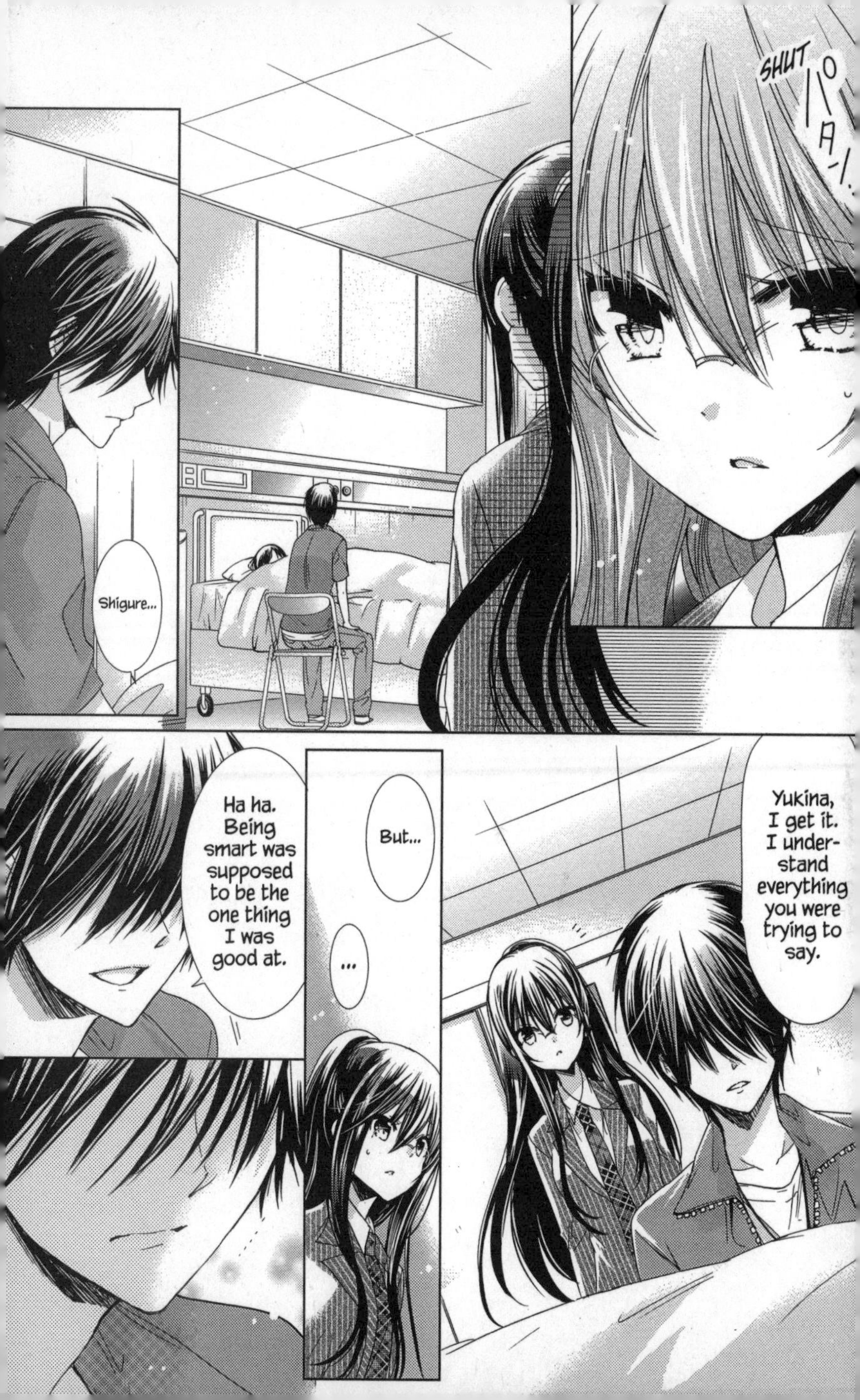
SHUT
Shigure...
Yukina, I get it. I understand everything you were trying to say.
But...
...
Ha ha. Being smart was supposed to be the one thing I was good at.

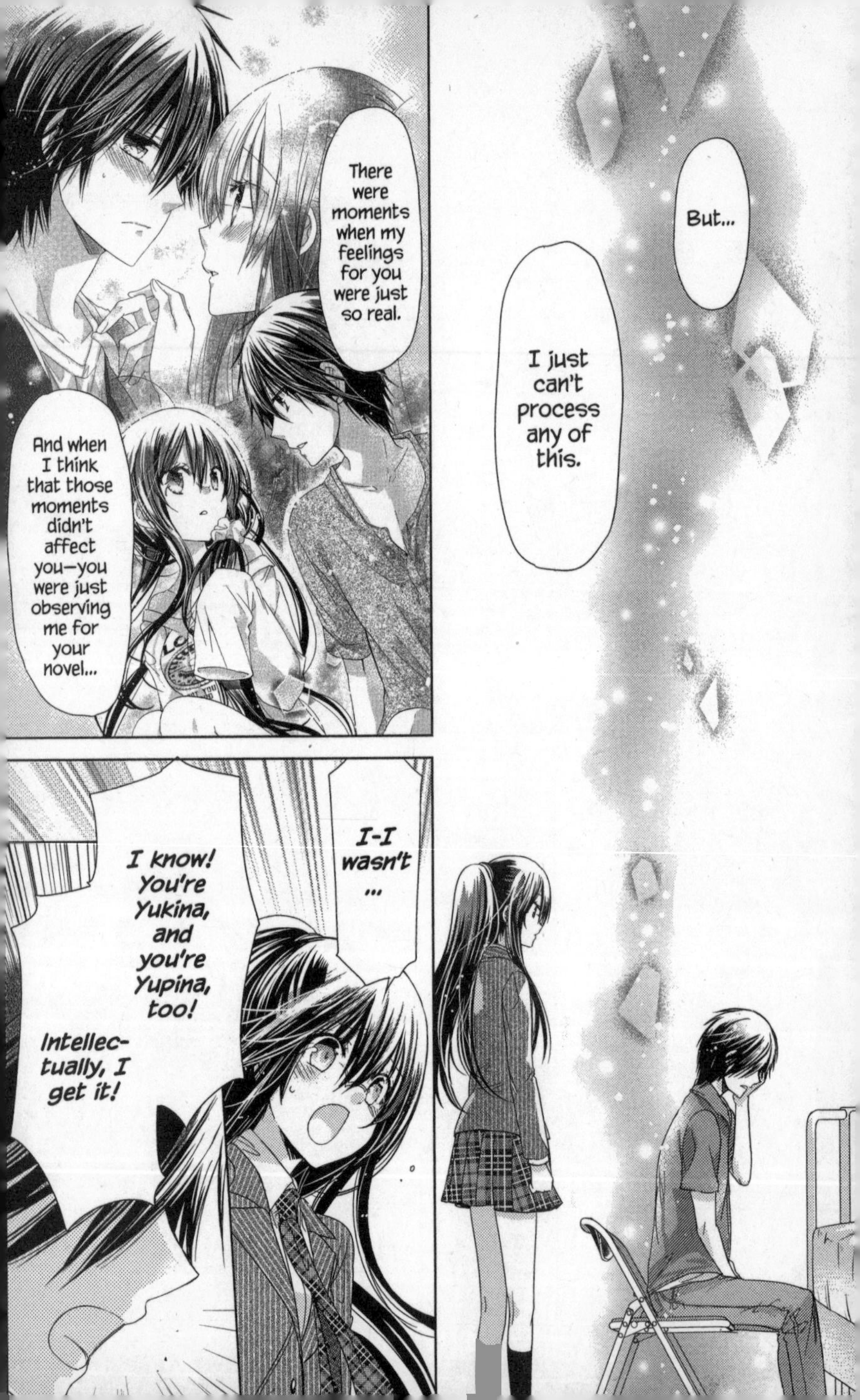
But...
I just can't process any of this.
There were moments when my feelings for you were just so real.
And when I think that those moments didn't affect you—you were just observing me for your novel...
I-I wasn't ...
I know! You're Yukina, and you're Yupina, too!
Intellectually, I get it!

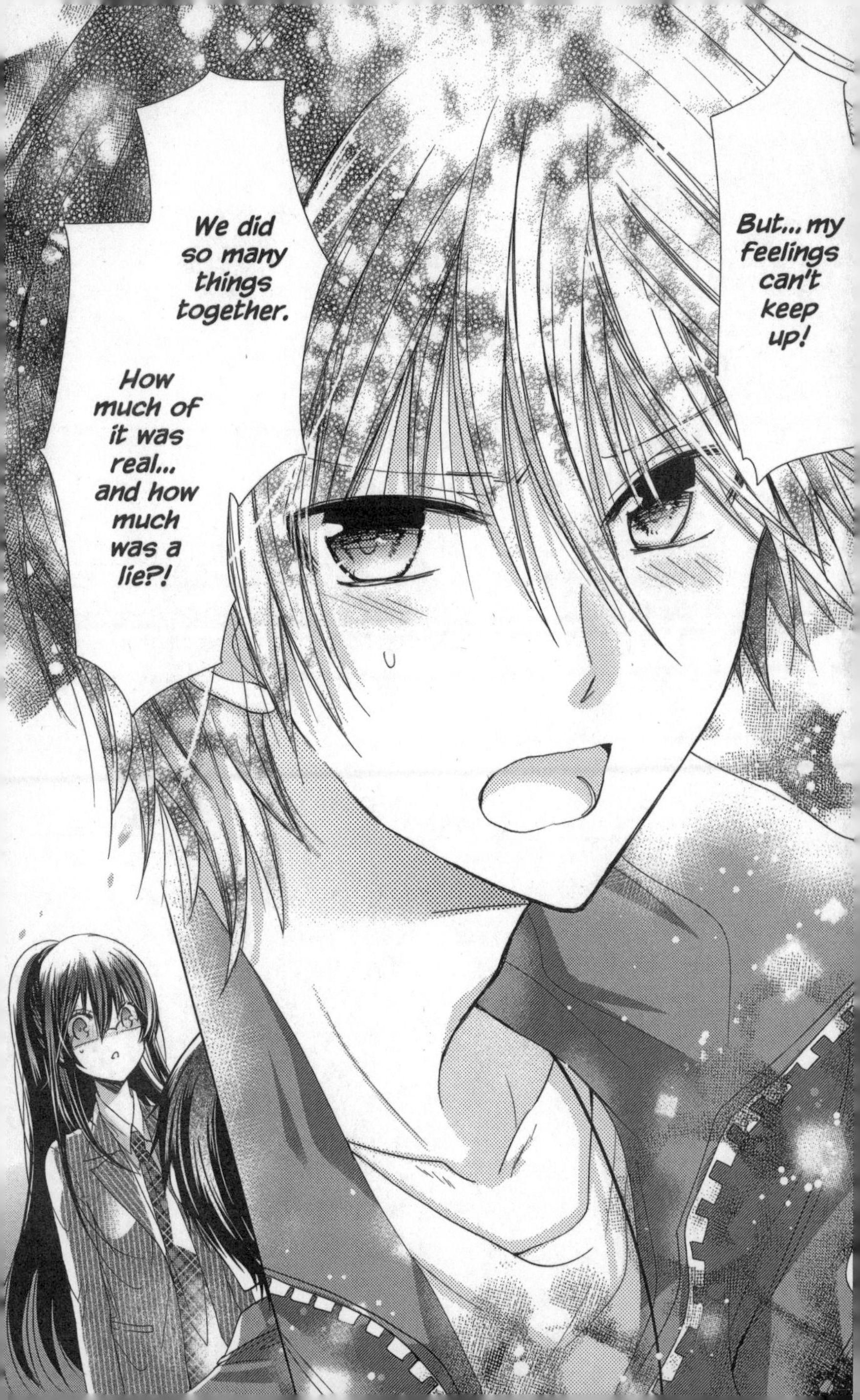
But... my feelings can't keep up!
We did so many things together.
How much of it was real... and how much was a lie?!

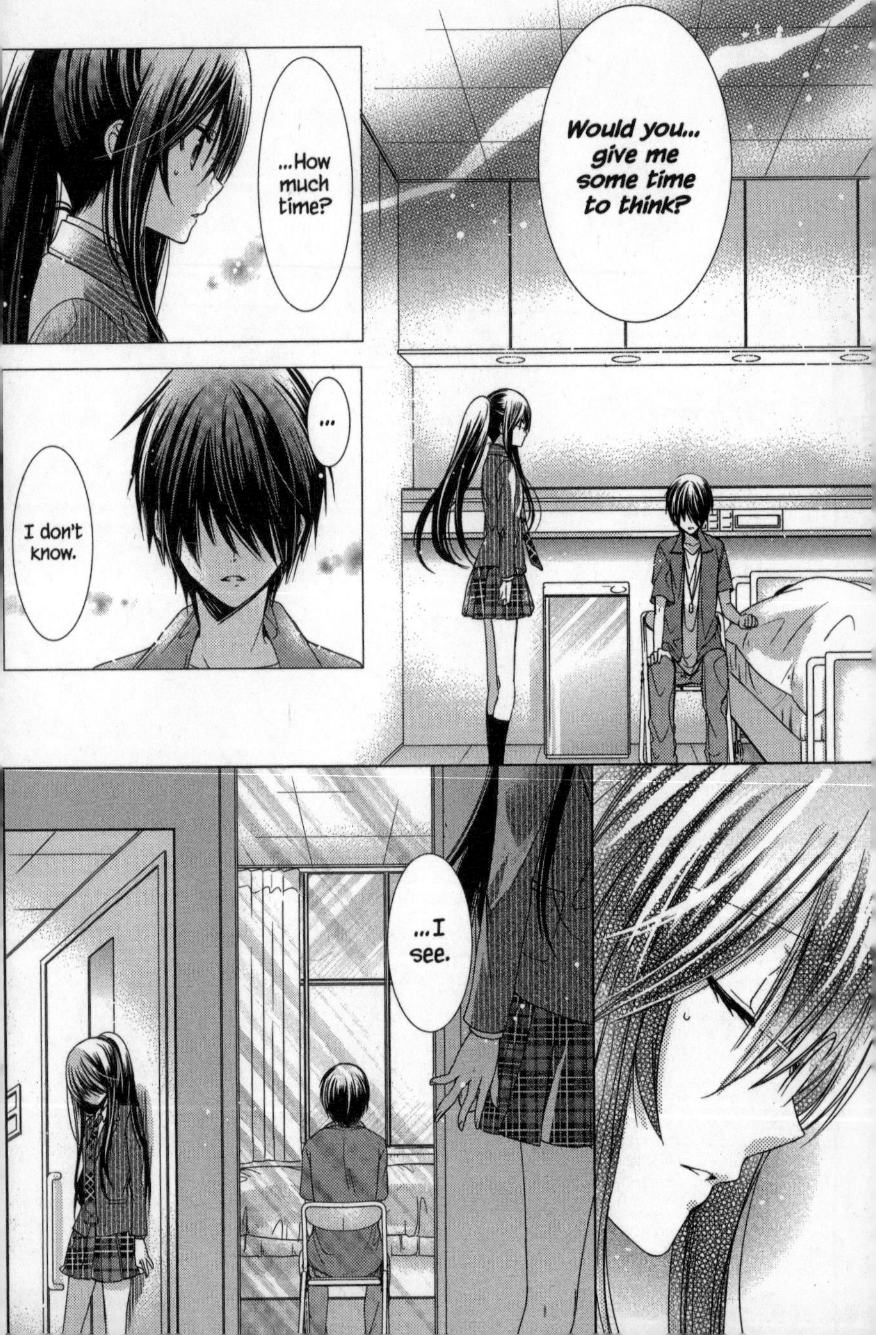
Would you... give me some time to think?
...How much time?
...
I don't know.
...I see.

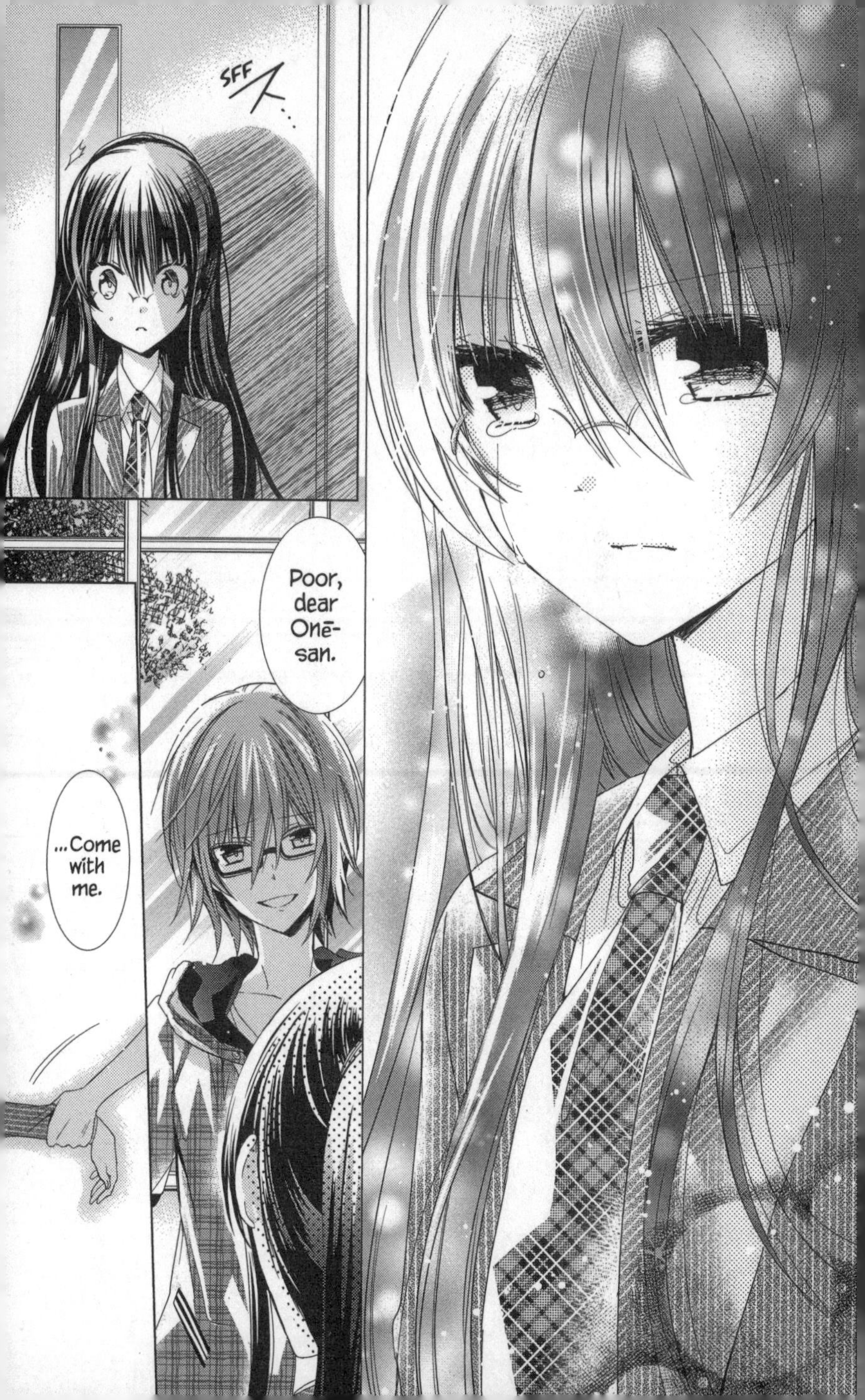
SFF
Poor, dear Onē-san.
...Come with me.

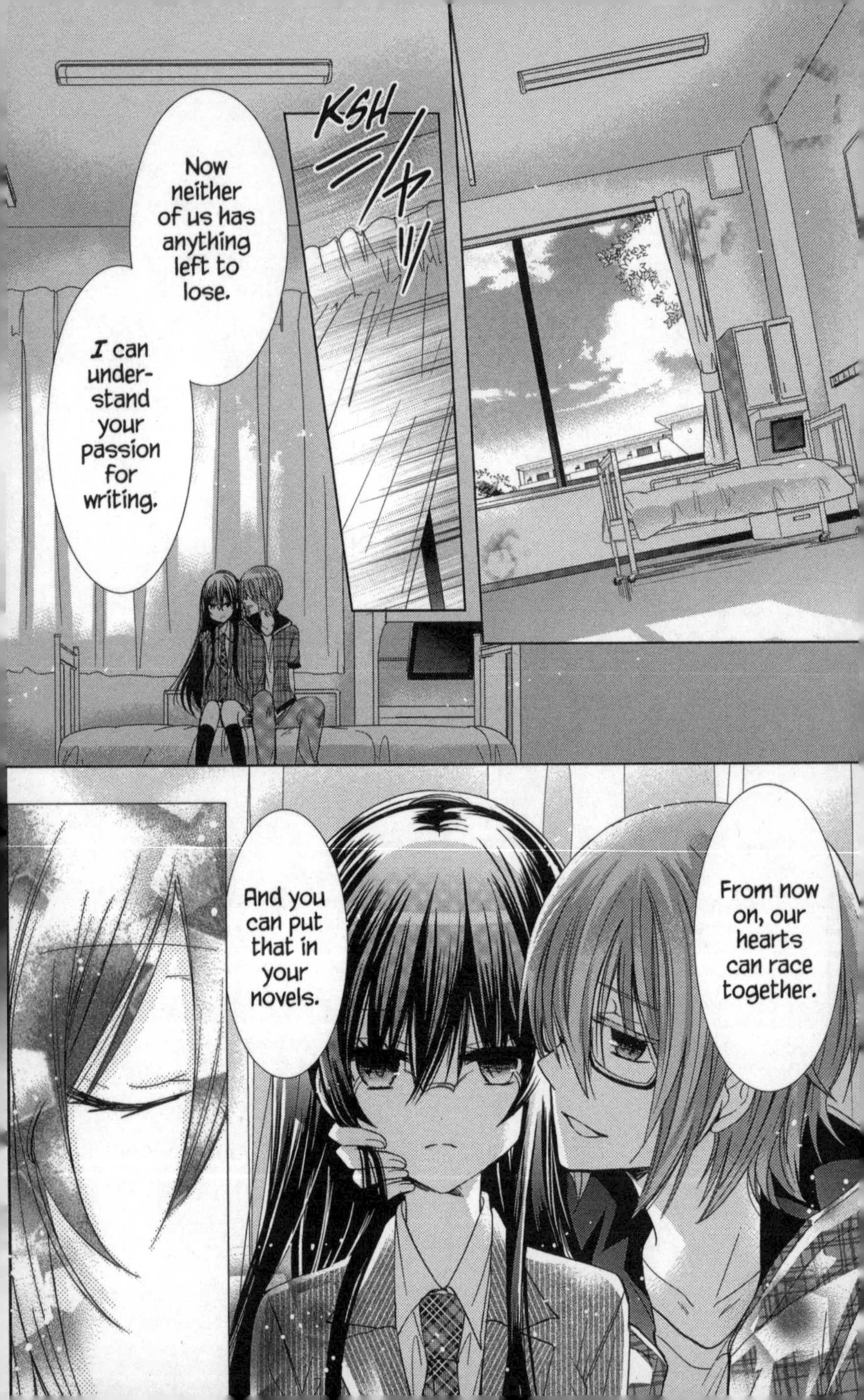
KSH
Now neither of us has anything left to lose.
I can under-stand your passion for writing.
From now on, our hearts can race together.
And you can put that in your novels.

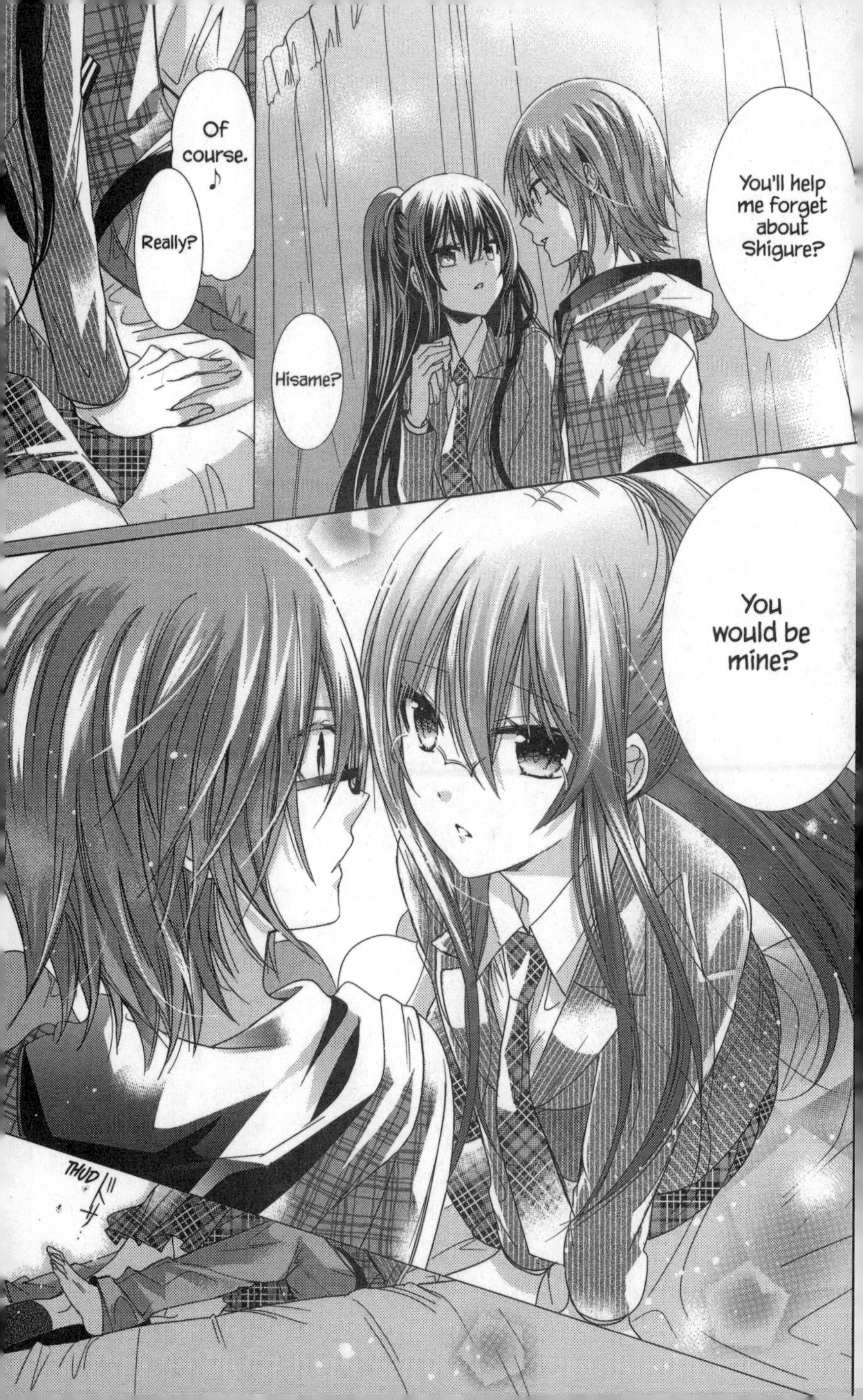
You'll help me forget about Shigure?
Hisame?
Of course. ♪
Really?
You would be mine?
THUD

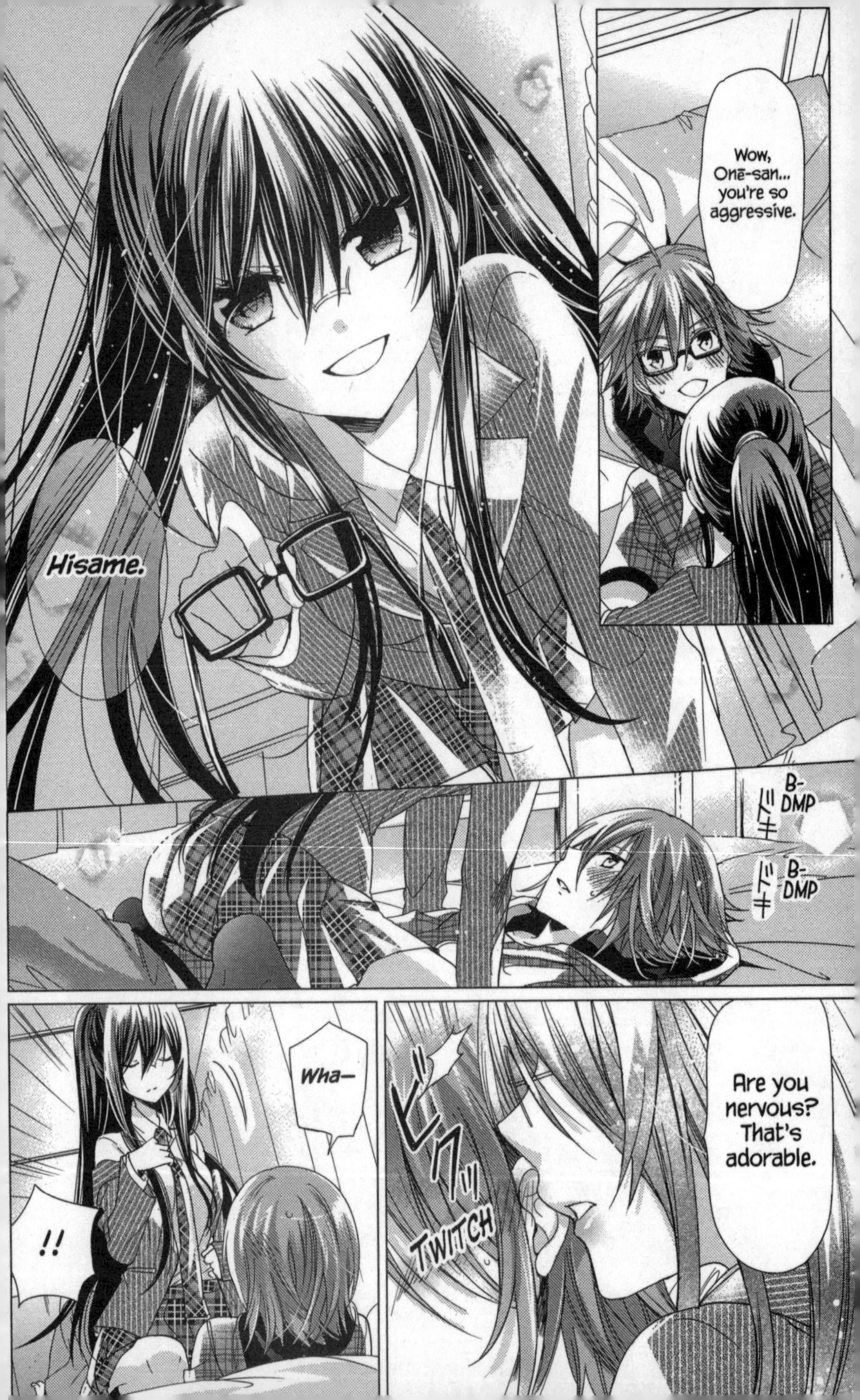
Wow, One-san... you're so aggressive.
Hisame.
B-DMP
ドキ
B-DMP
ドキ
Are you nervous? That's adorable.
ビクッ
TWITCH
Wha—
!!

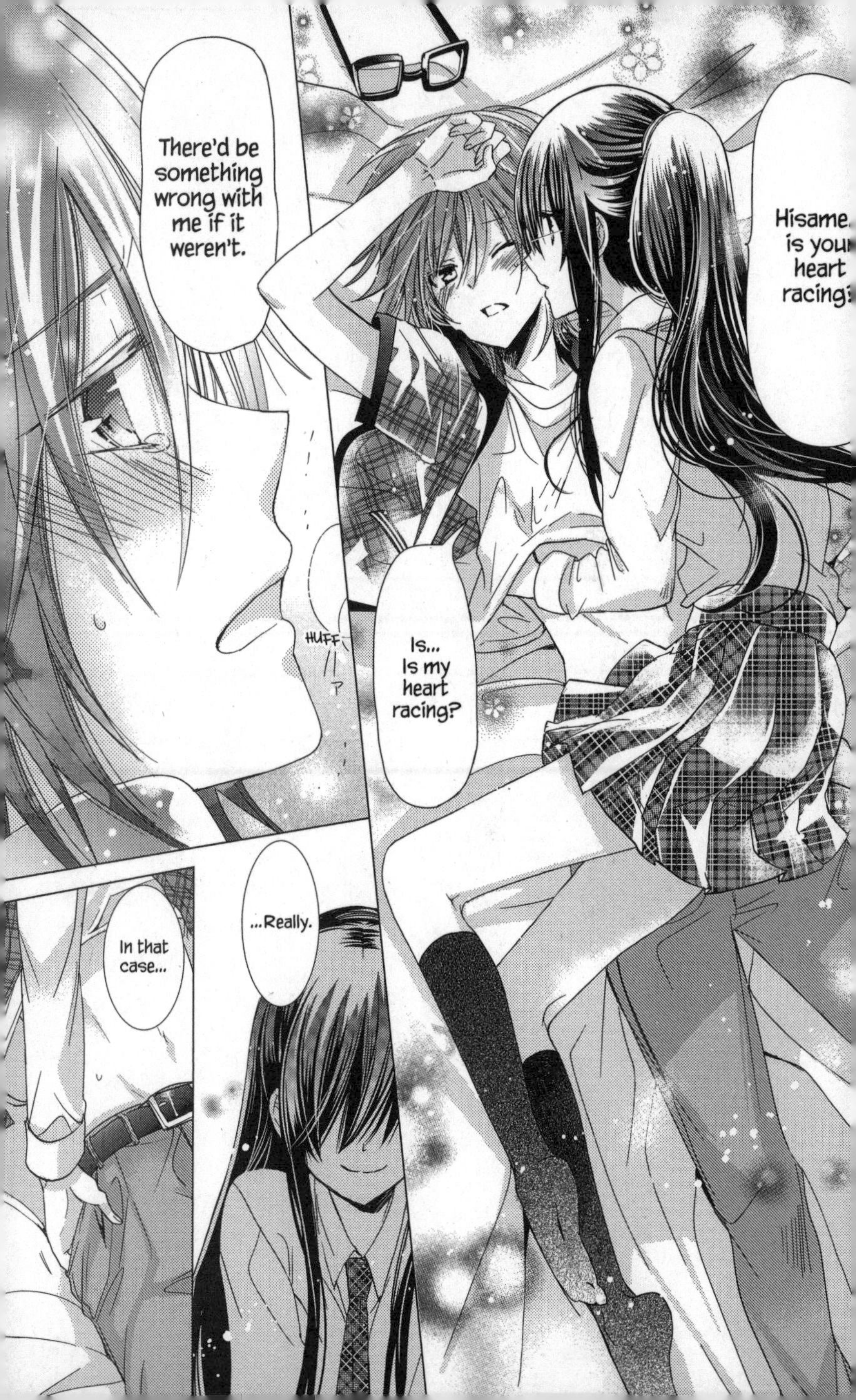
Hisame. is your heart racing?
HUFF
Is... Is my heart racing?
There'd be something wrong with me if it weren't.
...Really.
In that case...

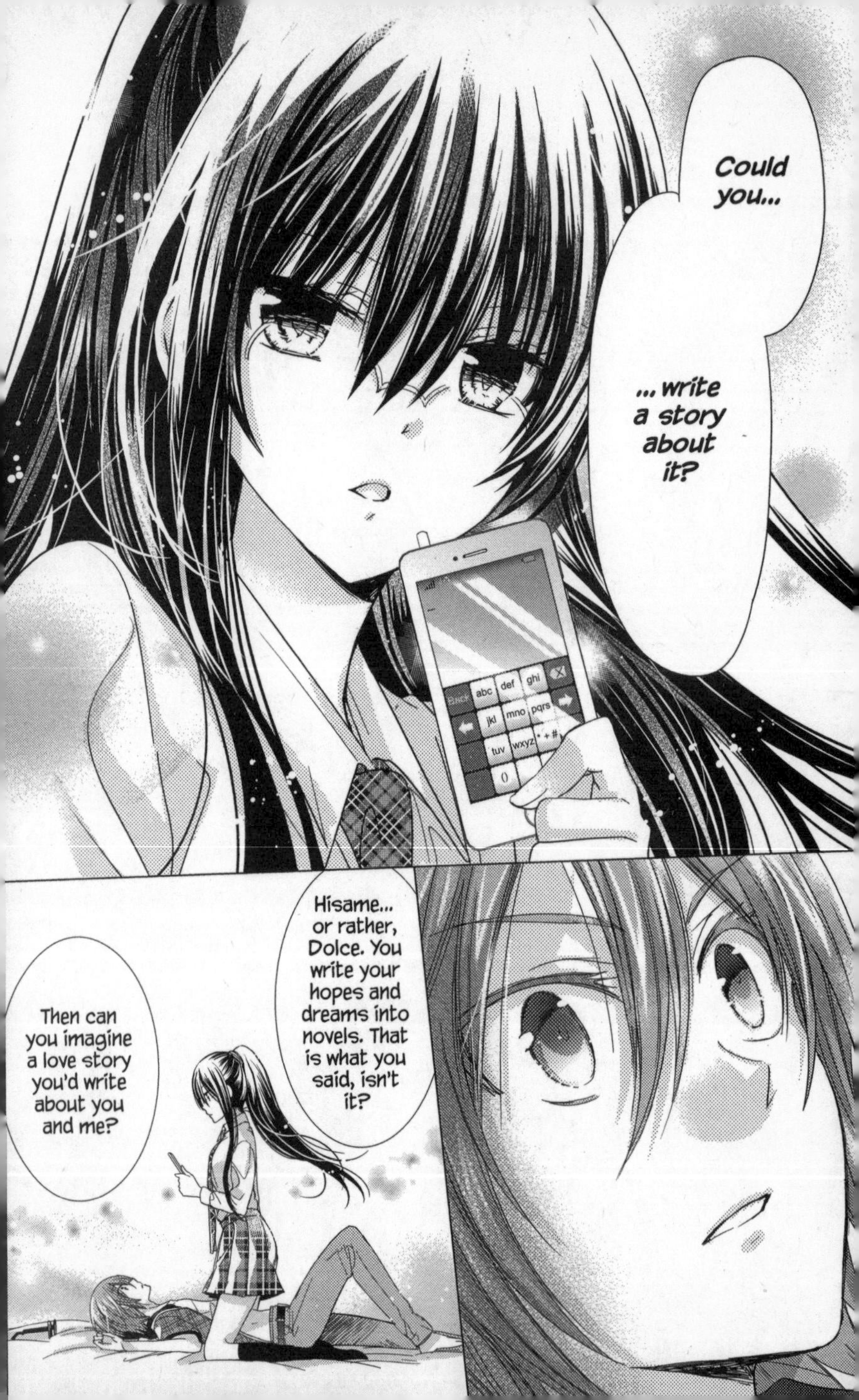
Could you...
...write a story about it?
Hisame... or rather, Dolce. You write your hopes and dreams into novels. That is what you said, isn't it?
Then can you imagine a love story you'd write about you and me?

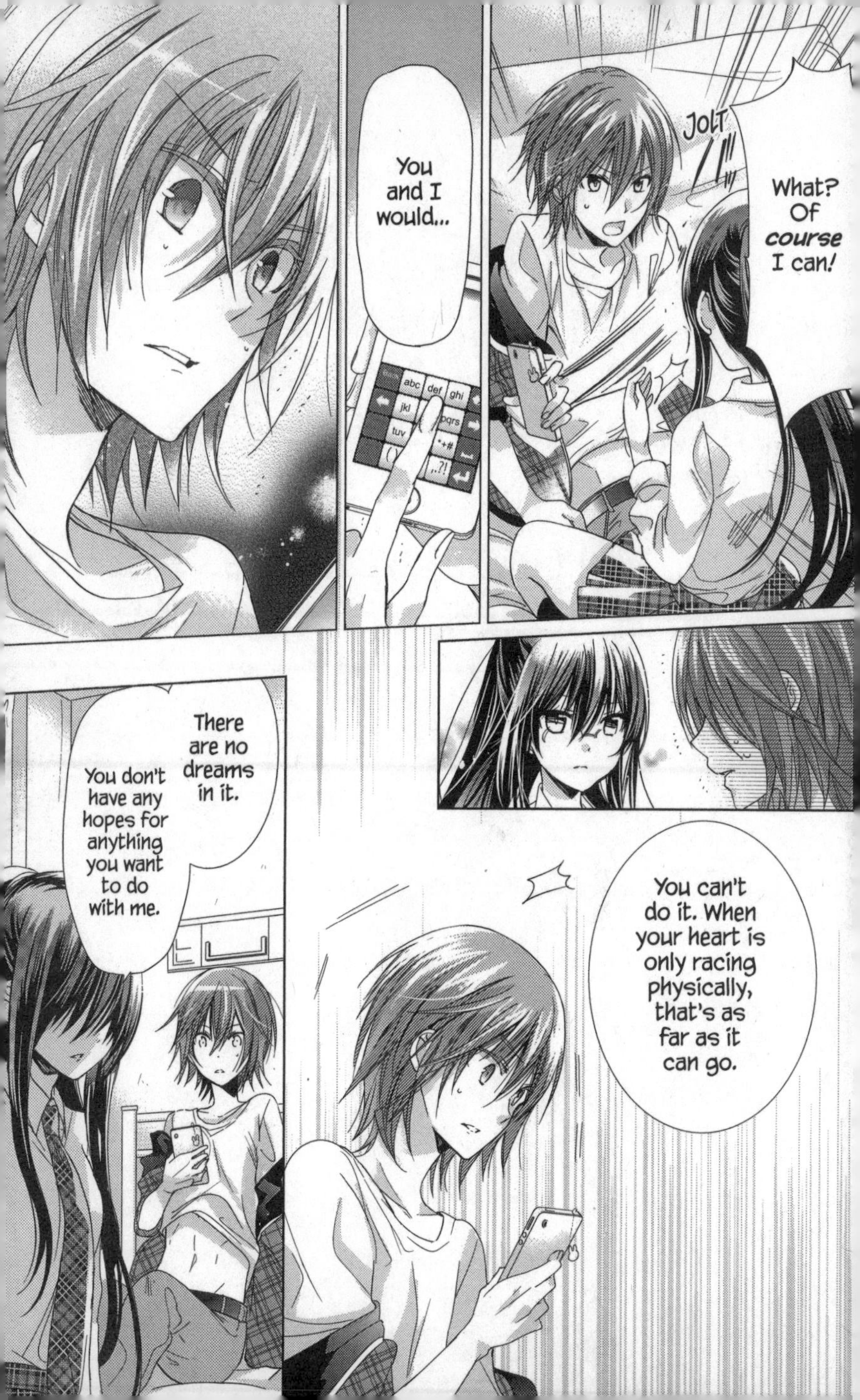
JOLT
What? Of *course* I can!
You and I would...
You can't do it. When your heart is only racing physically, that's as far as it can go.
There are no dreams in it.
You don't have any hopes for anything you want to do with me.

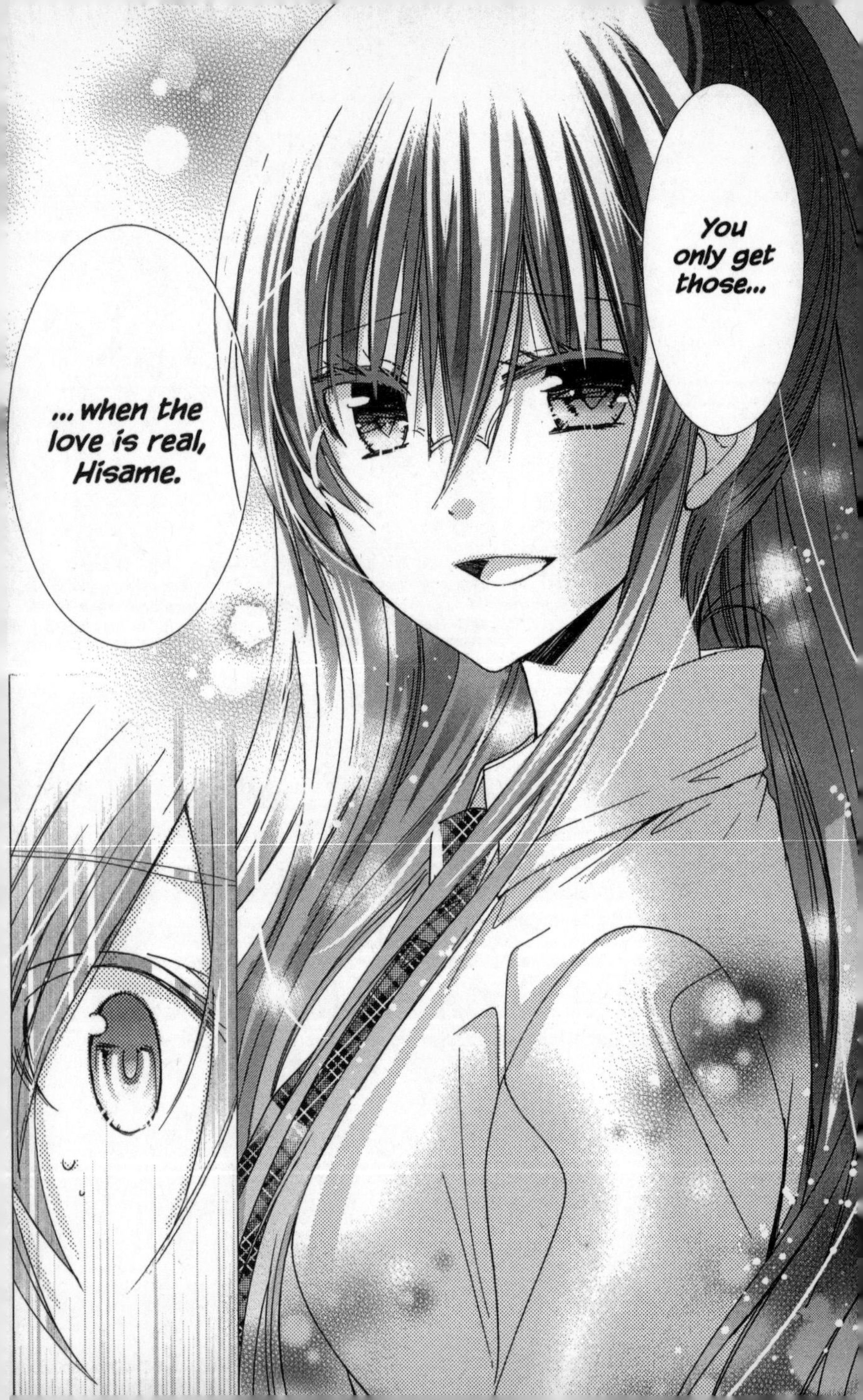
You only get those...
...when the love is real, Hisame.

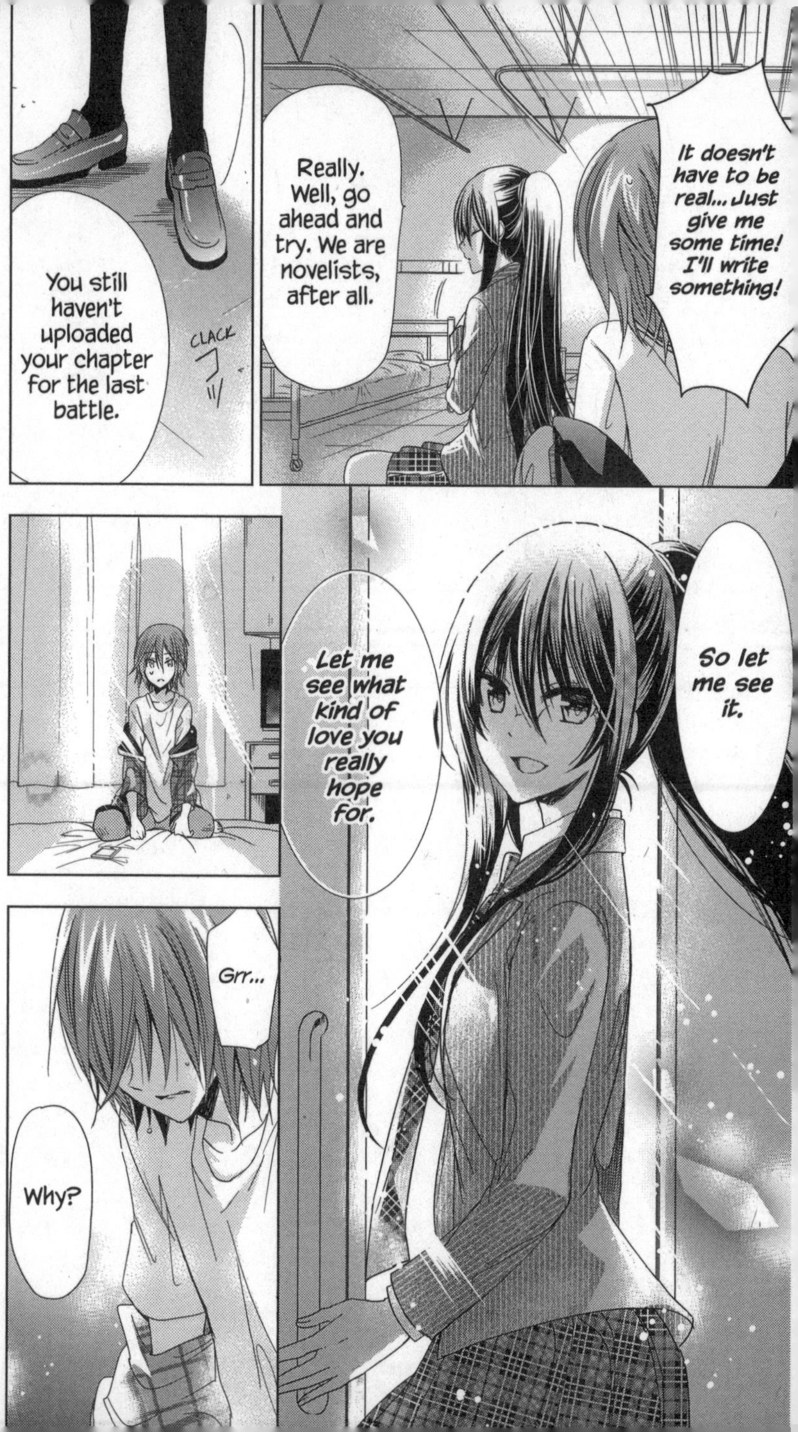
It doesn't have to be real... Just give me some time! I'll write something!
Really. Well, go ahead and try. We are novelists, after all.
CLACK
You still haven't uploaded your chapter for the last battle.
So let me see it.
Let me see what kind of love you really hope for.
Grr...
Why?

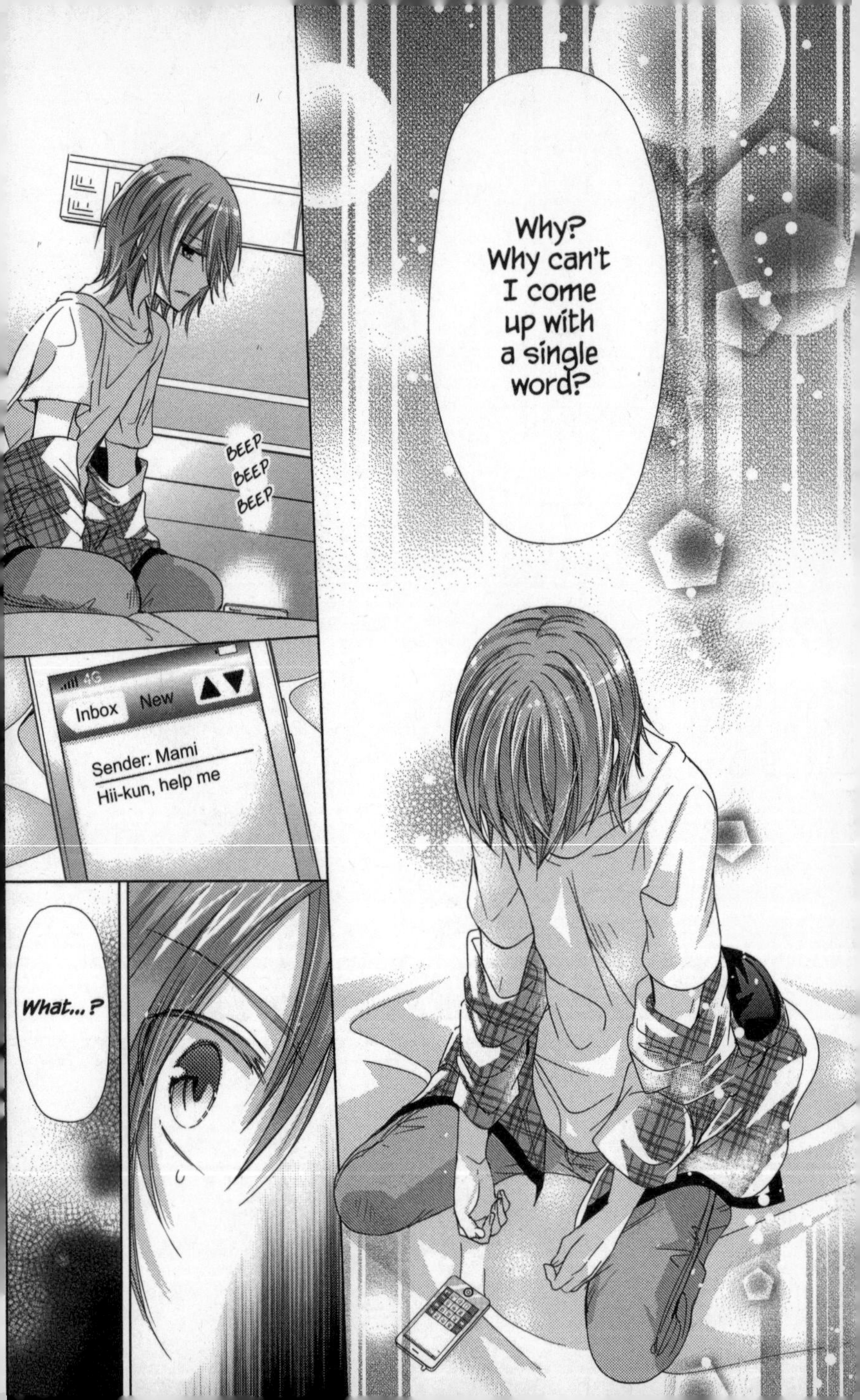
Why? Why can't I come up with a single word?
BEEP BEEP BEEP
Inbox
New
Sender: Mami
Hii-kun, help me
What...?

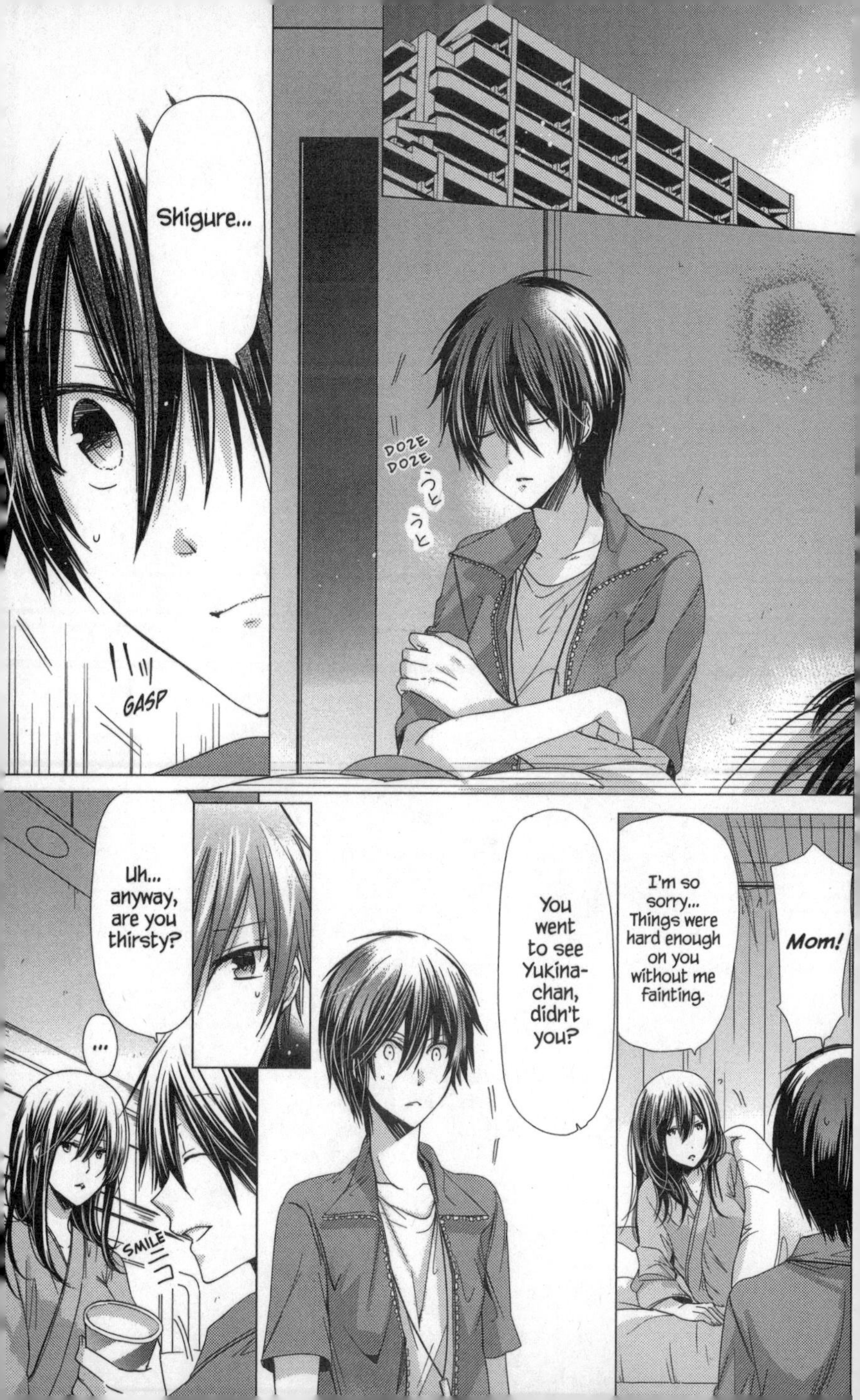
DOZE DOZE
うとうと
Shigure...
GASP
Mom!
I'm so sorry... Things were hard enough on you without me fainting.
You went to see Yukina-chan, didn't you?
Uh... anyway, are you thirsty?
...
SMILE

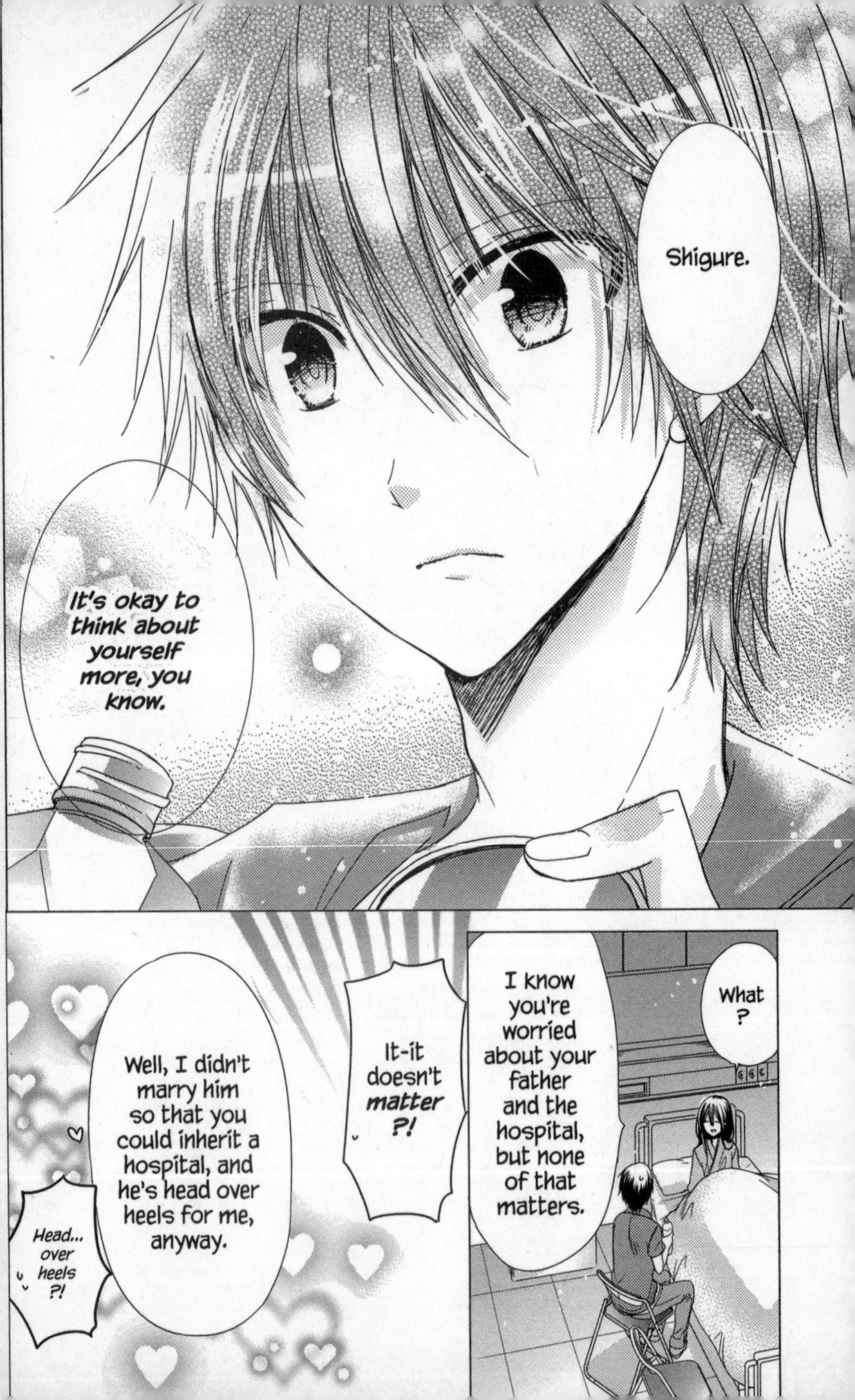
Shigure.
It's okay to think about yourself more, you know.
What?
I know you're worried about your father and the hospital, but none of that matters.
It-it doesn't *matter*?!
Well, I didn't marry him so that you could inherit a hospital, and he's head over heels for me, anyway.
Head... over heels?!

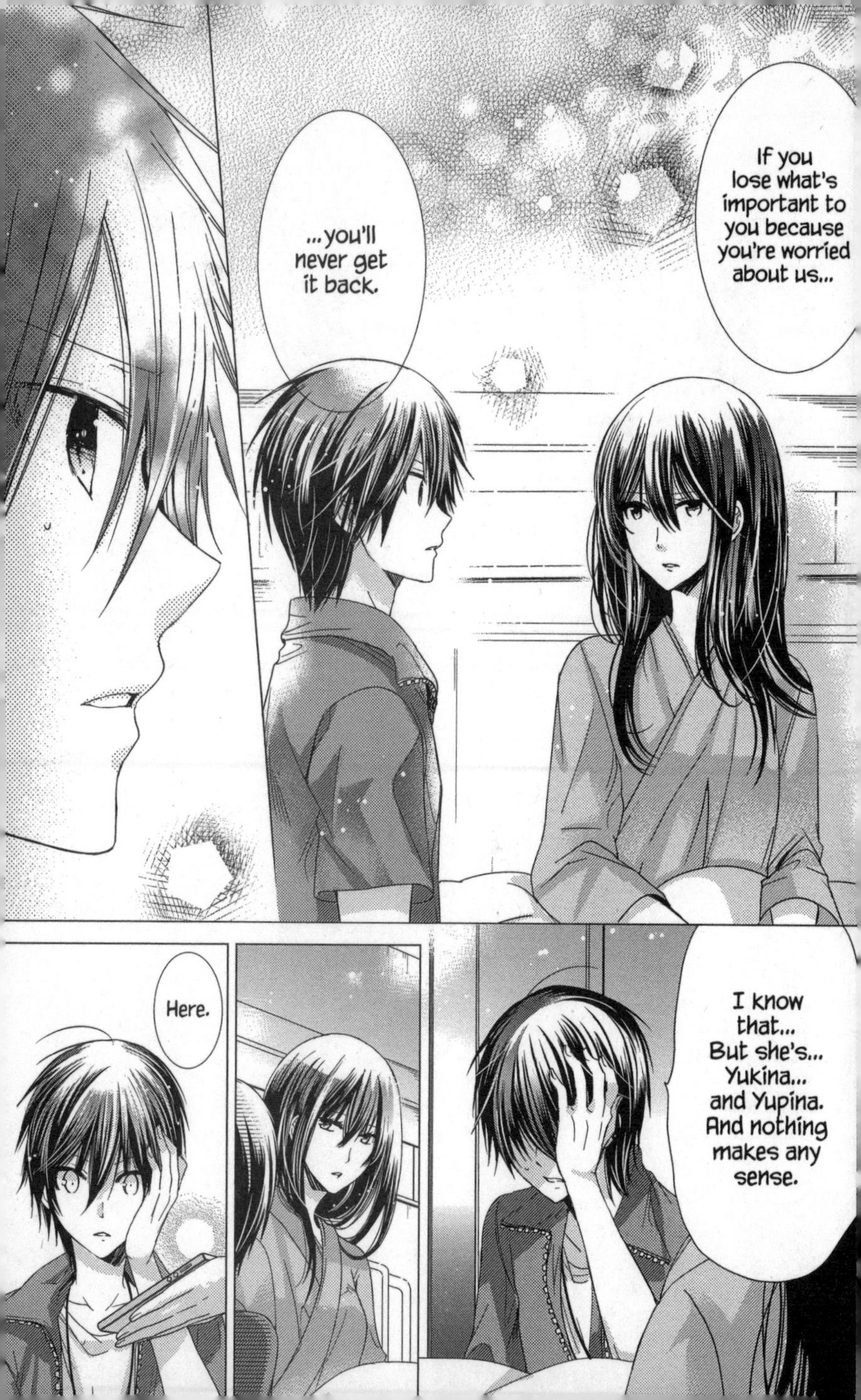
If you lose what's important to you because you're worried about us...
...you'll never get it back.
I know that... But she's... Yukina... and Yupina. And nothing makes any sense.
Here.

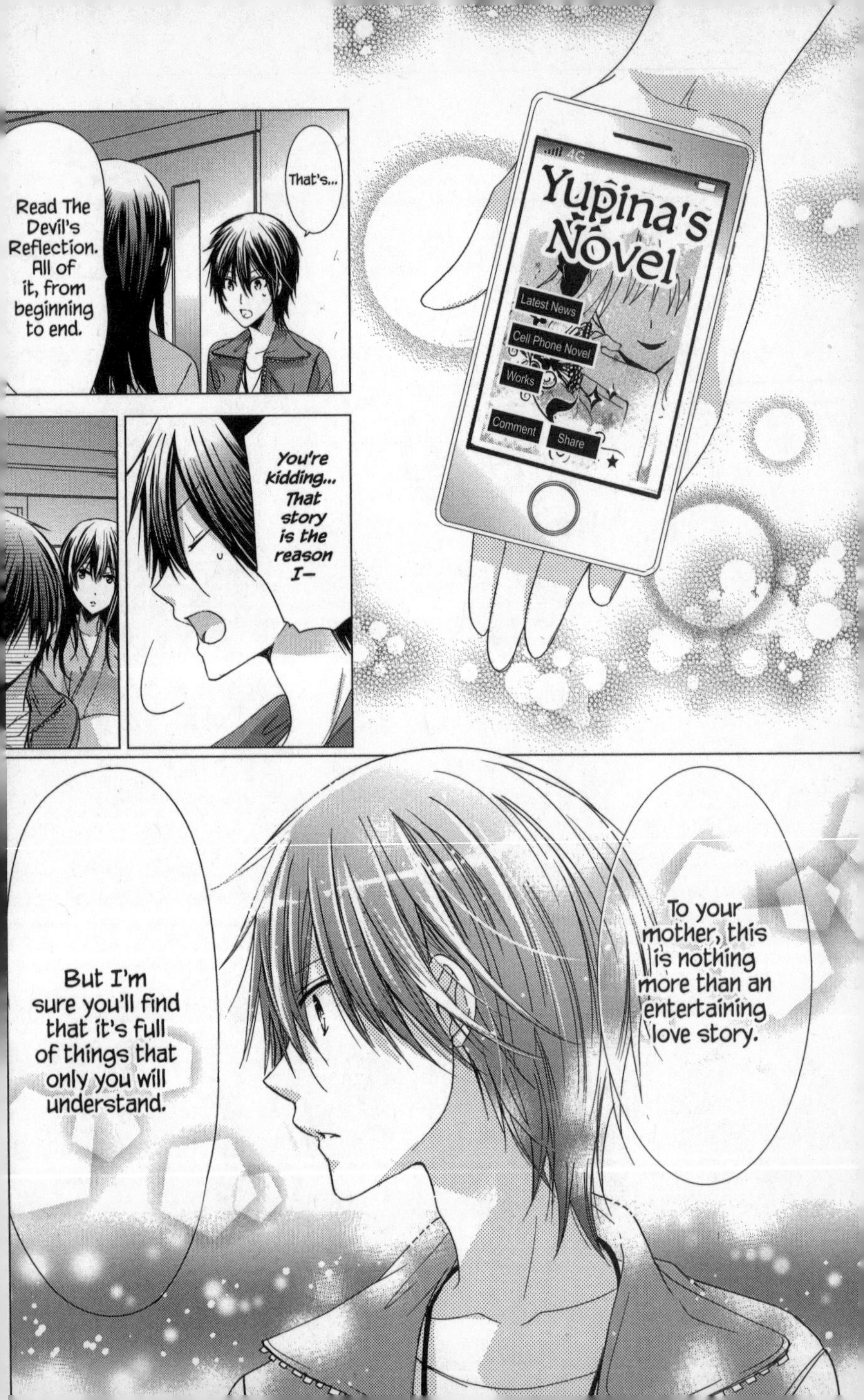
Yupina's Novel
Latest News
Cell Phone Novel
Works
Comment
Share
Read The Devil's Reflection. All of it, from beginning to end.
That's...
You're kidding... That story is the reason I—
To your mother, this is nothing more than an entertaining love story.
But I'm sure you'll find that it's full of things that only you will understand.

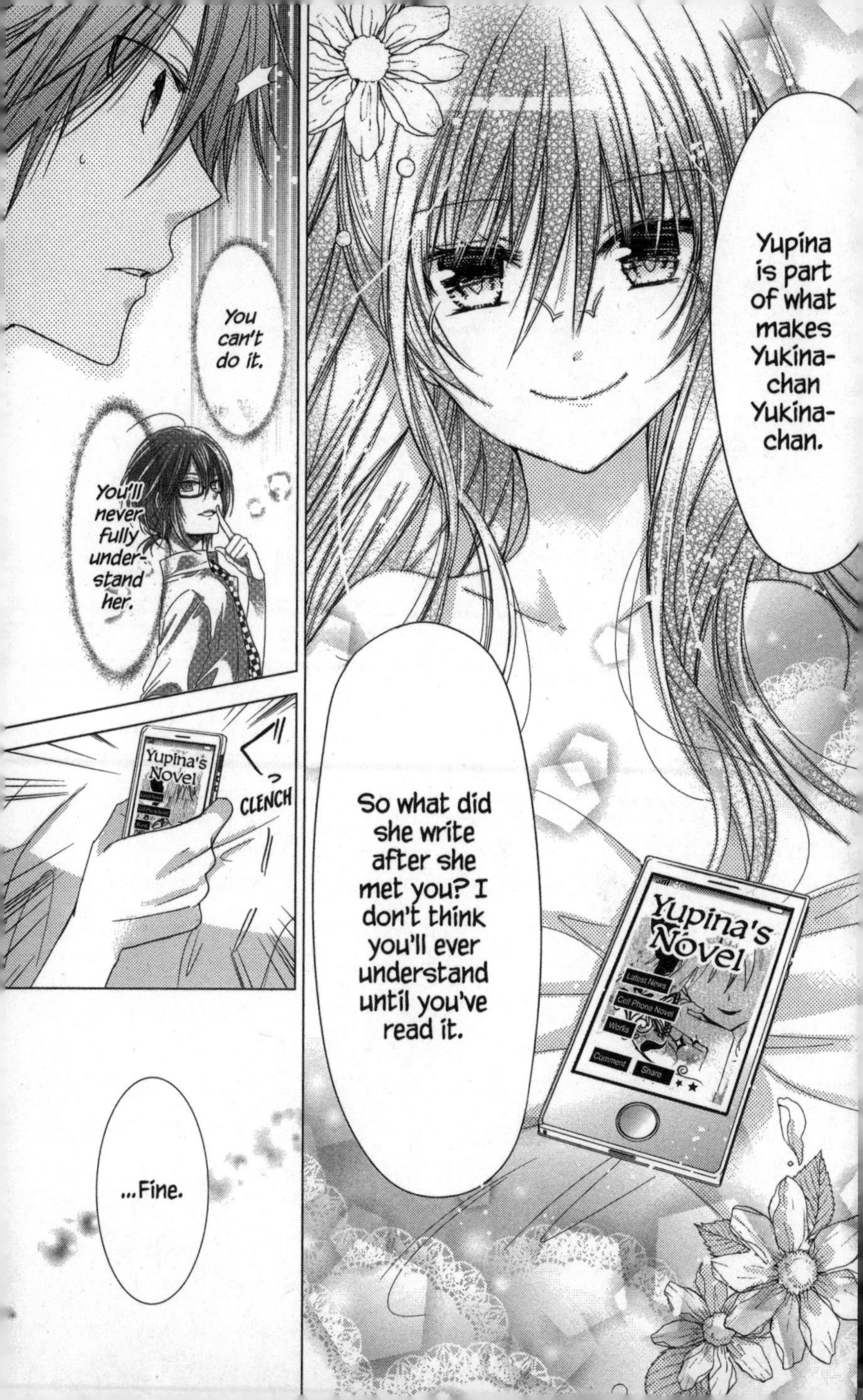
Yupina is part of what makes Yukina-chan Yukina-chan.
So what did she write after she met you? I don't think you'll ever understand until you've read it.
Yupina's Novel
Latest News
Cell Phone Novel
Works
Comment
Share
You can't do it.
You'll never fully under-stand her.
Yupina's Novel
CLENCH
...Fine.

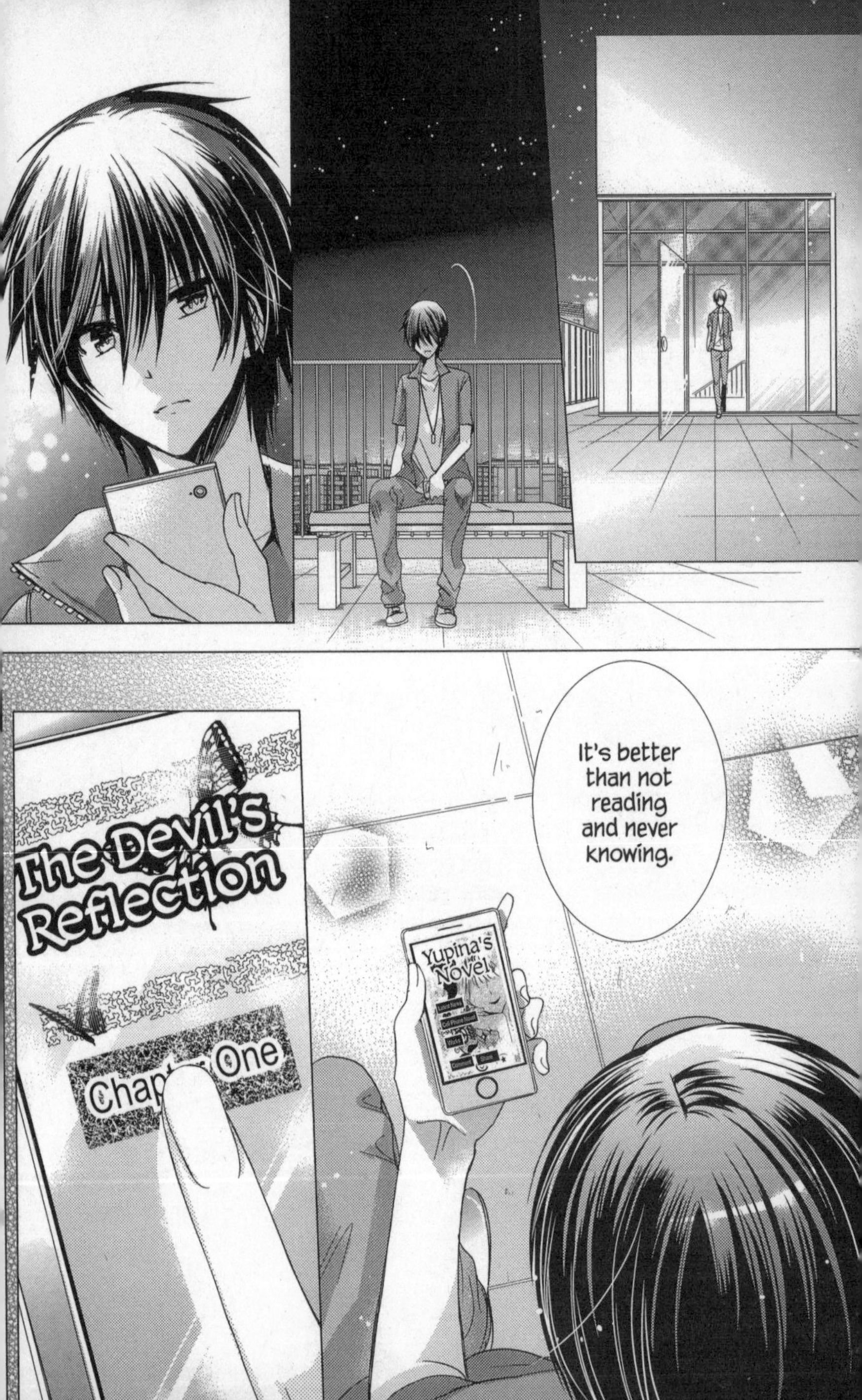
It's better than not reading and never knowing.
Yupina's Novel
The Devil's Reflection

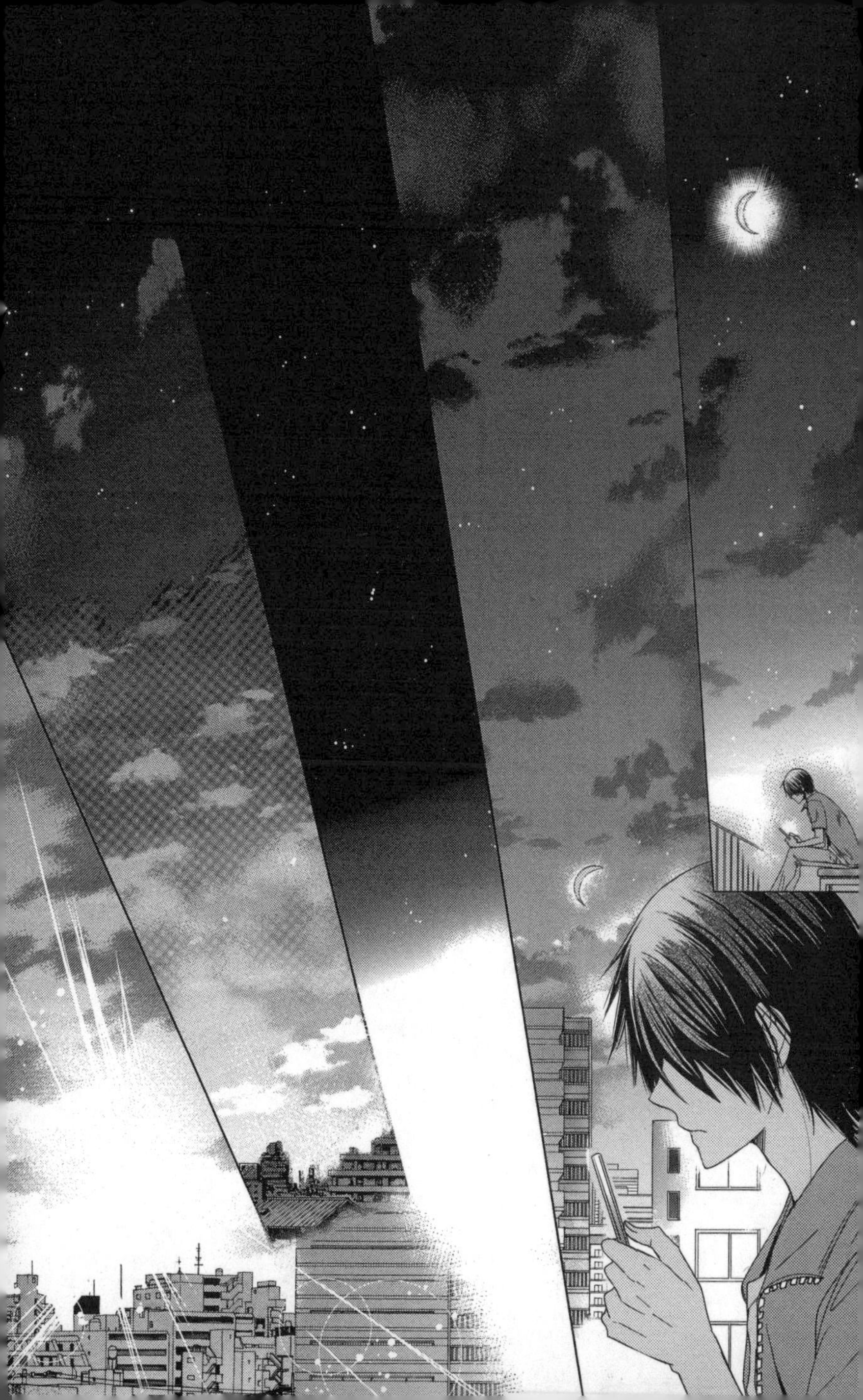

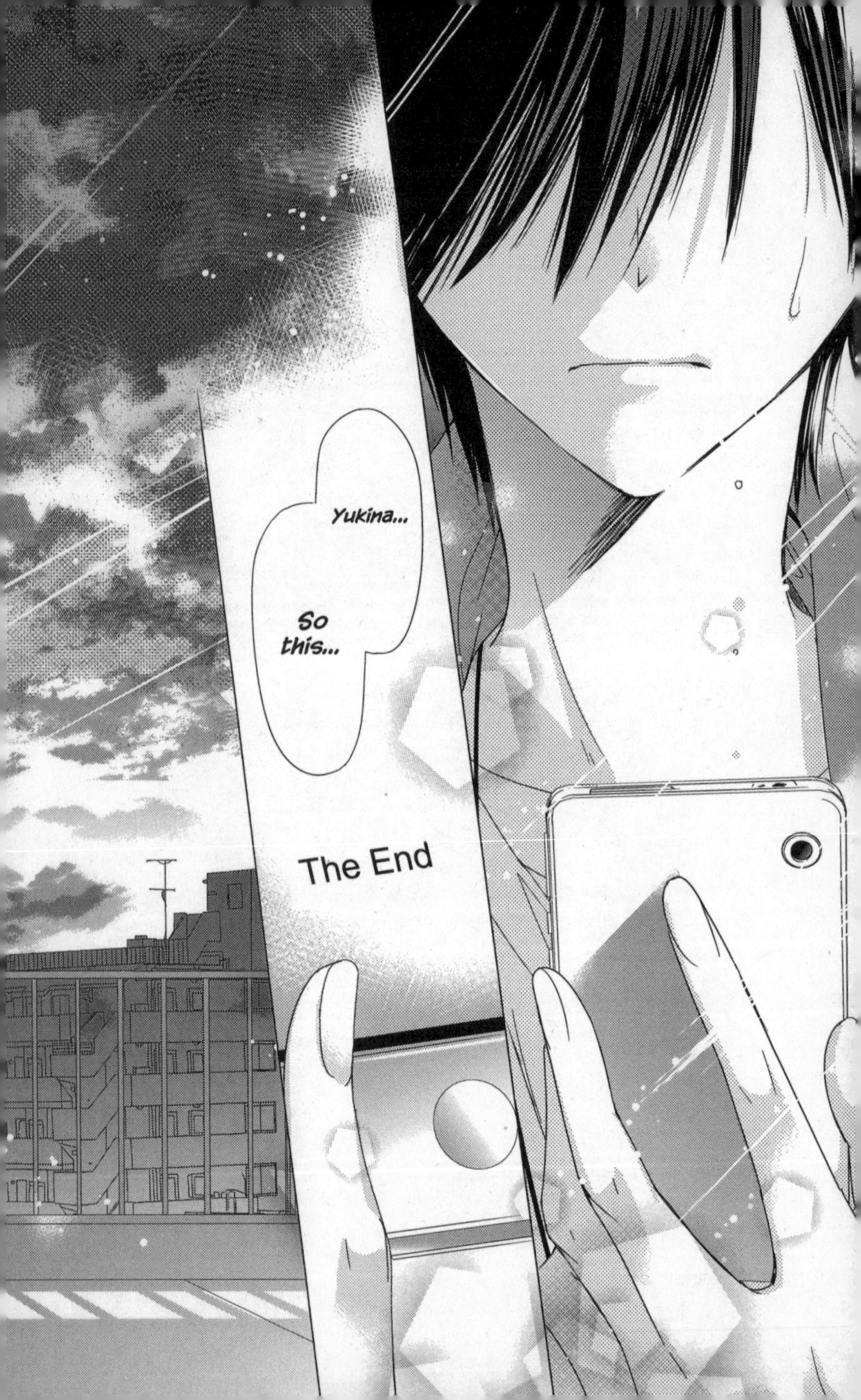
Yukina...
So this...
The End

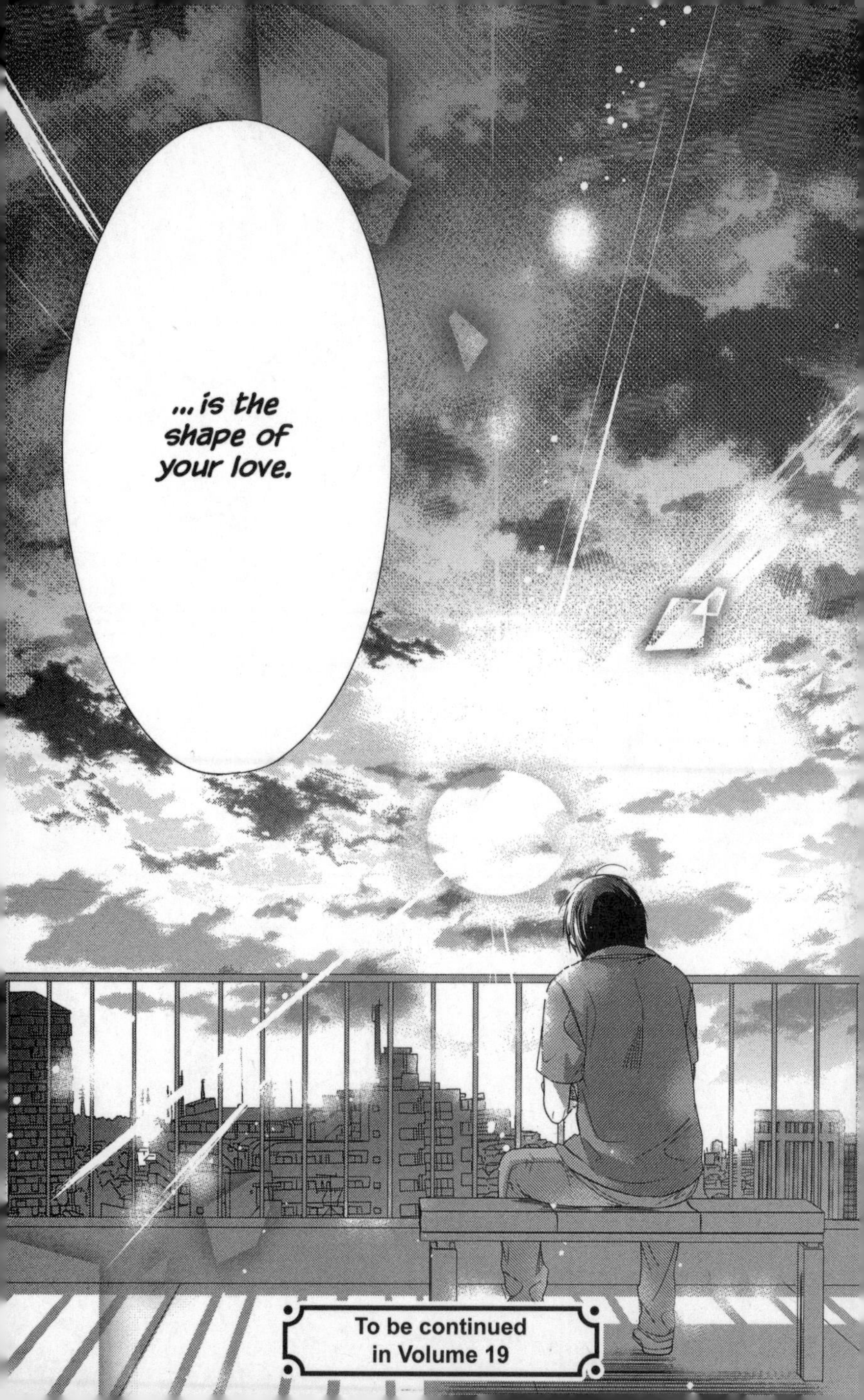
...is the shape of your love.
To be continued in Volume 19

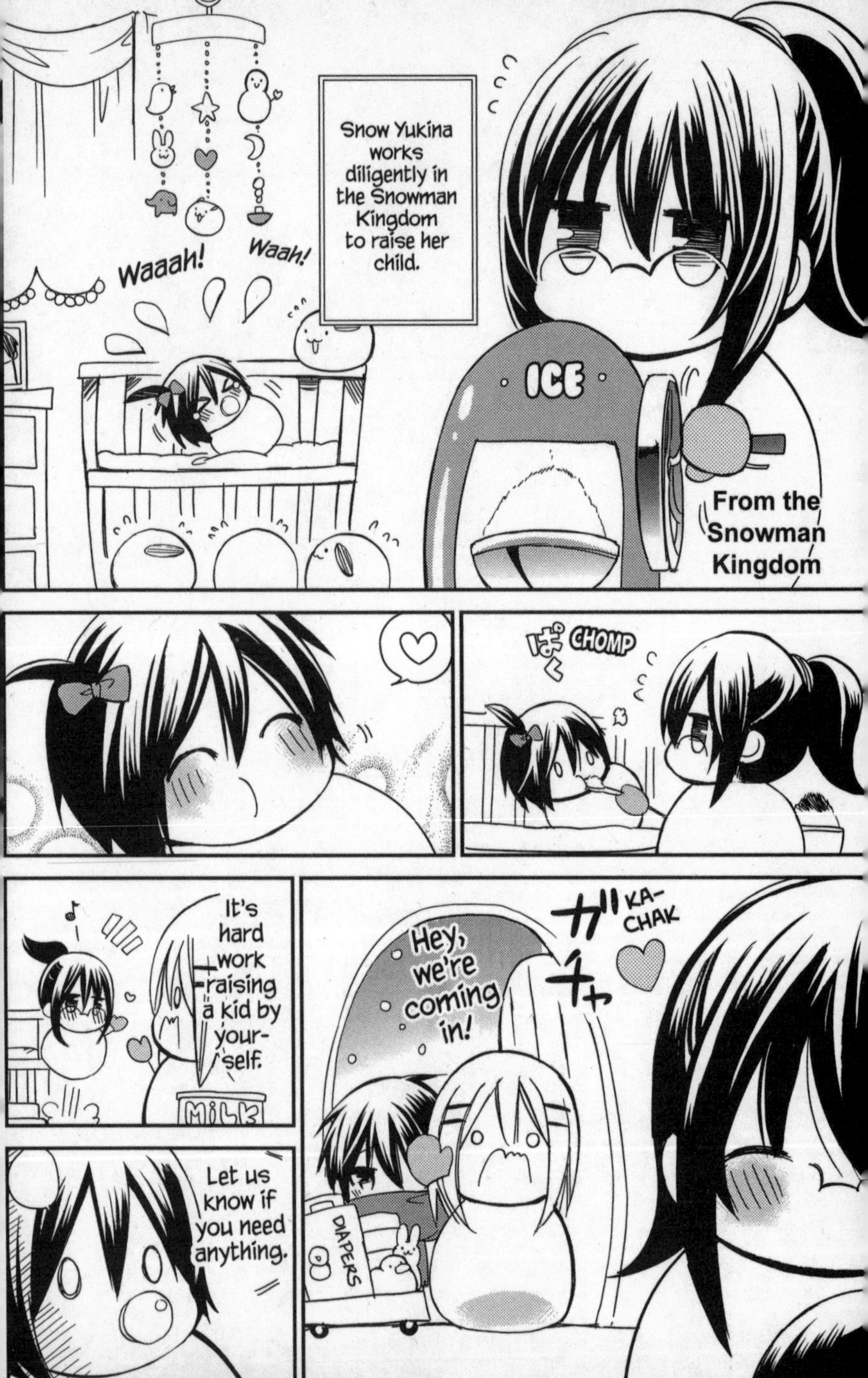
Snow Yukina works diligently in the Snowman Kingdom to raise her child.
From the Snowman Kingdom
ICE
Waah!
Waaah!
ぱく
CHOMP
ガチャ
KA-CHAK
Hey, we're coming in!
DIAPERS
It's hard work raising a kid by yourself.
MILK
Let us know if you need anything.

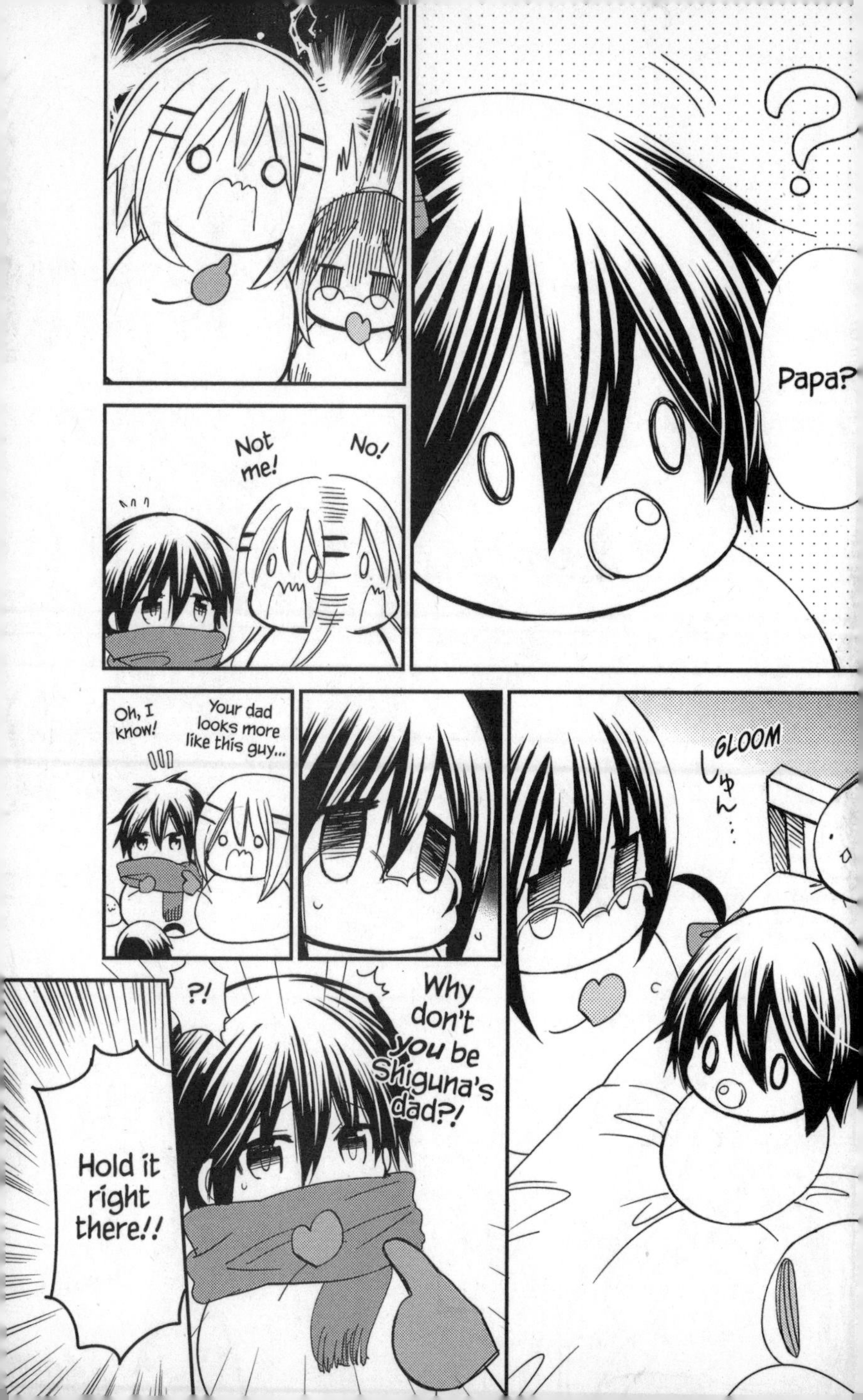
Papa?
No!
Not me!
GLOOM
しゅん…
Your dad looks more like this guy...
Oh, I know!
Why don't you be Shiguna's dad?!
?!
Hold it right there!!

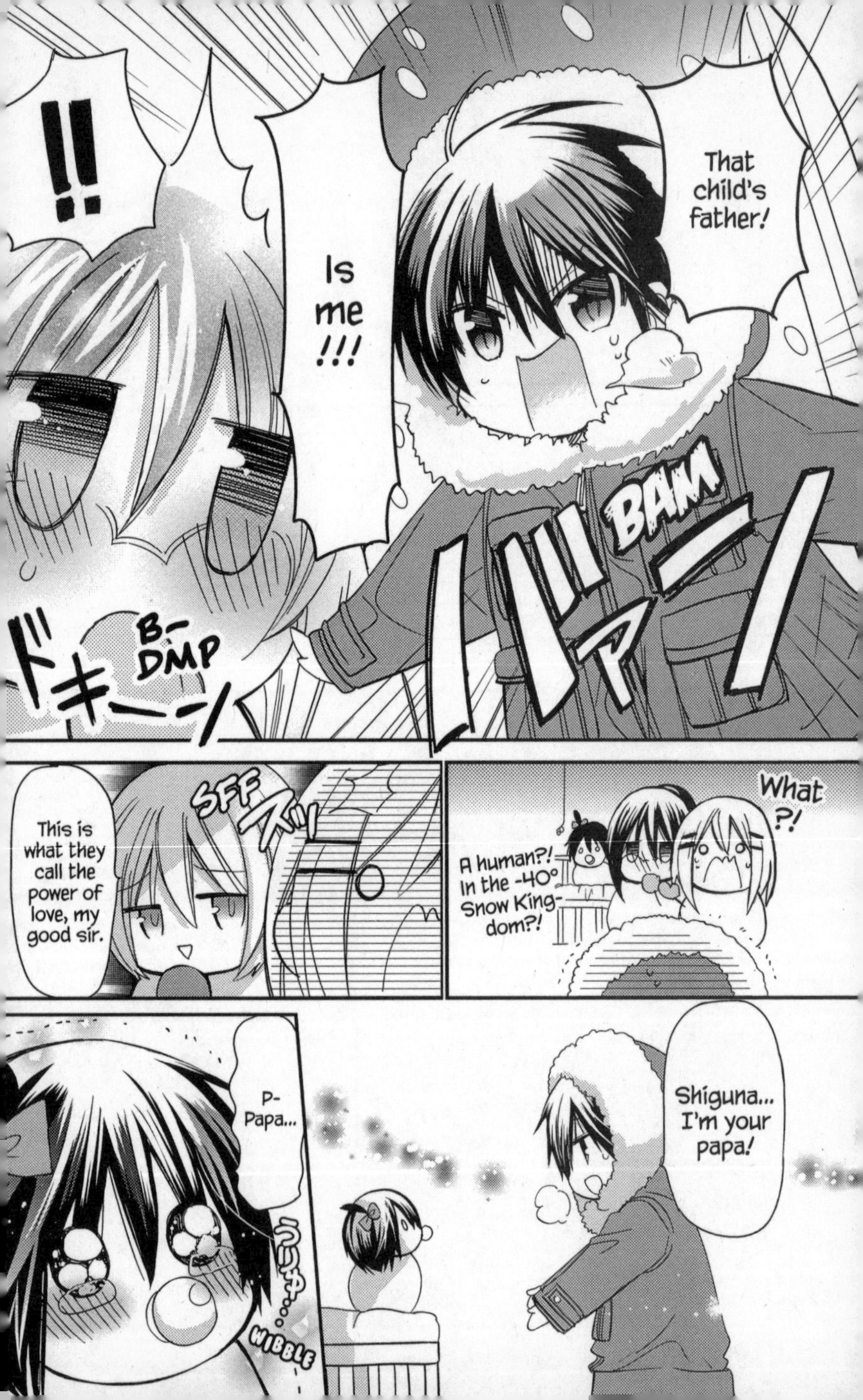
That child's father!
Is me!!!
!!
BAM
ドーン
B-DMP
ドキーン
What?!
A human?! In the -40° Snow King-dom?!
SFF
スッ
This is what they call the power of love, my good sir.
Shiguna... I'm your papa!
P-Papa...
WIBBLE

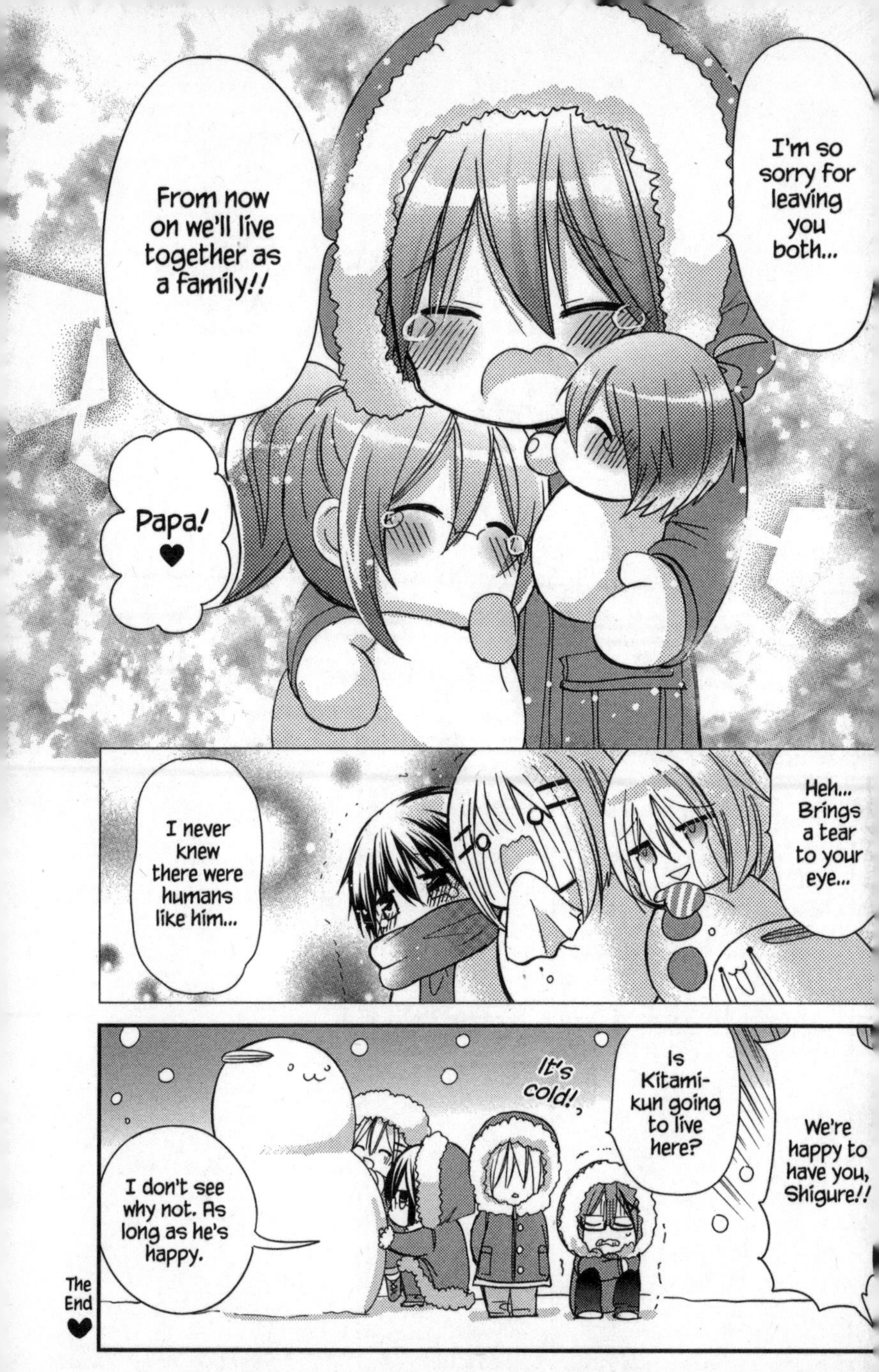
I'm so sorry for leaving you both...
From now on we'll live together as a family!!
Papa! ♥
Heh... Brings a tear to your eye...
I never knew there were humans like him...
We're happy to have you, Shigure!!
Is Kitami-kun going to live here?
It's cold!,
I don't see why not. As long as he's happy.
The End ♥

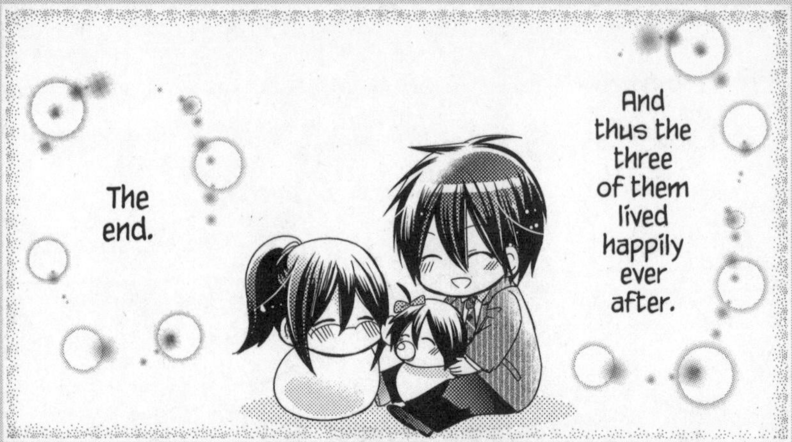
And thus the three of them lived happily ever after.
The end.

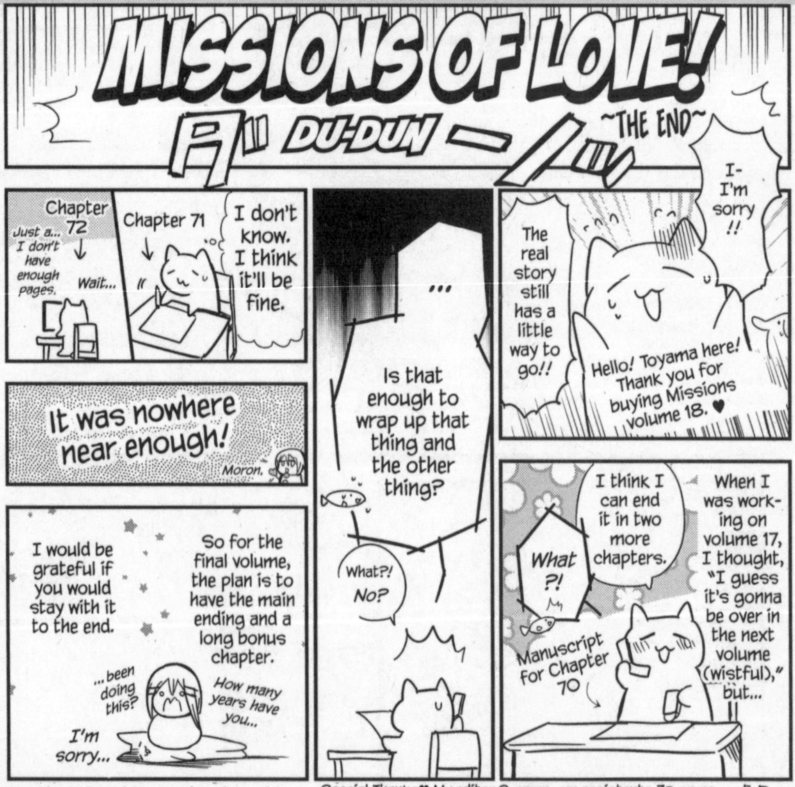
MISSIONS OF LOVE!
~THE END~
DU-DUN
I- I'm sorry!!
The real story still has a little way to go!!
Hello! Toyama here! Thank you for buying Missions volume 18. ♥
When I was work-ing on volume 17, I thought, "I guess it's gonna be over in the next volume (wistful)," but...
I think I can end it in two more chapters.
What?!
Manuscript for Chapter 70
...
Is that enough to wrap up that thing and the other thing?
What?! No?
I don't know. I think it'll be fine.
Chapter 71
Chapter 72
Wait...
Just a... I don't have enough pages.
It was nowhere near enough!
Moron.
So for the final volume, the plan is to have the main ending and a long bonus chapter.
I would be grateful if you would stay with it to the end.
How many years have you...
...been doing this?
I'm sorry...

(Incidentally, Shiguna-chan is a girl.)

Special Thanks♥ My editor S-sama, my assistants Zō-sama, Ryō-sama, Maruyama-sama♥

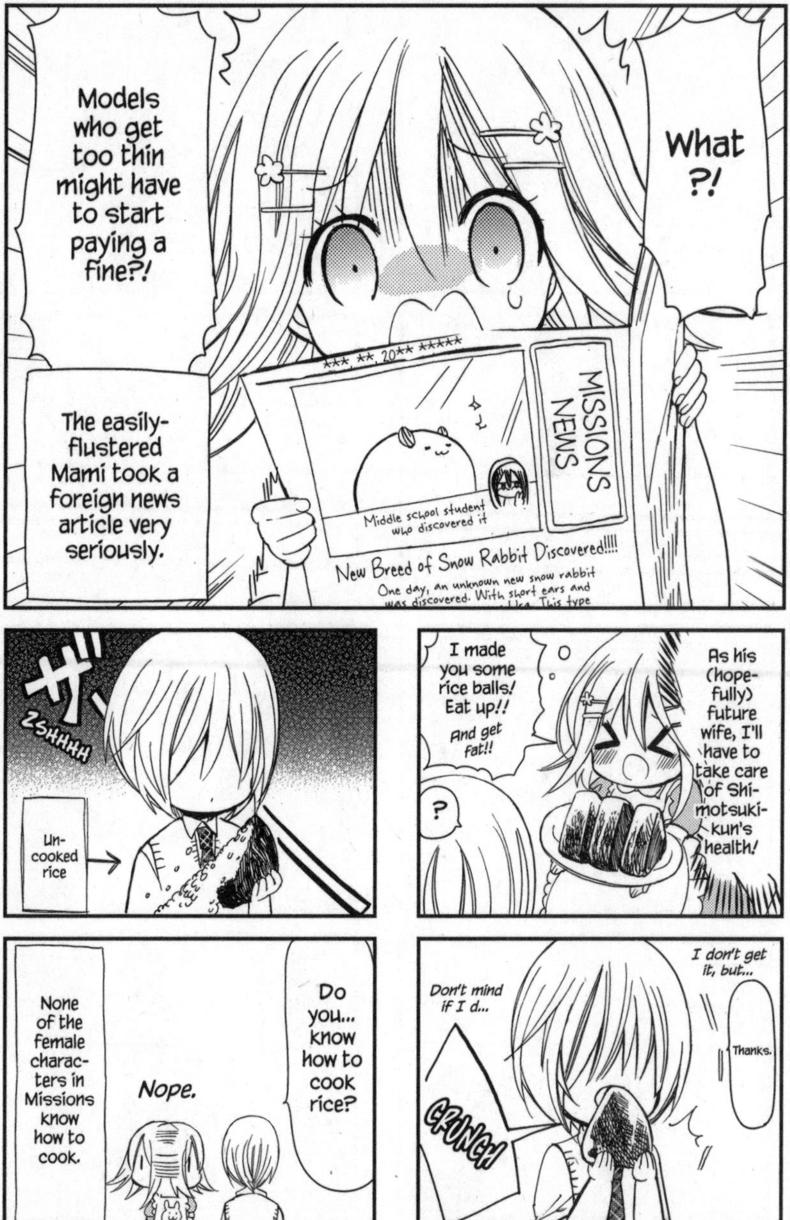
What?!
Models who get too thin might have to start paying a fine?!
MISSIONS NEWS
. **. 20** **
Middle school student who discovered it
New Breed of Snow Rabbit Discovered!!!!
One day, an unknown new snow rabbit was discovered. With short ears and
The easily-flustered Mami took a foreign news article very seriously.
As his (hopefully) future wife, I'll have to take care of Shimotsuki-kun's health!
I made you some rice balls! Eat up!!
And get fat!!
?
ザ
ZSHHHH
Uncooked rice
I don't get it, but...
Thanks.
Don't mind if I d...
CRUNCH
Do you... know how to cook rice?
Nope.
None of the female characters in Missions know how to cook.

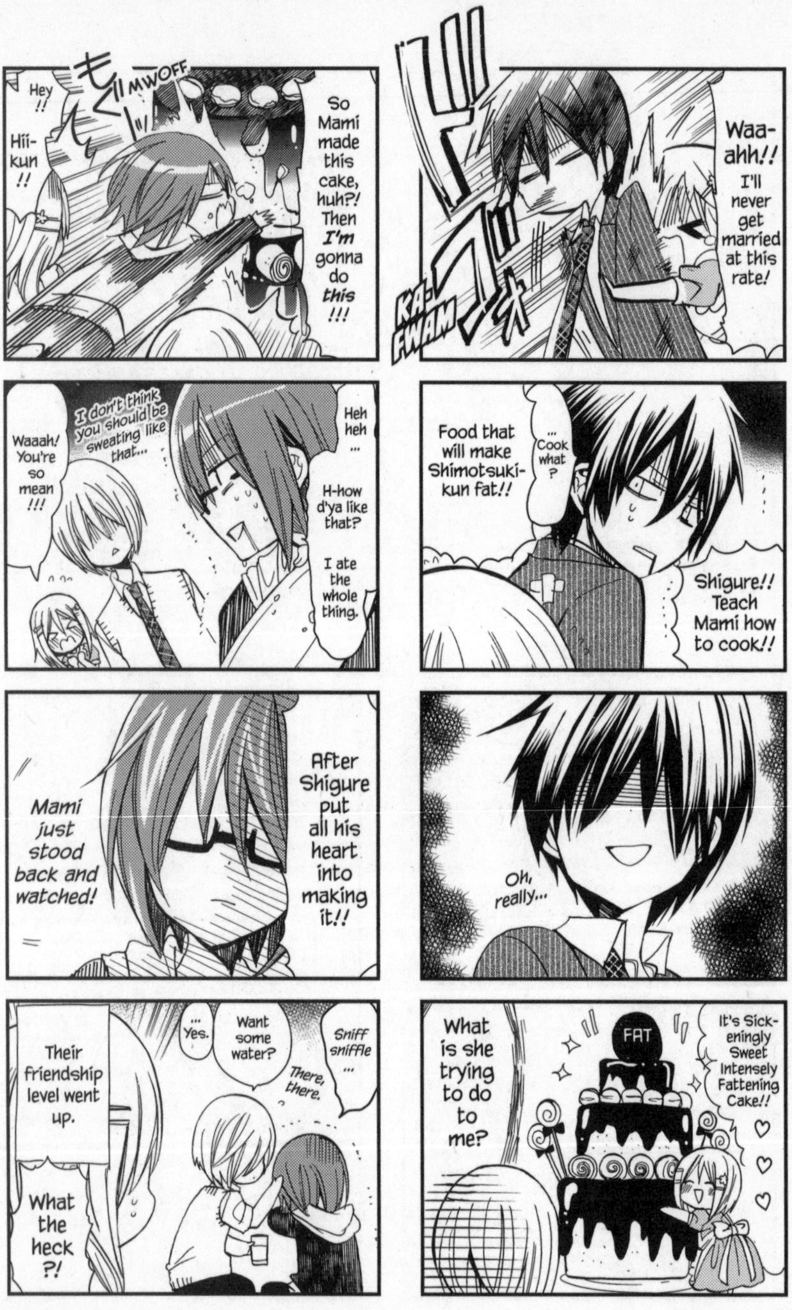
Waa-ahh!! I'll never get married at this rate!
KA-FWAM
Shigure!! Teach Mami how to cook!!
... Cook what?
Food that will make Shimotsuki-kun fat!!
Oh, really...
It's Sickeningly Sweet Intensely Fattening Cake!!
FAT
What is she trying to do to me?
So Mami made this cake, huh?! Then I'm gonna do this!!!
MWOFF
Hii-kun!!
Hey!!
Heh heh...
H-how d'ya like that?
I ate the whole thing.
I don't think you should be sweating like that...
Waaah! You're so mean!!!
After Shigure put all his heart into making it!!
Mami just stood back and watched!
Sniff sniffle...
There, there.
Want some water?
... Yes.
Their friendship level went up.
What the heck?!

Translation notes

Is she a celebrity, page 12

More specifically, these women are wondering if Yukina is a "talent," which is the English word used in Japan for people who appear regularly on things like game shows and talk shows, but aren't necessarily actors.

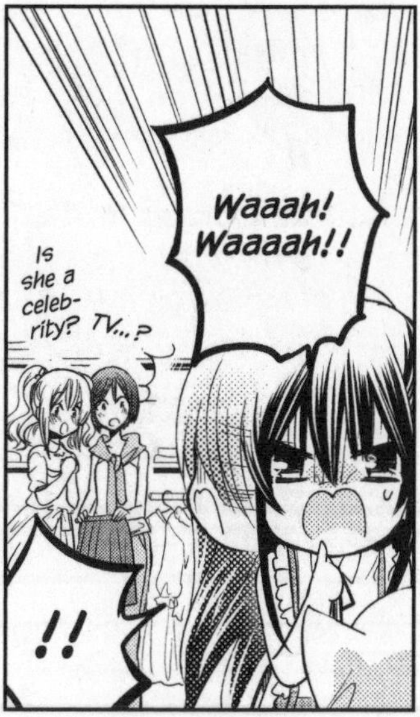
Waaah! Waaaah!!
Is she a celebrity?
TV...?
!!

Missions of Love volume 18 is a work of fiction. Names, characters, places, and incidents are the products of the author's imagination or are used fictitiously. Any resemblance to actual events, locales, or persons, living or dead, is entirely coincidental.

A Kodansha Comics Trade Paperback Original.

Missions of Love volume 18 copyright © 2015 Ema Toyama
English translation copyright © 2019 Ema Toyama

Published in the United States by Kodansha Comics, an imprint of Kodansha USA Publishing, LLC, New York.

Publication rights for this English edition arranged through Kodansha Ltd., Tokyo.

First published in Japan in 2015 by Kodansha Ltd., Tokyo as *Watashi ni xx shinasai!*, volume 18.

ISBN 978-1-63236-847-8

Printed in the United States of America.

www.kodanshacomics.com

9 8 7 6 5 4 3 2 1

Translation: Alethea Nibley & Athena Nibley
Lettering: Paige Pumphrey
Kodansha Comics edition cover design: Phil Balsman